INTERNATIONAL STUDIES

of the
Committee on International Relations
University of Notre Dame

INTERNATIONAL STUDIES

CATHOLICISM, NATIONALISM, AND DEMOCRACY IN ARGENTINA

CATHOLICISM, NATIONALISM, AND DEMOCRACY IN ARGENTINA

JOHN J. KENNEDY

UNIVERSITY OF NOTRE DAME PRESS

1958

Library of Congress Catalog Card Number 57-14970

FOREWORD

THE political and social role of Catholicism in the nations of Latin America has been frequently emphasized and rarely defined. There is a general tendency to regard Catholicism as a force, sometimes benign, other times oppressive, but at all times capable of determining a certain flow of human energy into the dynamics of society, as religious commitment may inspire either endorsement of or resistance to public policy. Critical and morbid situations seem most likely to evoke an attribution of decisiveness. Where a dictatorship falls and its fall has been preceded by a show of Catholic resistance, the claim is made that Catholicism produced the result. On the other hand, the chronically depressed condition of some Catholic countries has quite as readily been ascribed to the withering influence of theocratic insensibility to problems of material well-being. Assertions in these, and related, veins stress specific effects which are attributed to Catholicism. Corresponding specification about the cause, however, is usually lacking. The massive and central fact of the presence of Catholicism is apparently deemed sufficient explanation.

In the Argentine crisis of 1955, which led to the fall of Perón, press reports and commentaries placed a major emphasis on Catholic resistance as an element in the crisis. That Perón faced opposition in the Catholic laity, clergy and hierarchy is, of course, undeniable. Some commentators at the time went so far as to state that this was the opposition that had been decisive in Perón's downfall. Without it, they asserted, the regime could have survived all the other problems in the political and economic order that had contributed to the crisis. 14019

As a student of Argentine institutions who had earlier had some

vii

opportunity for close observation of certain aspects of the national political system, I found myself in at least partial disagreement with this claim. I did not question the underlying assumption that in Argentina Catholicism has a social importance, but I doubted that this importance had ever been sufficiently analyzed or measured to warrant the judgment that Catholicism had been the critically decisive element. In fact the judgment could be challenged, even though Argentina can be counted as a "Catholic" country in at least two ways. The vast majority of its population are members of the Catholic Church. Their commitment to the Catholic religious faith may range from nominal to devout, but more than nine-tenths of the Argentines will at any time claim Catholicism as their creed. Secondly, the Catholic religion has an official position in Argentina, which has been provided for in the Constitutions and the laws. In modern history, however, it does not necessarily follow that a Catholic country will have a Catholic government, as the history of other Latin-American countries illustrates. In Argentina at least two other administrations have survived without difficulty when they were at odds with the Catholic Church on specific issues. There is also evidence that Argentina had, without disturbing the official status of religion, gone sufficiently far in the direction of "secularization" to leave Catholicism in an exposed position and vulnerable to the attacks which a regime struggling for its survival would certainly level if Catholicism were regarded as a threat to its continued existence.

In other words doubts about the political role of Catholicism in the Peronist crisis seemed to be justified on two grounds. First, the claims on its behalf were for the most part so general that they ignored the strategic considerations which must be accounted for in evaluating a crisis of this magnitude. Secondly, Catholicism, in spite of its favored legal position, had lost earlier battles with secular authority. These doubts did not, of course, deny a very great political and social importance to Argentine Catholicism so much as they stressed the fact that the importance was still largely unmeasured.

This book has its origin in those doubts and is the result of a search for some means of more precise evaluation of the role of Catholicism in the life of the Argentine nation. The search has been focused not on the formal pattern of Church-State relations, which has been amply covered in several excellent studies, but rather on a considerable body of Argentine social and political thought that can be called Catholic. It is Argentine in the sense that it has been formulated under the stimulus of the various stages of national development. It is Catholic in that its authors have consciously drawn on Catholic doctrine and tradition as the sources of their political and social ideas. Its general significance is that it is an articulate reflection of the influence with which Catholicism has permeated, or has sought to permeate, the body politic.

I have undertaken to trace the main outlines of this thought from 1810, the beginning of Argentine national existence, down to the end of the Perón regime. Work on this project soon led to the discovery that the most noteworthy Catholic thought tends to concentrate in the two great formative periods of the nation's history, from 1810 to roughly 1830, and from 1853 to 1890. During the Rosas tyranny between these two periods there is some significant Catholic writing, but like most worthwhile Argentine endeavor of that time, it was the work of exiles. And after 1900 Argentine Catholic writing takes a different turn. It becomes more formally philosophic, and with a few exceptions it abandons the national orientation which had characterized the earlier periods. While this latter trend is undoubtedly of major importance in many ways, it does not offer many examples of a direct Catholic influence on the organic development of the Argentine political system. I have therefore made considerably less use of the product of this trend than of the earlier writing with its vitally national outlook. The continuum of this outlook in the present century seems better illustrated in the social action programs which have developed under Catholic influence.

The foregoing statement is not meant to suggest that the reader will find in these pages a social history of Argentine Catholicism. The writing of such a history with comprehensive exploration of the inter-relations between Catholicism and the factors which have produced modern urbanized, industrialized Argentina would undoubtedly be a most worthwhile task. Here, however, no more is intended than an exposition of the principal ideas, theories and trends which Argentine Catholic thought has produced.

Examination of that thought over the course of a century and a half has not produced definitive answers to all the questions involved in Perón's clash with Catholicism in 1955. The factual data which may eventually explain the specific role of Catholicism in that crisis are still unavailable and probably will be for some time to come. The history of Argentine Catholic thought, however, places that crisis in a perspective where the crisis *per se* takes on diminished proportions. It highlights the positions of peculiar strength and weakness from which Argentine Catholicism had to face that crisis. It also strongly suggests that despite an initial cordiality between the Perón regime and the Church a clash between the two was inevitable from the beginning.

As I have previously indicated, this is not a study in Church-State relations. Nor is it an attempt to explain the Catholic Church in Argentina, since that is the task of the theologian and the historian of religion. It is essentially a study of a body of political thought which owes its character to religious inspiration and guidance. Some of the thought is formally organized and systematically developed. Much of it is the product of isolated and sporadic efforts to apply a Catholic concept to a particular situation. Most of it, however, is directly related to the movements out of which the Argentine nation has grown and which have given it its unique character.

In the preparation of this study I have received invaluable assistance from both institutions and persons to whom I wish to express my thanks here. The University of Notre Dame generously arranged my teaching schedule so as to leave me with a maximum amount of time to pursue this work. The Rockefeller Foundation through its grant to the Notre Dame Committee on International Relations provided financial support for the project. To my colleagues Stephen D. Kertesz and M. A. Fitzsimons I am grateful for counsel, criticism and encouragement at various stages of the research and writing. To Mrs. Alvan S. Ryan I am indebted for typing and to Mr. Alvan S. Ryan for editorial work on the manuscript. Father Rubén de Hoyos, S.J., and Professor Arthur P. Whitaker read the manuscript and gave me the benefit of their discriminating judgment on many points. Needless to say, errors and deficiencies that may be found in the text are entirely the responsibility of the author.

TABLE OF CONTENTS

CATHOLICISM, NATIONALISM,
AND DEMOCRACY IN ARGENTINA

CHAPTER I

Catholicism in Argentina

THE role of Catholicism in a Catholic society is not an easy matter to identify and analyze. It is a commonplace to refer to Argentina and other Latin American countries as "Catholic" nations, but the word is rarely used with any precision. On many occasions the user may wish to indicate no more than that the Catholic Church is the only organized religious body of any significant size in a particular country. In other connections the term may signify that Catholic Baptism has been administered to the vast majority of the population to give them a nominal Catholicism which does not necessarily connote a life-long and active religious practice. Some Catholic countries have governments which are openly antagonistic to Catholicism, while a few others, including Argentina, accord the Catholic Church a special juridical status. At the same time in almost all Latin American countries some of the most vigorous intellectual and political currents, with important social consequences, challenge in varying degree Catholic positions of doctrine or discipline.

The element of the contradictory and the paradoxical in this general picture does not necessarily negate a Catholic character or cancel out an objectively recognizable Catholic influence, but it confronts the student of the public and social life of any one of these countries with a primary problem of determining what the commitment to Catholicism is on the part of the individuals, groups or institutions that are the objects of his study. Obviously, the problem is not the same for all disciplines. It is one thing for the cultural anthropologist and the sociologist, and something quite different for the historian of institutions. For the theologian it is still something else. The present study undertakes to examine

3

and evaluate Catholic social thought which has been formulated under the stimulus of the political growth and development of the Argentine nation. The purpose is a study of political ideas, but it should be noted at the beginning that the ideas are not of even quality. Some of them represent systematic development of comprehensive theories. Others are sketchy apologetics, while yet others are largely proposals for action. Within the scope which this purpose suggests the problem of a Catholic commitment may be approached in the following terms.

A CATHOLIC COMMITMENT

"Nominal Catholic" is an unpardonably ambiguous term. In a strict sense probably no one has a right to apply it to another, since the fervor with which one accepts a given creed is an internal matter of conscience beyond the judgment of another party. Nevertheless, in dealing with a country where almost every inhabitant may call himself Catholic, but where there are various degrees of outward manifestation of religious commitment, some term must be used to signify the minimal manifestation. For this purpose *nominal Catholicism* is probably as good a term as can be devised.

Nominal Catholicism has a political importance in Argentina. For example, the Constitution, both in the long-enduring 1853 version and in the 1949 revision, has required the President of the Republic to be a Catholic. This provision has never operated to demand more than a nominal credal commitment on the part of the Chief Executive. Nominal Catholicism is not, however, a force which generates ideas with a particularly Catholic stamp. However much practical importance nominal Catholicism may have in the realm of the political, it is not likely to be a source of social ideas that bespeak an inspiration in formal Christian doctrine. Therefore to argue that because the Argentine President must be a Catholic, ideas advanced by any particular President are Catholic in their inspiration is an absurdity.

A related and more complicated problem arises in connection with some of those Latin American clerics whose secular accomplishments have been more widely acclaimed than their sacerdotal careers. Presumably the priesthood indicates a commitment which is both precise and complete. Yet in the political history of Latin

America how many times is the ecclesiastical status of certain clerics ambiguous. For example, it is customary in the historical treatment of the Mexican struggle for national independence to identify both Hidalgo and Morelos as priests. But neither name is a symbol of a religious force in the development of the nation. The official Church, and especially the Tribunal of the Inquisition, dealt too harshly with them to permit it. Latter-day apologists are prone to minimize the disastrous action of the tribunal by questioning whether it was acting within its lawful sphere of competence. The doubt may be well-founded, but it does not change the fact that Morelos and Hidalgo, who represent so much in the history of their country, were priests whose actions were condemned, not approved. What they symbolize is Mexican nationalism, opposed by both the *ancien régime* and ecclesiastical power, not the force of Catholicism in society.

In Brazil, the priest Diogo Antonio Feijó was a powerful and influential leader from the time of independence down to 1843. He was Regent during two years of the minority of the second Emperor. Feijó's character was strong and upright. In an atmosphere of much laxity among the clergy, he was ever distinguished as one whose personal conduct was only that proper to the sacerdotal career. Yet Feijó's plans for the solution of the "Church problem" in the empire show an extreme concept of political authority which stands well outside even the broadest interpretation of Catholic orthodoxy.

Elsewhere in the history of Latin America other clerics have played prominent political and social roles. In many cases their priestly status did not guarantee a course of action that would be associated with a Catholic influence. This point is noted here not to arouse a general (and undeserved) suspicion of the orthodoxy of the Latin American clergy or to question the good faith of those clerics who have participated in the institutional development of their countries. Rather it is noted simply for the purpose of making clear that the problem of identifying a commitment to Catholicism is not readily obviated just because the person in question happens to be a priest or bishop.

On the Argentine scene this problem is most likely to arise in connection with the "liberal priests" of the Liberation period. The orthodoxy of such priests as Juan Ignacio Gorriti and Gregorio

Funes has been called into question, especially by secularist writers. Since the work of both these men will be considered in detail below, it is unnecessary to examine the question here. But it may be noted that the active political records of both men have given rise to the question.

These random examples suggest that the problem of identifying a commitment to Catholicism is not to be solved by establishing distinctions between positions and attitudes that have been taken by persons who for one reason or another could claim to speak as Catholics. The problem is more than anything else an historical matter, or more precisely a matter in the intellectual history of Western Civilization. It is necessary to appeal to the broad terms of history to explore the problem further.

During the Christian era Western man and his institutions have developed under many influences. Greece and Rome have had a primary importance. The folk customs of the barbarians of the North, modified and transmuted, are a part of the heritage. The culture of the Arabs left its mark where it came in contact with European culture through the Crusades and in the long occupation of the Iberian peninsula. The Renaissance brought both new and renewed secular forces into play. There have also been other forces too numerous to detail here, but throughout these centuries of growth (or at times, retrogression) there was until fairly recent times a single, dominant view of the nature of man, his origin and his destiny. Christian doctrine shaped and influenced both Western man and his social environment.

By the time of the Enlightenment, however, this doctrine had met with serious challenge. Indeed the very elements which made possible the advent of modernity seemed to combine to turn the hitherto dominant influence into an obsolete myth. Christianity had told the story of a special Creation with the earth as the focal point of the physical universe. Sixteenth century astronomy demonstrated that the world was a minor globe circling a not very brilliant star, inconspicuous in the infinity of space. In explanation of the contradictory nature of man with its capacity for good and evil, Christian teaching had emphasized the Fall of the human race and the Redemption by the God-man. In opposition to this, modern thought offered the concept of the natural goodness of man, corrupted only by institutions, from which mankind must be liberated so that it could assert its natural goodness. A widening view of history and increasing familiarity with non-Western cultures led to the doubt that a small Levantine nation could possibly have been chosen by the Creator as the special repository of truth, or that from its people could come the Salvation of the world. Christianity had taught that Revelation was the avenue to ultimate truth, but experimental science seemed not only to provide a more readily convincing approach to truth, but also to contradict much of what had previously been recognized as true.

On the basis of these new concepts of man and the world, statesmen and thinkers in many parts of Europe were to organize fundamental challenges to the existing social structure, whose pervasive element had been Christian doctrine. By no means did all of these challenges imply a rejection of Christianity. They were, however, directed against traditional ideas of social organization, and some of the defenders of tradition came to regard the new concepts as universally anti-Christian. In the eighteenth century these challenges were flourishing, and they came to a head in the French Revolution and its aftermath. The succeeding century saw the attack intensified on many fronts. Two conditions of this development ought to be noted here.

One is that the challenge was not always revolutionary in the sense of being offered by those out of power and seeking to gain it through overthrow of existing authority. The challenge could also come from the top, from those in power, as it did in the reign of the Spanish Bourbon, Charles III, who found his subjects superstitious and unenlightened and who set about to change their condition.

The other condition to be emphasized is that the attack leveled on the existing order could be based on an appeal to Christian principles as well as on a rejection of Christian teaching. This seeming anomaly is explainable by the fact that while the *status quo* could be defended and sustained by an appeal to religious belief, it also frequently contained elements of glaring injustice and corruption which themselves were often living contradictions of the very inspiration that the existing order claimed. A large part of the attempt to change the state of affairs, especially after 1789, was undeniably directed at abuse and injustice as much as against the conceptual bases of social organization.

These two conditions mark the difference between the ideal and the practical divisions in the assessment of the Christian content of the social philosophies that have developed in the modern period. Ideally and logically, it ought to be possible for the Catholic philosopher to say: Christianity has been the dominant influence in Western development. The social institutions constructed while this was the dominant influence are Christian institutions. The challenge to them rests on non-Christian philosophy. Therefore those who desire a Christian order will defend the traditional institutions and reject the new ones which an age of revolution and innovation seeks to establish. The logic leads to the de Maistre formula of "throne and altar."

It is seldom, and probably fortunately so, that the formula can be applied in practice. Often the throne has been too much the opponent of the altar to permit it; for example, Feijó. Another practical, and probably more important, obstacle to the logic is contained in the second condition noted above. There is no Catholic doctrine that holds that temporal institutions with human and therefore imperfect bases lie beyond the reach of criticism and attack. Especially when they give evidence of betraying in whole or in part the purposes for which they exist, they will arouse opposition in the name of justice. This is the reason why during the past two centuries tradition-minded Catholics have sometimes been allied with anti-traditional liberals, whose basic philosophy they do not share, but with whom they can be in agreement on programs of action. Specifically in Argentina it will be difficult to find prior to the twentieth century any significant Catholic thinkers who do not partake of this orientation in greater or lesser degree. (It probably should not be forgotten either that recent decades have witnessed the spectacle of tradition-minded Catholics joining with other quite anti-traditional forces, which are the very antithesis of liberalism, namely, the twentieth century fascists. Argentina has also had its share of these.)

What the foregoing résumé means in terms of a Catholic commitment can probably be summarized as follows: The commitment rests first of all on the unreserved acceptance of the traditional Christian teaching on the nature of man and his destiny, a position which stands in opposition to other, more recent explanations of human existence. It recognizes a divine, rather than human, character in both Revelation and the *Ecclesia Docens,* and acknowledges the super-human authority which this character establishes. This is in distinction from the position which may acknowledge a relative merit in either Revelation or the Church, but which rejects them as absolute authorities.

This commitment obviously conditions and limits the social thought and action of one who adheres to it, but it does not define either his thought or his action in the whole field of human relations. He may, in modern parlance, move right or left without abandoning it, although there are limitations on how far he may go in either direction. This latitude is something of which non-Catholics are frequently unaware, but this is not surprising, since very many Catholics are also quite ignorant of it.

This observation raises some question about the utility of undertaking a study of Catholic social thought. The Church has its dogmas, doctrines, and "official positions." It has a Body of Canon Law. These all establish obligations binding in conscience on the Catholic believer, and therefore a large part of his attitude would seem a cut-and-dried matter. Outside these areas of authority, however, if the Catholic is free to take any position that does not contravene a doctrine, can there be any unity in Catholic thought which will make it worthwhile to examine?

In an era of history in which the political were less important than it has been in the modern age, the answer might be in the negative. But for the past two centuries at least, the political has had a unique importance for Western civilization. The struggle over the questions of liberty and authority, of personal rights and duties in the increasingly complex form in which state and society are organized has been an endless struggle, and seems to grow ever more intense as the globe shrinks and the intricacies of the social pattern multiply. In the course of this process Christianity has retreated as a social force in some parts of the world, has extended its influence in others, and in still others it has experienced some degree of resurgence after an apparent defeat. In short, while Christianity has everywhere been challenged, it has hardly been eclipsed anywhere. The word continues to identify a social force to be reckoned with, though the force generally is not manifested in the same way in all places. What this force means to those who are dedicated to perpetuating it as one of the bases of social organization has therefore an importance which should not be ignored.

CATHOLIC SOCIAL THOUGHT IN ARGENTINA

The approach just outlined leads naturally to an emphasis on the extrinsic importance of Catholicism. Discussion of its intrinsic worth belongs in other pages and with authors claiming a different competence. It should also be noted that in this context the extrinsic importance of Catholic social thought immediately becomes a relative matter. In the intellectual history of Argentina, Catholic writers have not formed the majority in the ranks of the most influential. Nor can the Catholic ranks claim all of the most gifted of the Argentine political leaders.

Spokesmen who have sought to articulate Catholic positions in response to modern political and social problems have frequently been on the defensive. This has been especially true of some phases of Catholic thought and action in Argentina in the period since 1880. The defensiveness, however, has not shown the minority or "ghetto" mentality that Catholic thought has displayed in some other countries. A large part of Argentine Catholic thought seems rather to rest on the comfortable belief that tradition is on its side. There is a vital tradition, Catholics say, which is shown in the privileged juridical position of the Church and in the absence of any prolonged conflict between civil and ecclesiastical authorities such as other Latin American countries have experienced. Continual reassertion of the tradition seems a sufficient task for many, though certainly not all, Catholic spokesmen. It may be questioned whether this is a prudent trust in the force of historical inertia.

It would be wrong, however, to think of the mainstream of Argentine Catholic thought as being inert. Especially in the Liberation period and during the years between 1853 and 1880, Catholic spokesmen played major roles in influencing the course of Argentine development. Their spirit was essentially creative and only rarely defensive. Traditional Christian doctrine provided them with ideas that first strengthened the bases of revolutionary action. Later the same source was tapped to contribute to the consolidation of the new nation in the form of a federal republic. The long tyranny of Juan Manuel de Rosas set this movement back, in spite of a nominal spirit of cooperation between the dictator and the Church. After 1853, however, there came a Catholic intellectual revival that flourished throughout the period of the reorganization of the nation. Manifestations of this generally creative spirit have continued to occur even in the later period when Catholic thought has frequently been defensive in tone and character.

In the pages that follow an attempt will be made to identify the principal trends of Catholic thought as they have developed in response to the great questions involved in the political and social organization of Argentina. Most of these questions fall into two categories. In the first the central theme is nationalism as the force which promotes the political unity of the country and which is dedicated to preserving its integrity. The second arises out of the perpetual problem of the search for effective democracy. This is a problem which in its entirety is yet to be solved in spite of the fact that the best efforts of Argentine citizens have long been devoted to its solution.

Study of these trends will involve Catholicism in many of its aspects. The central interest of the study, however, is in ideas and attitudes, not in the formal pattern of Church-State relations, which is, of course, a separate matter. Nevertheless, since the juridical arrangements between Church and State in Argentina form a part of the background against which Catholic thought operates, it will be necessary to summarize here for reference in later pages the principal features of the arrangements.

CHURCH AND STATE IN ARGENTINA

Relations between the civil and ecclesiastical authorities have traditionally been determined by constitutional stipulation. The 1853 Constitution was revised in 1949 in many respects. The 1949 instrument was suspended by the Revolutionary Government that succeeded Perón. At the time that this is being written (1957) further revision by a Constitutional Convention is in prospect. Since the provisions on which the Church-State pattern depends have remained fairly stable through more than a century, reference in the following paragraphs is to the 1949 text. Even though this version is no longer valid, its stipulations largely

duplicate, in many cases *verbatim*, those of the earlier document.
Revision may, of course, be undertaken by the future convention.
The long persistence of the arrangements, however, probably indicates that any revision will be in word rather than in spirit.

Constitutional provisions and historical events and precedents
have combined to create at least three separate sets of problems
in the study of ecclesiastical-civil relations in the Argentine Republic. These can be identified as (1) the juridical status of
Catholicism, (2) the exercise of the *patronato*, and (3) relations
with the Holy See.

JURIDICAL STATUS

The major question that may be asked here is: Does Argentina
have an official religion?

Most Argentines would immediately reply in the negative.
They would maintain that Article 2 of the Constitution provides
"support" for the Catholic religion without making it the official
religion of the State. The decision of the 1853 convention was
definitely to "support" and not to "profess" Catholicism on the
part of the State. In this respect the 1853 decision was a deliberate departure from earlier constitutional essays, notably those
of 1819 and 1826, which had expressly recognized Catholicism
as the state religion.[1] The support, however, has been spelled out
in four articles which seek to extend the reach of the State so
far into ecclesiastical matters, that it is impossible for the State to
maintain that it is officially disinterested with respect to the
Catholic religion.[2]

The paradoxical situation of a State which concerns itself officially with the Catholic religion, but which is not a Catholic
State, is further accentuated by the fact that the Holy See has
never accepted *de jure* the extensive claims which the Argentine
constitution has asserted. A *modus vivendi* between Rome and
Buenos Aires has been accomplished, but settlement of the claims
has never been regularized in a Concordat. Thus Argentina for

1. Juan Casiello, *Iglesia Y Estado en la Argentina, prólogo de su Eminencia, el
Señor Cardenal Dr. Don Antonio Caggiana* (Buenos Aires, 1948), pp. 80, 95.
2. J. Lloyd Mecham, *Church and State in Latin America* (Chapel Hill, 1934),
p. 288, states that ". . . it certainly is the State religion just as much as is the
Established Church of England."

more than a century has "regulated" certain aspects of Catholicism in the latter's national existence and manifestation, and while the central authority of the universal Church has openly contested the regulation only on rare occasions, it has perpetuated a tacit protest, or reservation, in its official lack of recognition of the powers which Argentina claims.

Argentine secularist and Catholic students of the problem of Church-State relations both find much that satisfies their respective points of view in the existing arrangement. Secularists on the whole are happy with it because, they maintain, it keeps the religious question out of politics or at least reduces it to small proportions.[3] Catholics, many of whom in the past would have liked a closer approximation to a Catholic State, are consoled by the "Catholic orientation"[4] of the Constitution or by what Cardinal Caggiana has called the strong "Catholic stamp"[5] on the constitutional tradition.

The aspect of this tradition which appears to be most generous to the Catholic Church is found in Article 2 which states that the "Federal Government supports the Roman Catholic Apostolic Church." While there have been differences of opinion about just what *support* in this context entails, there seems to be no disagreement over the interpretation that it includes economic support. José Manuel Estrada has suggested that it may also oblige the Federal Government to protect the Church against possible Provincial despoliation.[6] Does the support call upon the State to

3. President Nicolás Avellaneda (1874–1880) paid tribute to the system with the assertion that it "has avoided among us those questions between Church and State which so deeply disturb the peace and the conscience of other South American Republics." Ricardo Rojas, *Obras de*, Vol. XIV (*La Literatura argentina, ensayo filosófico sobre la evolución de la cultura de la Plata, Los Modernos, Tomo I*) (Buenos Aires, 1925), p. 34.
4. Casiello, *op. cit.*, p. 98.
5. *Ibid.*, p. 19.
6. *La Iglesia Y El Estado, prólogo del* Dr. Rudolfo Rivarola (Buenos Aires, 1929), p. 43. (This is Volume XXVII in the series *Grandes Escritores Argentinos*, Director, Alberto Palcos.) Estrada was the outstanding Catholic intellectual of the second half of the nineteenth century. (See below, Ch. III, pp. 98–104.) The article cited was written originally in the 1870's, and probably shows the influence of the French Catholic writer, Montalembert, on Estrada. When it first appeared other Catholics in Argentina attacked it as unorthodox. They thought that it urged too much of a break with tradition in the claim that the Church should be "freed" from the State. The intra-Catholic controversy that had raged around the essay later embarrassed the editors of Estrada's works, and they omitted

provide religious instruction in the public school system? Does the pledge of support prohibit public authority from taking certain actions which might infringe upon ecclesiastical jurisdiction over Sacraments, notably matrimony? These are questions which have been the subject of prolonged disputes.[7]

During the 1860 Constitutional Convention (called to reincorporate the province of Buenos Aires into the Argentine federation) Félix Frías led a Catholic movement to resolve these and related questions through an amendment of Article 2. The text of Frías' proposal was: "The Roman Catholic Apostolic Religion is the religion of the Argentine Republic, whose government defrays the cost of worship (costea su culto). The government owes it the most effective protection and its inhabitants the greatest respect and the most profound veneration." [8] The proposal was rejected, largely as a result of a strong protest voiced by Sarmiento, who was to become President eight years later. From that time until Perón's unsuccessful and incompleted maneuver to "separate" Church and State in 1955 there was no serious undertaking to revise this article.

There is probably also a suggestion of pro forma support in the credal qualification that Article 77 establishes for the President and Vice President who must "belong to the Catholic Church." [9] The condition of eligibility does not appear to have been very strictly enforced at any time. While it has been suggested that a self-declared non-Catholic might be barred from either office, the provision seems to have been treated with the same breadth of interpretation with which the vast majority of Argentines are recognized as Catholics by virtue of having been baptized in the Church. At least one leading Freemason has not been considered ineligible for the Presidency in terms of the article.[10]

Two other articles seek to establish the power of the government to control important ecclesiastical appointments and other

---

the article from his collected works. An ironical fate overtook the piece in 1955 when Peronist sources reissued it to support a proposal to "separate" Church and State; see Hechos E Ideas, Año XVI, Tomo XXVII, Nos. 134–135 (June–July, 1955), p. 581 et seq.

7. These questions will be examined in detail in Chapter VI.

8. Casiello, op. cit., p. 95.

9. The qualification applies to no other federal officials.

10. Sarmiento was a Mason. See William Rex Crawford, A Century of Latin America Thought (Cambridge, 1944), p. 43.

arrangements within the Church. Article 68, section 19, authorizes Congress to "arrange the exercise of the ecclesiastical patronage in the whole nation," and section 20 of the same article provides the means for control of the admission of religious orders into the national territory. Article 83 vests important powers in the President. Under section 8 he "exercises the rights of the national patronage in the appointment of bishops for the Cathedral Churches, selected from three names proposed by the Senate." (In practice this appointment is a *presentation*, aspects of which will be considered below.) According to section 9 the President "makes effective or withholds the decrees of the Councils, the Bulls Apostolic, and Rescripts of the Roman Pontiff, subject to the approval of the Supreme Court; a law, however, being required when they contain general and permanent provisions." [11]

The Papacy has never acknowledged the existence of these powers, but the lack of recognition has not inhibited the Argentine government in exercising them. Moreover, in general they have not resulted in any lack of working harmony between the Holy See and Argentina. The harmony is generally considered to be the result of a *modus vivendi* which covers the most important issue at stake between the two, namely the appointment of bishops.[12] Appointments are achieved in the following manner.

When an episcopal see becomes vacant, the President transmits official notice of the vacancy to the Senate. The Senate then submits to the President the names of three clerics whom the Senate considers suitable for the post. The President selects one of the three names and *presents* it to the Holy See through diplomatic channels. Rome then normally extends a bull of *nombramiento* which authorizes the person presented to become bishop of the vacant see. This is done without any reference to the fact that the person has been presented by the President. Under Section 9 of Article 83 the President must then submit the bull to the Supreme Court. The Court generally responds with an *exequatur* approving the appointment but with specific reservations regarding the "rights of patronage," which, of course, the Holy See has in no way acknowledged in the bull. The President then

11. Casiello, *op. cit.*, p. 142 suggests that this section has become mainly a dead letter, except for the processing of episcopal appointments.
12. *Ibid.*, pp. 135–142.

issues the decree of appointment, and the appointee takes an oath to support the Constitution, with reservations regarding the "laws of God and the Church."

All this may seem like too much and too elaborate face-saving, but the *modus vivendi* keeps two theoretically irreconcilable positions from coming into general conflict. Under the Constitution neither the President nor the legislative and judicial authorities can avoid an obligation which is imposed on them by law. The Roman Catholic Church cannot condone a system of "lay investiture," and accordingly has found the means of keeping the canonical institution of bishops within its own jurisdiction without directly challenging the Argentine State.

The only modern case of a breakdown in these arrangements illustrates the peculiar resources which each party commands. The difficulty arose in 1923 during the Alvear administration.[13] The government presented in that year for the Archdiocese of Buenos Aires the name of Dr. Miguel de Andrea (then as now Titular Bishop of Temnos). Rome did not follow with the customary response, and after some delay the Nuncio at Buenos Aires informed the President that the Holy See found difficulty in conferring canonical investiture on the candidate. The President's reply was a renewal of insistence upon the appointment. Bishop Andrea publicly withdrew as a candidate, but the government refused to accept his resignation. The government continued to press for Andrea's appointment, and the Vatican's reply was that it was not obliged to make public the reason for its decision since the question was wholly within its own competence. After a lapse of a year and a half the difficulty was resolved with the presentation of another candidate whose investiture was authorized by Rome late in 1925.

A subsidiary problem arose before that date, however, when the Nuncio authorized an administrator *sede vacante* to take possession of the Archdiocese. The administrator came into conflict with the Minister of Foreign Affairs and Worship over the question of whether his temporary appointment should be processed through the Supreme Court in accordance with section 9. Eventually the Attorney-General ruled that since the documents

13. The case is discussed by Casiello in the pages just cited. See also Mecham, *op. cit.*, pp. 297–298.

had not come from Rome but only from the Buenos Aires Nuncia-ture, the section did not apply. The Supreme Court held other-wise, claiming jurisdiction under the section. The *de facto* posses-sion of the see by the administrator was not disturbed, however, and he continued in office until the permanent successor was agreed upon.

What this incident seems to show is that though the *modus vivendi* has been a useful device, it can prove inadequate to cer-tain situations. It leads both parties to respect each other's posi-tions, but it does not oblige either of them to concede any part of its own interest. Its history on the whole suggests that each party has taken and continues to take careful measure of the other, and this may explain why the system has worked so gen-erally well. Breakdowns in the system are obviously possible, but the record of the Andrea presentation indicates that a breakdown need not be fatal to the system.

Modern Catholic practice does not, of course, exclude the possibility of government presentation of candidates for episcopal and other Church offices. But a fundamental theoretical objection on the part of Catholics to the Argentine practice is that it rests on a unilateral assertion of the right of presentation. The Ar-gentine system is regalistic in that it involves an assumption that the power to appoint to ecclesiastical office inheres in the national sovereignty. The exercise of the power as a function of sovereignty becomes then a continual challenge to the view that the power to appoint rests with the Pope as head of the universal Church.

THE PATRONATO

Regalism is a centuries-old problem for Catholicism throughout the Iberian and Ibero-American nations. Its origins are medieval, but it was transferred to the American scene at the beginning of the Spanish and Portuguese colonization. The long-abiding issues which regalism involves cannot be settled in the present study. Nevertheless, the influence of a long regalistic tradition in Ar-gentina should be noted here.

The influence begins certainly with Ferdinand and Isabella who sought from the Pope a validation of their titles to the newly discovered lands. Alexander VI's response came in the so-called *bula de donación* of May 4, 1493. Under the Pope's grant the sovereigns were charged to organize the work of evangelization of the American natives. This was followed by other grants from Alexander VI, Julius II and Paul III, who awarded further responsibilities and privileges to the Spanish monarchs. On these grants is based the claim that Rome recognized from the beginning a right of patronage, or *patronato*, in the sovereign, because there was no other way of organizing the Church in the New World.[14]

Disputes between regalists and anti-regalists have centered in the issue of whether the *patronato* is an inherent right of sovereignty which various Popes have *recognized* or whether it is a right which the same Popes have *granted* to specific rulers. Modern Catholic authorities refer to the *Corpus Juris Canonici* which in Canon 1448 recognizes the *patronato* only as existing by *concession of the Church*. Some of them, however, recognize that prior to this formulation two views did exist and that the historical reality is that the regalistic thesis dominated Spanish colonial thought, and in Argentina the thesis has continued to operate from the beginning of the republican period.[15]

Argentine public authority began to concern itself with problems of the *patronato* at a very early period, even before the Republic as such had been formed. The Revolutionary *Junta* in August 1810 desired to fill a canonicate in the Buenos Aires Cathedral which had become vacant. This was during the period in which the exterior relations of both civil authority and the Church were somewhat ambiguous. Civil authority rested nominally on a resistance to the Bonapartist usurpation in the Peninsula, and the position of the Church was accordingly clouded. The *Junta* sought originally from Dean Gregorio Funes an opinion on whether it could fill the vacancy. The *Junta's* question was whether the *patronato* pertained to the person of the King or the *sovereignty* of the Crown. If the *Junta* was exercising the sovereignty of Napoleon's captive, could the *Junta* fill the canoni-

14. A standard Argentine work on the *patronato* is Faustino J. Legón, *Doctrina Y Ejercicio del Patronato Nacional* (Buenos Aires, 1920). Its juridical significance is treated from a frankly regalistic point of view in the classic nineteenth-century work by Dalmacio Vélez Sarsfield, *Derecho Público Eclesiástico* (Buenos Aires, 1871). Casiello, *op. cit.*, pp. 23–55 and p. 125 *et seq.*, offers an anti-regalistic view. See also Mecham, *op. cit.*, pp. 12–44.
15. Casiello, *op. cit.*, p. 53.

cate?[16] Funes' reply was that the *Junta* could not. The *Junta* then consulted another priest, who gave a largely identical answer. Ricardo Rojas has pointed out that the *Junta* was anxious to establish its own authority, but at the same time its members did not want to offend against Catholic orthodoxy.

The situation remained clouded for many years, but the full force of regalism came to flourish in the period of Argentine history that was dominated by Bernardino Rivadavia after 1820. By the end of 1822 Rivadavia had established state control over the Church in almost all of its personnel and property aspects.[17] Churches and Church property came under the jurisdiction of the government, and not only the diocesan clergy but also the religious orders were subjected to the most detailed regulation by public authority. At the same time the cost of maintaining Churches and their clergy was assumed by the government.

Some students see in the Rivadavian moves the logical extension of the *patronato* into the creation of a national Church with its clergy firmly tied to the national authority rather than to Rome. Catholic writers on the whole take a different view. While they are critical of Rivadavia's reforms,[18] they are reluctant to see in them an anti-Roman intent or a purpose of severing the Argentine Church from the universal body.[19] Rivadavia is for them an historical figure who was personally a sincere, practicing Catholic, but who erred in subjecting religion to an excess of state control. According to this view he sought to correct abuses which had grown up because of the unsettled condition of the Church, and if his remedies were not good, they merely show a mistake in judgment not an intention of weakening the position of the Church in Argentine society. Whatever Rivadavia's motives may have been, there seems to be little doubt that the effect of his ecclesiastical reform was a consolidation of regalistic strength which has continued in uninterrupted sway ever since. Though the liberal, centralist political system that Rivadavia constructed dissolved

16. Rojas, *Obras,* Vol. 14, pp. 36–37.
17. Mecham, *op. cit.,* pp. 276–277.
18. Félix Frías, *Escritos Y Discursos* (Buenos Aires, 1884), Vol. III, p. 110. Frías was a major Catholic politician between 1860 and 1880. (See below, Ch. III, p. 77 *et seq.*) In numerous other passages, however, Frías treats Rivadavia more kindly.
19. Casiello, *op. cit.,* p. 76.

later into the chaos on which was eventually built the long dictatorship of Rosas, the claims of the *patronato* suffered no diminution as a consequence, just as earlier they had survived intact in the violent transition from royal to republican government.

Rivadavia's actions, for all their vigor, failed to settle the question of appointments to episcopal sees then vacant. Bishop Lue of Buenos Aires had died in 1812, and no successor had been named. An appointment was finally achieved at the beginning of the Rosas period, with Bishop Mariano Medrano taking possession of the diocese. Medrano's occupancy did not pass without challenge. Pope Pius VIII had first appointed Medrano Bishop of Aulon *in partibus* in 1829. He was constituted by the Pope *motu propio* as Vicar Apostolic over the Buenos Aires diocese. Three years later Gregory XVI, again *motu propio,* named Medrano Bishop of Buenos Aires. In the regalistic view of the Buenos Aires rulers both papal actions were an affront to the claims of the *patronato*. Rosas, not yet a full dictator, had given pragmatic sanction to the first appointment in 1831. The second, however, was regarded as a more serious matter. If the government accorded recognition to Medrano as the appointee of the Pope in full possession of an Argentine see, the recognition would, of course, be a total abandonment of the claims of the *patronato*.

The government wished neither to postpone any longer the already overdue settlement of the Buenos Aires diocese nor to concede any portion of its claim to patronal rights. Accordingly, the chief legal officer of the Rosas regime, Pedro Agrelo, established in 1833 a commission of 39 "citizens, theologians, canonists and jurists" to consult and advise the government on the rights of the *patronato*. The commission reported early in 1834 with a completely regalistic recommendation. The report was not quite unanimous, two lay members dissenting entirely from the recommendation, while a third member, the Friar, Buenaventura Hidalgo, insisted on reservations to protect the interests of the Holy See. On the basis of the report two months later, the government recognized Medrano as Bishop of Buenos Aires. (This was nearly 22 years after the death of his predecessor in the see.) The reason offered by Agrelo was that Medrano had originally, some years before, been proposed by the government and consequently his appointment did not violate rights of the *patronato*. Thus the papal authority asserted *motu propio* in 1829 and 1832 was simply not acknowledged.[20]

After Rosas had consolidated his dictatorship he issued in 1837 a decree which made null and void all documents coming from the Roman Pontiff after the date of May 25, 1810 which had not received the *pase* or *exequatur* of the Foreign Ministry. The only exception allowed was for documents "whose content relates solely" to the Sacrament of Penance.[21]

Late in the Rosas regime Bishop Medrano died. The dictator apparently felt that he was in a position to present the successor. He met opposition from the Pope's representative at Buenos Aires, and to overcome this opposition Rosas turned to Vélez Sarsfield for legal advice. Vélez reaffirmed the right of presentation, and the dictator pressed his claim.[22] Rojas states the nationalist view of this affirmation when he says: "Vélez had to choose between recognizing the supremacy of the Pope over the Argentine State by virtue of his universal power or recognizing the supremacy of the Argentine State over the Church, by virtue of the *patronato* conferred by the Holy See to the Kings of Spain and assumed by independent America as an attribute of its own sovereignty. He chose the latter with patriotic ability." [23]

From this it was but a short step to achieve the incorporation of the *patronato* into the Constitution of 1853. Indeed any other eventuality would have been surprising. A militant nationalism had from the beginning claimed the right, and the Constitutional Convention of 1853 was thoroughly nationalist in spirit. That its members were in large part practising Catholics, some of them clerics, who would not have wanted to challenge papal supremacy in the Church, did not change the situation. Regalism had acquired a firm hold in the River Plate region long before the Argentine Republic was born, and it had easily weathered the tumultuous early decades of national existence.

Since the adoption of the 1853 Constitution, however, some serious Catholic opinion has been critical of the baldly assumed

20. José Ingenieros, *La Evolución de las Ideas Argentinas* (Buenos Aires, 1925), Vol. IV, pp. 61–62.
21. *Ibid.*, pp. 86–87.
22. Casiello, *op. cit.*, p. 80.
23. *Obras*, Vol. 14, p. 33.

rights of the *patronato*. Some Catholics began to resist the adoption of the Constitution immediately after it was drafted because of their objections to the assumption of the right. But most of the Catholic resistance of this period was overcome through the efforts of the saintly Fray Mamerto Esquiú.[24] Esquiú's spirit of compromise probably set the precedents which Catholic opinion has since followed. Individual Catholics may from time to time attack the *patronato*, but their attacks do not stir up strong antagonisms in the Catholic population.

Moreover, individual Catholic positions in relation to the *patronato* shift from time to time as circumstances may determine. Frías, the most versatile politician in defense of Church interests, wanted at one time, as we have seen, a closer union between Church and State. Failing that, he leveled a strong journalistic and parliamentary attack on the *patronato*. His grounds were that the *patronato* was a violation of the freedom of religion in that it produced direct State intervention in only one creed and therefore was a discrimination against Catholics.[25]

However, when Estrada published his work on Church and State,[26] it was Frías who led the Catholic attack on Estrada. Estrada was then arguing—with more skill in logic than Frías ever commanded—that the *patronato* amounted to a discrimination against Catholics and that the Church itself should be freed from its hold. Frías had once also contended that it was a discrimination, but he now saw in Estrada's essay the beginning of a move to "separate" Church and State. This was an entirely unacceptable prospect to Frías, and probably to most of the Catholics of his times. His energetic counsel then became to leave well enough alone. While recent Catholic judgment does not agree with Frías' evaluation of Estrada's position and holds that all the latter wanted was to get rid of the *patronato*,[27] the leave-well-enough-alone attitude seems to have dominated Catholic thought since Frías' times. A kind of oblique authoritative confirmation of this attitude may even be seen in the statement which the Argentine hierarchy has issued on various occasions since 1931. The

24. Casiello, *op. cit.*, p. 91 *et seq.* See also below Ch. III, pp. 91–97.
25. *Escritos Y Discursos,* Vol. III, p. 108 *et seq.*, Vol. IV, p. 108 *et seq.*
26. See footnote 6.
27. Casiello, *op. cit.*, p. 95 *et seq.*

statement has offered specific condemnation of movements to "separate" the civil and ecclesiastical powers.[28] This does not indicate episcopal approval of the *patronato*, but since it is an essential part of the "union," such as it is, Catholic attacks upon the *patronato* would probably not receive encouragement.

RELATIONS WITH THE HOLY SEE

From the Catholic point of view the desirable solution for the problem of the *patronato* and related difficulties would be in the form of a Concordat between the Holy See and the Argentine Republic. A Concordat might not change very much the present Church-State pattern of relations, but it would put them on a different basis. It would end the unilateral determination of certain features by the civil power and transfer them to an area of mutual agreement reached through the voluntary action of two parties.

From a strictly nationalist point of view, however, such a transfer would be an infringement on sovereignty. This point of view asserts that Argentina solved its "Church problem" all by itself through an insistence on its inheritance of the complete regalistic prerogative of the Spanish monarch. Nationalists argue that the Argentine State could have done nothing else, since at the beginning the Pope refused to recognize the new governments of Spanish-America. This resulted in a period of "incommunication" with Rome, and during this period the Argentine authorities alone were able to provide for governance of the Church. They cite the brief of Pius VII of January 30, 1816, to his "venerable brethren, Archbishops, Bishops and dear sons of America, subjects of the King of Spain," recommending "due obedience to your King." [29] If Rome refused to recognize the fact of the Argentine Revolution, the nationalists ask, what else could have been done other than the assumption of the full prerogatives of the *patronato?* The American *patronato* was still claimed by the King of Spain. Rome had a choice between continuing to recognize his rights and recognizing the new national sovereignties. The prevailing political and ecclesiastical trends apparently left little room for a

28. See below, Ch. VI, p. 184.
29. Casiello, *Iglesia Y Estado en la Argentina*, p. 58.

third possibility, which was that Rome might deal directly with the Church within a given geographical territory in disregard of the question of sovereignty.

Nationalists also refer to the later brief of Leo XII in 1824 calling upon the bishops to work for the return of peace in the regions under the rule of the King of Spain. Casiello reflects a recent Catholic doubt that this brief was intended for the American regions. It was, perhaps, intended only for Spain, then emerging from the internal disturbances of 1820–23.[30] The same author insists that the Papacy was at no time hostile to the idea of American independence, but that it had no means of informing itself about the situation in the New World. It was therefore waiting for clearer developments before it committed itself. Casiello points out that this was the course of action followed by nearly all the European governments at the time.

That the Papacy was then being pressured by Spain seems certain. Yet that the pressure was being resisted seems equally certain. Pius VII received in two private audiences the Friar Luis Pacheco, who had come as an emissary from Buenos Aires to plead for the appointment of bishops and for other acts to take care of the spiritual necessities of the country. Pacheco was vilified by the Spanish Embassy at Rome, and it was announced that he had not been received in any official capacity. The fact is, however, that he was received and the Pope listened to him.[31]

Argentina's neighbor, Chile, meanwhile was having slightly better luck at Rome. Chile's representative was received by the Pope in 1822, and the protests of the Spanish Ambassador were given the reply that the Common Father of Christianity could not deny attention to anyone who came to plead in the name of "spiritual necessities." At the same time the Ambassador was assured that no intention to offend against the claims of the Spanish King was involved. Out of the Chilean negotiations came the mission to Chile headed by Monseñor Juan Muzzi in 1824–25. (In Muzzi's party was the priest Giovanni Mastai Ferreti, who two decades later was to become Pius IX.) Muzzi visited Buenos

30. *Ibid.*, pp. 58–59; Mecham, *op. cit.*, pp. 94–95, supports a contrary view. See also Mecham, p. 93, for a long quotation by Cardinal Consalvi containing his views of the problems of the Church in America.
31. Casiello, *op. cit.*, p. 61.

Aires in 1824, but without any practical results, the government refusing to recognize any validity in his mission so far as Argentina was concerned.[32] After 1825 the incommunication between Buenos Aires and Rome was not absolute, but it was not fully terminated until the first negotiations over the Medrano appointment in 1829.[33]

This year also marks the beginning of the rise of Rosas. During his long tyrannical regime the regalistic principle continued to be asserted, as has already been noted. In 1855 the new Argentine Confederation sent one of its most eminent figures, Juan B. Alberdi, to Rome. Alberdi sought to negotiate a Concordat and President Urquiza apparently was in favor of it. The negotiations continued until 1859 but without result.[34] In 1882–83 there was a revival of the attempt to negotiate a Concordat. President Roca and Pope Leo XIII exchanged personal correspondence on the subject, but again without result. On this latter occasion the Pope desired to have the negotiations undertaken between plenipotentiaries meeting at Rome. Roca preferred, instead, to have the negotiations conducted at Buenos Aires. The Pope's letter of August 30, 1883, is quite conciliatory, however, on this point, indicating the Papal preference for Rome as the site of negotiations, but recognizing that this might not be possible for the Buenos Aires government to accept. In that case he suggested the Apostolic Delegate at Buenos Aires might be instructed to begin negotiations of a preliminary character with Roca's government.[35] This was not apparently the point on which the correspondence broke down, however. The nationalist tradition of unilateral determination received fresh impetus in the immediately following years, and a laicist movement within the government came into sharp conflict with groups of Catholic citizens. This gave rise to a political crisis, which eventually produced a break with the Vatican which was to last for several years.[36] Later Presidents were

32. Mecham, *op. cit.*, pp. 277–278.
33. *Ibid.*, p. 280.
34. *Ibid.*, pp. 290–291.
35. José Manuel Estrada, *Obras Completas de,* 12 vols. (Buenos Aires, 1899), Vol. XI, pp. 120–122.
36. At the root of this crisis was the great struggle over the secularization of education. The struggle and some related crises are discussed below, Chapter VI, pp. 190–193.

not disposed to open negotiations for a Concordat even after the breach had been healed.

In recent years the only open advocacy by Argentine authority of a Concordat has been that voiced by Provisional President Lonardi in September, 1955.[37] Lonardi's tenure in the Presidency was brief, and it is alleged that among the causes of his downfall was his position on a Concordat, which is supposed to have offended the strong nationalist view of the Church-State question.

RELIGIOUS LIBERTY IN ARGENTINA

As the foregoing suggests, a great deal may be said on the subject of the status of Catholicism in Argentina without arriving at a precise determination of what that status is in its entirety. Between the Catholic Church and the Argentine State a general harmony has prevailed which has rarely been broken. But ambiguities persist, because neither State nor Church is able to recognize *de jure* the respective full claims of the other. If the religious preoccupation of the Argentine State is chiefly with the Roman Catholic Church, where, it may be asked, does this circumstance leave the non-Catholic creeds? What is the position of other Churches, and how does the public law of the nation affect their adherents?

Most Argentines would reply that their country has a long record of observance of the principle of freedom of belief and worship. The earliest evidence of religious toleration was probably in the Constitution of 1819 which guaranteed "freedom of conscience." This Constitution also made Catholicism unequivocally the religion of the State. The President of the convention which produced this Constitution was a priest, Gregorio Funes, and eight other priests were members.[38] Freedom of conscience is not necessarily the equivalent of freedom of worship, and at the time there were hardly any persons professing a non-Catholic creed in the River Plate region. Freedom of worship seems, however, to have been the practical intent of the guarantee. For in the treaty with Great Britain in 1825 the Buenos Aires government pledged British subjects resident in Argentina the right to wor-

---

37. Arthur P. Whitaker, *Argentine Upheaval* (New York, 1956), p. 36.
38. Mecham, *op. cit.*, p. 276.

ship in their own Churches. The first Protestant Church in Buenos Aires was built in 1829.[39] Casiello identifies the earliest example of a formal guarantee of freedom of worship for Argentine nationals as that contained in Governor del Carril's Constitution for the Province of San Juan in 1825.[40]

The 1853 Constitution reiterated in Article 19 the earlier guarantee of freedom of conscience, while the right of freedom of worship was made specific in the same instrument in Article 14. This guarantee passed into the 1949 revision as a part of Article 26, which includes the freedom among the rights which all inhabitants of the nation enjoy "in accordance with the laws which regulate the exercise thereof." The phrase quoted probably indicates that at no time has the Argentine State regarded any creed, Catholic or non-Catholic, as being absolutely beyond its power to regulate or otherwise affect in its public manifestations. At the same time the important aspect of the guarantee is that it perpetuates the tradition according to which the Argentine government does not impose the observance of a particular creed on anyone.

While Argentina has had in practice a long history of religious tolerance, a genuine diversity of creeds such as exists in the United States has never fully developed. The immigration pattern in the nineteenth century simply did not produce it, as it did in the United States, although some German and English Protestants entered the country and there has been a significant Jewish immigration from eastern Europe. Questions of freedom of belief and worship, where they have arisen, have not grown out of the problem of tolerance of diversity, but out of arrangements between the Catholic Church and the civil authorities. Some of these will be examined below in Chapters V and VI.

Though the pledge of tolerance has been given to all creeds, Catholicism is clearly on a different footing from the others. The difference is formalized in the Constitutional provisions which have been referred to, but beyond that there is the fact that Catholicism has had a peculiar place of its own in the organic development of the nation. The stresses and strains of national

39. *Ibid.*, p. 279.
40. *Op. cit.*, p. 113.

growth have directly involved Catholicism in the major issues of almost every important stage of political and social evolution. A study of the inter-action between the main currents of nationalism and Catholicism in the nineteenth century helps to explain not only the character of Argentine Catholicism but also of Argentine nationalism itself. To this study the following two chapters will be devoted.

CHAPTER II

The Evolution of Argentine Nationalism

THE forces which were to give Argentine nationalism its unique character were first set loose by the revolution which separated the colony from the Spanish Crown. The continual play and influence of these forces on the River Plate society throughout most of the nineteenth century make of Argentine nationalism an historical process marked by distinctive stages of development. The purpose of this chapter is to present a summary of the process. In the following chapter an analysis of Catholic thought bearing on Argentine nationalism will be undertaken. For these purposes the terminal dates may be fixed as the years 1810 and 1880.

The roots of nationalism probably go back beyond 1810, but the date marks the emergence of a political entity which, though it was vague and ill-formed, nevertheless grew into the modern Argentine state. The Buenos Aires *cabildo* and the *cabildo abierto* in that year represented the stronger and better organized elements in the colonial society. In the acceptance of political authority, the *cabildos* were in a position to make a conscious choice between the several alternatives offered as a result of the Napoleonic occupation of the mother-country. They chose to reject for the time being any ties to an extraterritorial sovereign and to establish executive power in the three-man *Junta,* which in turn was expected to be responsible to the broadly representative *cabildo abierto.*

This action did not sever the nominal relations with the legitimate and deposed monarch, and the arrangement had a basic internal weakness in that it failed to recognize the rights and interests of the provinces other than Buenos Aires. Nevertheless, the decision was the beginning of the Argentine nation. This claim rests not on the particular decision itself, even though it virtually resulted in the national independence which was proclaimed six years later. It rests rather on the fact that the action showed that the River Plate society contained elements sufficiently strong and sufficiently organized to produce a free decision in terms of its own interests at a time of crisis. The trans-Atlantic leading-strings had begun to weaken.

The other terminal date, 1880, may be more symbolic than absolute. It has been selected because it is the year in which the city of Buenos Aires was brought under the jurisdiction of the national government. Argentine independence had begun with the city playing a dominant role. The political and economic strength of Buenos Aires—city and province—gave it dominance over the rest of the nation at various times in the first seventy years of national existence. The city of Buenos Aires achieved an even greater political importance after 1880, but if the nation had not grown as a whole and if it had failed to acquire an integrated character, "federalization" of its most important social unit could never have taken place. For this reason it appears that the process of nationalism was essentially complete by 1880, and the completion is symbolized by the new position of the city of Buenos Aires.

THE ELEMENTS OF NATIONALISM

During the seventy years between 1810 and 1880 Argentine nationalism offered a very lively drama on the stage of history. It was marked by conflict between good and evil with heroes and villains playing major roles. It revealed to the nation the deep internal contradictions present in its own character, as violence and brutality contended with chivalry and honor, and the country alternated between decency and degradation.

Two basic concepts of the Argentine nation were held by the most influential leaders in this period. While these concepts were in sharp conflict, the conflict seemed capable of resolution. Whether full resolution of the conflict ever was achieved is an open question. It is certain, at least, that the great efforts of many men were expended to that end, and it is equally certain that the conflict left its permanent mark on the national character.

From the one side the idea of an Argentine nation seems to

have been originally the exclusive product of learned and in-
quiring minds. Nationalism's early spokesmen may have been of
differing ideologies, but they were united in their respect for
human dignity. At the beginning they were genuine liberals on a
rationalist basis like Moreno, or liberals with autocratic tendencies
like Rivadavia, or arch-conservatives like the priest Castro Barros.
In later years the natural continuum of these and many like
figures would be found in such men as Echeverría, Alberdi, Zuviría
and Sarmiento. In neither period were all these men drawn from
the uppermost economic stratum, but they formed a kind of
natural aristocracy in the sense that they were leaders who were
more likely to act on principle than on interest, on reason more
than emotion, and with a sense of the long-range objective in preference to the immediate and temporary success.

Contrast these examples of integrity, however, with some of the
unprincipled scoundrels who have also contributed to the making
of the Argentine nation: Juan Manuel de Rosas and Fray Félix
Aldao, to cite both a major and minor example. The question
immediately arises whether Rosas, Aldao and the numerous other
demagogues and *caudillos,* great and small, can be dismissed as
unrepresentative of Argentina. Can they be canceled out of the
formula of Argentine nationalism on the ground that the good
which their opponents upheld eventually triumphed, and that
therefore these men lack real significance? The answer is, probably not. For if the men of integrity have won the struggle most
of the time, these other less laudable persons have not ceased to
be important. They too represent something real and effective in
the character of the nation.

In seeking to identify what it is that they represent—as well as
what their opponents have stood for—we can follow the analysis
offered in various forms by many Argentine authors, from whose
ranks we can draw three examples, each distinct in his approach
but in substantial agreement with the other two: Sarmiento, José
Manuel Estrada and Ricardo Rojas.

Sarmiento defines the problem in his classic work *Facundo.*[1] As
is well known, Sarmiento's book was a biographical study of the

1. Buenos Aires, 1933. It was originally published at Santiago in 1845 and has
gone through numerous editions. A fuller title is *Facundo; civilización y barbarie
en las pampas argentinas.*

caudillo Quiroga. The author was less interested in biography *per se* than he was in using his work as a vehicle to carry an explanation of his country to the rest of the world. It was written in exile and in wrath, which circumstances acccount for the numerous errors of detail in which the work abounds. Yet for more than a century no attempted criticism has disproved the basic validity of the main theme which Sarmiento was endeavoring to expound in this book. The theme was that Argentina represented a violent struggle between *la civilización* and *la barbarie*. Civilization and barbarism in the fourth decade of Argentine existence were engaged in a deadly warfare which pitted the city against the plain, armed ignorance with weapons to destroy science, and made savagery the fearful challenger of law and order. It was this warfare between the two great forces that Sarmiento saw as the central issue in his nation's history. It has been pointed out that the terms of definition of the conflict, *civilization* and *barbarism*, may not have been original with Sarmiento.[2] It was, however, Sarmiento's original and forceful intelligence that put the problem of Argentine national existence into a focus that made the problem comprehensible. Sarmiento saw in his society all the elements of civilization: wealth, learning, honor, and self-discipline. He also saw poverty, ignorance and brutality, in a word *la barbarie*. He was unique among the leaders and leaders-to-be of his times in realizing that barbarism, as long as it remained a vital element in the social complex, could as readily control and direct Argentine society as could civilization.

Thus it is that the barbarous enters into Argentine nationalism as a major force. It explains Rosas, Aldao, Quiroga and the host of other *gaucho* leaders. They were the spokesmen for the uncivilized masses and the fearful conditions under which the masses lived. Earlier political leaders, whether rationalist liberals or traditional conservatives, seem to have assumed that in solidifying the new Argentine society order could be established through the use of trained intelligence, through law, through a social system controlled from the principal urban centers. They forgot or ignored the prevalence of the plainsmen and their semi-savage way of life. Sarmiento recognized the error and gave to this uncivilized

2. Allison Williams Bunkley, *The Life of Sarmiento* (Princeton, 1952), pp. 210–211.

element the importance that it deserved in the growth and construction of the Argentine nation.

One can speculate about why previous leaders ignored this
force of the masses. Perhaps it was because the leaders had hoped
too naively to transform the character of the masses in the process
of constructing an independent nation. If that is so, however,
why did the masses find their spokesmen in the butchers and
tyrants of 1830–50 rather than in the civilized leaders who had
hoped so well for them? Why did the Argentine plainsmen elevate
Rosas to the dictatorship at almost the same time that the North
American frontiersmen were raising Jackson to constitutional
leadership? José Manuel Estrada suggests some answers to these
questions in *La Política Liberal Bajo La Tiranía de Rosas*.[3]

Estrada takes the problem back to the period in which the national independence was being won. The Argentine Revolution,
he says, was the product of two distinct, great forces. On the one
hand he identifies a primary force as the leaders of the Revolution, the intellectuals who conceived the idea of national freedom
and of a national society. On the other, was the force that turned
the ideas of the leaders into reality: the masses who were willing
to bear arms, to fight, and to die in order to establish a new nation.

Once national existence was assured, however, the intellectuals,
according to Estrada, sought to exclude the masses from participation in the public affairs of the new state.[4] There were many
reasons for this attitude: natural distrust and lack of effective
communication between the two groups; on the part of one an
emphasis upon order, stability, and science, and on the part of the
other an emphasis on strength, freedom and superstition. But
whatever the reasons, the masses felt deprived of something that
was rightfully their own. Their power had already been made
evident in the battles of the Revolution. In time they found the
leaders who could turn their raw and unrefined power into the
dominant force in society.[5]

3. Published as Volume LXXXIII in the series *Grandes Escritores Argentinos*,
Alberto Palcos, ed. (Buenos Aires, 1925), *prólogo de* Pedro Goyena. It was first
issued in Buenos Aires in 1873, and forms Vol. IV of Estrada's *Obras Completas*
(Buenos Aires, 1899). References in this text are to the edition first cited.
4. *Ibid.*, p. 6 *et seq.* This is a principal theme of Estrada's first chapter.
5. Estrada himself would have to concede some exceptions to his blanket indict-

Estrada wrote 25 years after Sarmiento had published his *Facundo,* and a different terminology is characteristic of each book, but the parallels between Sarmiento's *civilization* and *barbarism* and Estrada's *intellectuals* and *masses* are obvious.[6] Estrada is no more the friend of barbarism than is Sarmiento. He is perhaps more severe in his judgment of the intellectuals, however. He implies that the *clase pensadora* should have recognized that the great problem following liberation was to maintain a balance between the two forces and that it was the obligation of this class to solve the problem. They chose, on the contrary, to ignore it. This was dangerous because both forces had been responsible for bringing the nation into being, and in its development one could no more be ignored than the other.

A somewhat similar view of the historical content of Argentine nationalism is offered by the twentieth-century Argentine writer, Ricardo Rojas. In his history of Argentine literature Rojas suggests at one point an analysis of the problem in terms of military versus civil power.[7] He says that the liberation movement of 1810 had two objectives: (1) the independence of the nation to be achieved through military action, and (2) the establishment of Argentine democracy through civil action. The military action, Rojas suggests, was a centrifugal force and it constantly operated out toward the periphery of the republic, away from the centers of civilization. The civil action, on the contrary, was centripetal, and its appeal was to what Rojas has called the "historic conscience" of the nation. It is implied that the centrifugal force tended to fragmentize order and responsibility and to make for chaos, while the civil action, the appeal to the "historic conscience" was lost on the masses who could not properly comprehend it.

Rojas does not leave this problem without a solution. He sees in the *"ideal de Mayo,"* promulgated by the young exiles of the

---

ment of the intellectuals; Moreno is specifically exempted by name and others who shared his democratic orientation, by implication.

6. At the time of the writing of Estrada's work, Sarmiento was President of the Republic, while Estrada was the first occupant of the Chair of Civic Instruction in the *Colegio Nacional,* a chair which Sarmiento had created and which established Estrada as Argentina's first political scientist.

7. *Obras de Ricardo Rojas,* Vol. 13, pp. 853–854. The reference by no means exhausts Rojas' great systematic evaluation of the Argentine national character. This particular citation is offered, however, because of its congruence with the views of Sarmiento, Estrada, and many other Argentine writers.

1830's, the "genetic clay" from which the Argentine nation emerges and in the molding of which both powers are effective. Treatment of the "*ideal de Mayo*" is reserved for subsequent pages in this chapter. For the present it need merely be noted that Rojas, like the other two authors cited, acknowledges the presence of two contradictory forces in the evolution of the Argentine nation.

Whether these forces are called *civilization* and *barbarism* or whether they are given some other labels, both seem to be universally recognized as basic factors in the making of Argentina. The difference between them helps greatly to explain the ups and downs of Argentine national development and renders credible the vivid contrasts that have appeared within the Argentine cultural complex.

BLENDING THE ELEMENTS

If these two vital forces had remained constantly at war with each other, the history of Argentina would be a quite different thing from what it is. The years between 1810 and 1820 were characterized by the general, but by no means successful, dominance of the one force. After 1830 the second, barbarism, came into its own and held sway until 1852. Conceivably this pattern of alternation could have been perpetuated. If it had been, Argentina would have come into modern times as underdeveloped and as "backward" as many other Latin American states.

This, however, is not what happened. The two forces continued to be at work, but meanwhile Argentina grew from a small, sparsely populated country on the outer fringe of Western civilization into an important modern nation. While never large in terms of population, Argentina emerged as one of the integrated and responsible nations of the world before the nineteenth century was finished. In the middle of the century there was much in the internal structure of the nation that would have warranted a forecast to the contrary. The evolution, however, turned in the direction of civilization.

In seeking to locate the critical point in the evolutionary process, one turns necessarily to the group of exiles of the 1830's and to the loosely formed, perhaps merely nominal, organization in which many of the younger ones were banded together. The organization is known under the various names of *La Joven Argentina*,

La Joven Generación Argentina (both labels borrowed from Mazzini's *Young Italy*) or *La Asociación de Mayo*. The association was a clandestine lodge which had acquired some rudimentary organization in Buenos Aires during the early years of the Rosas tyranny. Its members were extremely young, perhaps too young to be taken seriously by the dictatorship. Nevertheless, in due time it became safer for most of them to be out of the country. Montevideo became their center, and it was there that their most notable document was published in 1839. This was the *Código* or *Creencia*, or, as it has come to be more generally known, *El Dogma Socialista*.[8] Its purpose was to present a systematic outline of bases on which a workable form of government could be constructed to avoid both the chaos and the tyranny which Argentina had experienced to date.

The *Dogma's* principal author was the poet Esteban Echeverría, who may have received some collaboration from Juan María Gutiérrez, the critic and future educator, and from Juan Bautista Alberdi, the "Father of the Constitution of 1853." The work is built around the fifteen "Symbolic Words," which the lodge had previously adopted as the outline of its social creed.[9]

The word *Socialista* in the title does not mean *socialist* in any modern sense of the term. More than anything else it probably represents the general reaction of the young Argentines to the extreme individualism of the preceding generation of intellectuals. The latter, under the influence of eighteenth century philosophy, had focused its political ideas on the individual. The focus of the new generation's thought was society, not the individual. On this basis the term *socialista* becomes little more than an affirmation of a point of interest for the group.

This does not, of course, exclude the possibility that the authors of the document had been influenced by the early pre-Marxian socialist writers in Europe. Echeverría had spent a good deal of time in France. He had been exposed to the works of Saint-Simon

8. The *Dogma* has gone through many editions. Probably the best documented is that issued by the University of La Plata in 1940. It carries a long introductory comment by Alberto Palcos and contains a host of documents related to the history of the work.

9. José Ingenieros, *La Evolución de las Ideas Argentinas* (Buenos Aires, 1925), Vol. IV, p. 259, suggests that the association perhaps never formally approved Echeverría's draft. Whatever the merits of the question raised, the *Dogma* remains the principal document historically linked to the group.

and Comte, although Ingenieros asserts that during Echeverría's European sojourn he remained a firm disciple of the doctrines of Condillac.[10] Ingenieros on the whole seems willing to dismiss the socialism of the *Dogma* as not much more than fashionable literary declamation.[11] He does, however, recognize that there are points of similarity between the *Dogma* and the *Exposition de la doctrine saintsimonienne*, which was published by Saint-Simon's followers after his death.[12]

Alberto Palcos attributes the major inspiration of the *Dogma* to Lamennais. He suggests that Echeverría made a conscious choice between the doctrines of Lamennais with their proven popular appeal and those of Saint-Simon and Comte, which were still "too much intellectualized" to attract a numerous following.[13] Ingenieros too accords a certain influence to the work of Lamennais, but he does not give it the all-inclusive scope that Palcos recognizes in it.[14]

Most students of the *Dogma's* origin and history agree that its contents were greatly influenced by European sources which Echeverría had absorbed between 1826 and 1830. The real purpose of the work, however, is the reconstruction of Argentine society. Its aim is not to Europeanize Argentina, but to develop the means whereby the resources of the new nation may be organized to provide a decent life for its inhabitants.

The long-range influence of the *Dogma* itself—considered apart from the subsequent influence of its supporters—is somewhat elusive. It was presented originally as a social creed which was subscribed to by many of the men who were to shape Argentina after 1853. But these men were not of a character that was likely to be limited or restrained by a profession of faith given many years earlier. While they undoubtedly continued to adhere to much of the spirit of the *Dogma*, it is not always possible to identify its direct consequences in later developments. If, however, one ac-

10. *Ibid.*, pp. 245–246.
11. *Ibid.*, p. 314: "El socialismo de la *Creencia* era una simple declamación literaria, una actitud personal conforme con la última moda."
12. *Ibid.*, p. 247.
13. *Loc. cit.*, p. xl.
14. *Op. cit.*, p. 262. "Para quien haya leído *las Palabras de un Creyente*, y sobre todo *El Libro del Pueblo*, fácil es advertir que esta declamación preliminar es una glosa, no mejorada de los anátemas de Lamennais contra las tiranías europeas."

cepts Rojas' judgment that the emergence of the *Joven Argentina* marks the beginning of the resolution of the conflict between two opposing forces, the *Dogma* then becomes the most logical point of departure for analysis of the work of the generation of 1853.

In this connection a primary inquiry should be directed to whether the *Dogma's* authors and subscribers recognized the two vital elements which have previously been identified as the sources of Argentine nationalism. The text of the document shows that they did, although the recognition was in narrower and more strictly political terms than those which Sarmiento was to employ a few years later. The *Dogma* acknowledged that the first quarter-century of the new nation had been filled with the strife of two opposing camps, the Federalists and the Unitarists. It would be an oversimplification to say that the Federalists had represented barbarism and the Unitarists, civilization. Nevertheless at the time of writing the Federalists in power were behaving like barbarians, while the defeated Unitarists by comparison appeared on the whole to have been greatly better. Echeverría, however, did not choose sides. In the fifteenth "Symbolic Word" the association had called for an "Abnegation of the sympathies which might link us to the two great factions which have disputed power during the Revolution." In developing this "word" in the text of the *Dogma*, Echeverría threw out the question of which side had been right. What appeared to him as wrong was the internal warfare which the struggle between the two had visited on the nation. Therefore he and his associates refused to join either camp. If they were to do anything for the nation they would have to rise above the strife.[15]

The practical political instinct of the inexperienced authors of the *Dogma* should be noted. Although they condemned both sides, they realized that any workable solution in the future would require some cooperation from those who had been bitter antagonists. Thus Echeverría left the door open for the survival of the federal form, even though he did not approve of the Federalists.[16] He was also aware that the Unitarist ranks included some impor-

15. In the Palcos edition of the *Dogma* Echeverría's treatment of this theme is found on p. 219 *et seq.*
16. *Ibid.*, p. 224.

tant elements which any future non-dictatorial government would want to attract. Ingenieros points out that the Unitarists who shared an exile in Montevideo with the *Joven Argentina* were sharply antipathetic to Echeverría. He in turn attacked them in later writings, but through the *Dogma* he hoped to "seduce them, if possible." [17]

There are other portions of the *Dogma* that tend to support an attitude reminiscent of "a plague on both your houses." Thus the lodge's eighth "Symbolic Word" had called for a reexamination of the "glories" and "reputations" that the brief history of the nation had so far produced. What is implied is a rejection of the *status quo* as seen through the eyes of either contending group, to be followed by a "revision of values," which would have resulted in a deflation of the claims of both sides. The Federalists in power under Rosas would have been the most obvious target of such a revision, but Ingenieros asserts that the revision would have challenged primarily the claims of the opposing camp.[18]

A second important inquiry regarding the *Asociación de Mayo* relates to what its members did to produce a solution when they became in large part the rulers of Argentina after 1853. Of their general influence on the course of national history there seems to be little doubt. Estrada, who undertook the first comprehensive criticism of the *Dogma*, asserted that its significance lay in the fact that there was scarcely a major figure of the later nineteenth century who had not contributed in some way to the content of the statement or who had not subscribed to its creed. Estrada also judged that it contained the key to Argentine public policy for the time in which he was writing, when *La Joven Generación* had become the "governing generation." [19] Estrada's evaluation is limited to the strictly political elements in Argentine life at the time. A later scholar, Ingenieros, has suggested the broader scope of the association's influence on all of Argentine society by singling out the six major figures of the lodge whose names are associated with the social and cultural history of the second half of the cen-

17. Ingenieros, *op. cit.,* Vol. IV, p. 320.
18. *Ibid.,* p. 266. "La revisión fue, aquí, contra los unitarios, lo que no es de sorprender en jóvenes que no desesperaban de regenerar al país bajo los auspicios de la Federación."
19. *Op. cit.,* p. 31.

tury: Echeverría,[20] Alberdi, the historian López, Mitre, the historian, military leader and politician, Juan María Gutiérrez, the literary figure, and Sarmiento.[21]

Not everyone will agree with the implication that these are the six "greatest" of the association. But Ingenieros' judgment delineates the greatly expanded scope of the lodge's influence on future Argentine life. Its members formed what was essentially a political group, but in their maturity they came to direct and influence much more than the political system alone. Letters and art and learning, statesmanship, industry, and military affairs all came under their sway. In a word it was the *nation* that they took hold of and which they organized into a definite form.

If theirs was a work of over-all social organization, as it is generally conceded to have been, this fact intensifies the importance of the question suggested above, namely, what did the organizers do to reconcile and bring into a manageable system the two contradictory forces that had been at work in Argentina since 1810? The answer probably lies in three features which characterized the Argentine state and the national society after 1853.

The first of these certainly is a tactical shift of liberalism toward a course of realism and away from the doctrinaire idealism which liberals had avowed down to 1829. The early liberals, from Moreno to Rivadavia, had, with some exceptions, labored to create the ideal state within the ideal society. They had been imbued with the spirit of the Enlightenment, and their guides to action had been books, written constitutions, statutes. They thought of Argentina in terms of the city of Buenos Aires, which since 1776 had increasingly dominated the regional development and which had become the scene of a great intellectual ferment. For the most part the rest of the country weighed much less in their consideration.

The authors of the *Dogma*, however, came to regard the earlier liberal position as one of sterility. In their exile they argued that

20. This would have to be a posthumous influence, since Echeverría was dead long before 1853.
21. *Op. cit.*, Vol. IV, p. 255. These men were all members of the association, but the intensity of their relationship to it during exile was not uniform. Sarmiento, for example, was not in close contact with the others for much of the time, and Ingenieros notes, p. 314, that he was regarded by his associates as a "loco sin remedio."

future liberal leaders could not return to it, but must strive to construct a government in accord with the "necessities of the country." They were no less devoted to the idea of a free society, but they refused to find a basis for it in the abstract logic of philosophers and legalists.

When they came to power in later years, the new generation of liberals showed themselves to be realists. They recognized the contingent nature of the political process. They did not seek to impose a system from above, but to construct from the ground up. Their shift in tactics greatly diminished the doctrinaire factor in Argentine liberalism. This circumstance in turn gave a more realistic recognition of the condition as well as of the power of the Argentine masses.[22] It produced the first workable unity between the divisive elements of Argentine nationalism.

This development is attested to by many events of the organization period. It is apparent in the attitude of the victors in the battle of Caseros, which spelled the end of Rosas' barbarism. There it was promised that there would be no reprisals and that the future Argentine state would not differentiate between those who had fought the tyranny and those who had suffered it. It is shown in the political combinations of *caudillos* and intellectuals in this period. It is also demonstrated in the leadership tactics of such genuine intellectuals as Mitre and Sarmiento. These men in the Presidency displayed energy and decisiveness in a hardly less robust way than that of the traditional *caudillos*. They were not above an appeal to the masses, and they won from them admiration and support which their prototypes of an earlier generation would have scorned.

Respect for the accomplishments of these men is not meant to suggest that they ushered in the millennium in Argentina. All the crooked and twisted paths could not be made straight in a single generation. The political processes were not always conducted with scrupulous honesty, and the leaders suffered, like most men, from human faults and imperfections. Sarmiento, for example, with his extraordinary vanity and ego-centricism could be a liability for national unity as readily as an asset. Mitre for all the demonstrations of his "civilization" and in spite of his professed disdain for the role of *caudillo* could on occasion behave as badly

22. The implications of this move will be treated in Chapter IV.

as any of the leading barbarians. His tenure of the presidency in 1861–62 was patently illegal and had been achieved through force of arms. Urquiza, the "reformed" *caudillo*, had played a genuinely useful role in uniting the nation and in holding it together in spite of Mitre's machinations between 1852 and 1860. Yet Mitre and Sarmiento treated him with contempt, and failed unpardonably to comprehend the contributions that Urquiza's leadership was making to national unity. On the other hand, Alberdi and many of the lesser intellectuals stood firmly on Urquiza's side.

With due allowance for human frailty and for the magnitude of their task, it is still to the men of 1853 that credit must be given for creating the modern Argentine nation. They not only pulled down an oppressor, but they also cut the notion of a free society loose from its doctrinaire moorings. Time has shown that they were probably guilty of errors of judgment and of mistaken zeal, and the strife that broke out among them from time to time reflects no great credit on any of them. They did, however, guide Argentina into an abundant realization of her own potentialities.

The second feature to mark the accomplishments of this period is the emergence of the vital institutions that characterize a free society. In the fragmented nation of the previous period, dominated by *personalismo*, no such development was possible. But the period following 1853 is marked by the formation of institutions, official and non-official, which had been the dreams of the earlier liberals: a free press and a great publishing industry; banks to further the economic development of the country; revitalized universities and technical and scientific institutes to serve the population.

However, it is probably in the establishment of the institutions of government that the generation of 1853 showed their real genius. They recognized, as many of the earlier liberals had failed to do, that the governance of Argentina must take a federal form. The significance of this decision might easily be undervalued. Rosas had headed a federal organization—of a sort. After his fall the various provincial governors had made in 1852 a pact known as the *Acuerdo de San Nicolás*. The pact called for a Constitutional Convention and it also indicated that a federal constitution should emerge from the convention. Therefore it might be said that the new organizers of the country were confronted with a *fait accompli* and really had no choice in selecting between the federal and unitary forms.

To say this without qualification is to neglect the question of whether the federalism of the Constitution of 1853 was real or nominal. It could have been merely nominal, if the traditional dominance of Buenos Aires had been perpetuated. In times past both Unitarists and Federalists had attacked this problem of the dominance of the port city over the rest of the country, but the problem had never been solved. Among the causes of the collapse of Rivadavian centralism had been the resistance of the largest province to sharing its resources with the others. Under Rosas the federal form had been merely a convenience for extending the hegemony of Buenos Aires. In the interior provinces, however, where the desire for protection against the all-absorbing centralism of Buenos Aires had a long history, there had always been agitation for a genuine federalism. This agitation had never achieved very much, because Buenos Aires' overwhelmingly greater wealth and population offered a natural base of operations to any government, and the early liberals had sought to use it for domination of the country, whether they espoused a federal or unitary form.[23] After 1852 Buenos Aires refused for nearly a decade to join the new federation, and it was finally brought in only at the price of warfare. Buenos Aires' attitude in the 1850's undoubtedly helped to harden the federalist sentiments in the rest of the country, but the result of the new organization under the 1853 Constitution was something much closer to a genuine federalism and offered greater possibilities for provincial autonomy.

The weaknesses of Argentine federalism, as they have subsequently been made evident, should not be passed over in silence. A spirit of fair play in maintaining its essential character has not always been present: liberals and conservatives alike, when they have been in power in the national government, have frequently abused the system to the detriment of the provincial autonomy that the Constitution was established to safeguard. Yet the test of the wisdom of the decision of 1853 probably lies less in these abuses than it does in the fact that the federal form has survived for more than a century and that it is honored in the constitutional

23. There were, of course, exceptions in the liberal ranks, e.g., Gorriti who will be treated below, Ch. III, p. 50 *et seq.*

revision of 1949. The survival of the form has retained some vitality in the provinces, as is shown by the wealth and distinctive culture of such centers as Rosario, Santa Fe, Córdoba and Mendoza. It is true that the provinces do not have an autonomy comparable with that of the states in the North American union. Yet, in spite of these weaknesses which frequently operate to the detriment of provincial interest, the federal arrangement has probably saved the national government from the insupportable top-heaviness which would have resulted, if the power of the largest, single province had been left unchallenged by any other forces.

In this view Argentine federalism is in its origins quite dissimilar from the North American. In the latter case the federal form was used to weld together several independent units which voluntarily submitted themselves to a paramount authority of their own construction. With Argentina, however, federalism was a means of establishing a counter-balance to the power of a single unit which was capable of absorbing the whole direction of the nation. Only a partial success may be claimed for the means. Yet the degree of its success was probably sufficient to contribute to resolution of the conflict between the two opposing forces from which Argentine nationalism has arisen. *Civilization,* so far as it was represented by the educated, urban classes, was protected by the strength of the central government. The vitality and energy of the masses, the force that Sarmiento had called *barbarism,* found their natural channels in the internal development of the country, which provincial autonomy helped to make possible.

The third distinguishing feature of the organizing period between 1853 and 1880 is the emphasis upon universal education. An emphasis on education was not new to the River Plate area, but the note of universality was. The area had had a long history of higher education beginning with the University of Córdoba in 1619. Yet at the time of independence the vast bulk of the population was ignorant and illiterate. The independence leaders included in their ranks some men who, as will be apparent below,[24] saw the need for a system of popular education. From the beginning some efforts had been made in this direction, but the early days of the nation were too turbulent to permit any wholesale attack on this problem. In the Rosas period no genuine educa-

24. See Ch. III, pp. 54–55.

tional system could develop for many reasons, among them the fact that the regime itself could thrive only on the ignorance of the people.

After 1853, however, there was a deliberate policy to place education within the reach of all the people. The policy may have lacked unity in formulation and execution, since various jurisdictions, national and provincial, were involved, and private as well as publicly supported systems grew up. Yet there was a kind of unity in two aspects of this development.

First, there was the conscious drive of the new leaders to overcome the illiteracy and ignorance of the masses and thus cut down the assets of barbarism. This move is symbolized by Sarmiento, the "schoolmaster President," but he was not alone in the field. During his residence in the United States Sarmiento had come in contact with Horace Mann and was greatly influenced by the latter's ideas.[25] As a result he tried to transfer much of the North American development to the Argentine scene. Toward this end he was instrumental in establishing normal schools for the training of teachers and in bringing North American personnel to staff them. Sarmiento could be an interfering busy-body as readily as he could be an effective leader.[26] His methods, particularly the use of foreign personnel, were not always popular. Nevertheless, the drive which Sarmiento symbolizes did produce the desired results. Argentina came into the twentieth century with a substantial part of the battle against illiteracy already won.[27]

Secondly, it may be noted that the Argentine education movement acquired unity through the fact that it sought to embrace the whole population, not just the rising generation. It would be an exaggeration to claim an "adult education" character for this aspect of the movement. But special institutes, public libraries and other innovations, such as the voluntary offering of instruc-

25. Bunkley, op. cit., p. 280.
26. For example, while he was President he plunged into details of educational work that might better have been left to teachers and school administrators. He was capable of establishing by presidential decree the exact text-books to be used in given courses, even though logic would seem to require that these decisions be made at a lower executive level.
27. At the close of Sarmiento's presidency, there were 103,000 persons in school out of a total population of less than 2 million. See Ysabel F. Rennie, The Argentine Republic (New York, 1945), p. 116.

tion to working-men, helped to bring education to some segments of the mature population.

The significance of this general movement for helping to settle the conflict between civilization and barbarism is obvious. The latter's strength had its chief roots in the ignorance of the people. While education as a single factor did not put an end to barbarism, the education movement was nevertheless a successful long-range attack, and the increasing literacy of the people brought Argentina constantly closer to the civilization its leaders desired to cultivate.

SOME CONCLUSIONS ON ARGENTINE NATIONALISM

To single out these abstract concepts which have been used by Argentines to explain the contradictory nature of their own national character has been an aid in identifying the sources of Argentine nationalism. Because they are abstractions, however, they must not be understood to exclude many positive and concrete factors which ran a contemporaneous course through Argentine history. The heavy stream of southern European immigration into Argentina in the second half of the century is one of these factors. The various undertakings which resulted in skillful exploitation of the country's economic resources form another. The post-1853 influence of the power structure known as the "oligarchy" is still another.[28]

A key to the understanding of the institutions and movements of nineteenth century Argentina, however, is most clearly offered by the broadly sweeping abstractions which Sarmiento first formulated and which have been examined in the foregoing pages. Nationalism starts with the two great forces which he identified as civilization and barbarism. These forces may join together, as Estrada says that they did during the Revolution. They may struggle against each other as they did in the Rosas period. After 1853 the means of bringing them back together are: (1) a dominant realism in the new ruling class, which leads to abandonment of purely intellectual positions; (2) the establishment of institutions devised in accordance with the "necessities of the country"; and (3) an intensive movement in popular education.

28. The oligarchy will be treated in detail in Chapter IV, pp. 110–112.

CHAPTER III

Nationalism and Catholic Attitudes

THE powerful drives of Argentine nationalism touched many interests of the Catholic Church, and throughout the nineteenth century various spokesmen voiced the concern and reaction of Catholicism in the face of nationalism's succeeding developments. To understand the positions of these men some preliminary consideration of the relationship between the institution of the Church and the forces of nationalism is necessary.

THE CHURCH AND NATIONALISM

The basic challenge which a growing nationalism offered to Catholicism was one of adjustment to a radically changed power structure in society. It has been suggested earlier that the Church itself was too fraught with social potentialities to be ignored in any rearrangement of power after the collapse of the Spanish Empire.[1]

Until the beginning of the nineteenth century the system of power had centered in the Spanish Crown. If the ecclesiastical relations of the Crown were not always harmonious, they were at least traditional and familiar. They produced no staggering surprises and, with the exception of the expulsion of the Jesuits in 1767, no revolutionary changes.

Moreover, the fact that the political system, however weak, had a recognizable center of power, however imperfect, helped to bulwark the universality of the Church. The Spanish power system extended over six million square miles of territory. Its center was in Europe, but it touched Asia and engulfed the larger part of America. Its subjects represented most of the races of mankind.

1. See Ch. I, pp. 17–21.

Within the system flourished almost every stage of culture from Stone Age to modern European. This human diversity was matched in degree only by the dispersion of the empire over global distances that in an age of sailing ships made communication difficult and precarious. Within this far-flung and heterogeneous realm the Church had a single consistent mission, which was to Christianize the people and instruct them in faith and morals.[2] This mission had to operate on a geographic scale infinitely greater than that on which any previous evangelization had ever been carried out. It is therefore not surprising that the Church and Crown, the only two entities interested in introducing into the empire any element of homogeneity, should be closely linked and that the Crown should provide the channel through which the Church might carry out its universal mission.

But the vast hegemony of the Spanish Crown, of three centuries' standing, disappeared from the world in a decade. In a sudden cataclysm of such huge proportions no traditional institution could avoid a certain dislocation. For the Church with its claim to universality the threat of dislocation was extreme: the diversity of power in the new nations replaced the imperial unity to which the basic mission of the Church had been linked.

The purely formal question of Church-State relations in the new situation could be settled in some such way as has been outlined in Chapter I.[3] If, however, the new society was to remain in turmoil, as it did, a merely formal settlement offered little encouragement to those who hoped that Christian social thought would play a major role in the formation of the new society. Catholic political thinkers in Argentina have consequently been less concerned with Church-State relations than with the means to permeate the national society with Christian teaching. Especially is this attitude true of the clergy who participated in the independence movement.

If this is the abiding interest of Catholic thinkers, it must be asked why so many of the clergy joined the revolutionary movement at the beginning of the nineteenth century, a movement

2. This is not the place to evaluate the degree of zeal on the part of the Church in carrying out this mission. It is enough to acknowledge that the Crown-Church relation provided for no other.
3. See above, Ch. I, pp. 12–16.

which sought to overthrow the system with which they were familiar, and why they led and supported a cause which held no definite promise for a continuing or expanded role for religion. What did they hope to gain for the doctrines of which they were the custodians and teachers? Was there something in the old system which had become oppressive to religion, and did they hope to exchange it for something better?

Any answers to these questions must be somewhat speculative. For the action of the nationalist clergy, if they are looked upon only as clergy, remains somewhat puzzling. Their roots were in America, and they must have shared some of the *criollo* antipathy toward *peninsulares,* but there were no basic doctrinal conflicts between the clergy and the Crown. There were, however, some grievances and complaints which might have affected the Churchmen's attitude. Charles III and his liberal reforms, culminating in the suppression of the Jesuits, had probably won no allies for the Metropolitan power among the colonial clergy, even though other religious orders were consoled with inheriting the privileges and possessions of the suppressed order. The creation of the new viceroyalty in Buenos Aires in 1776, another act of the Enlightened monarchy, may have contributed obliquely to clerical dissatisfaction. Hitherto the dominant center of River Plate society had been the "theocratic" city of Córdoba, whose ancient university had set the intellectual tone of the whole region. The new viceroyalty, however, meant that the domination of Buenos Aires would supplant that of the old university town. This in turn signified that commerce and trade would replace religion as a major concern of society, while the spokesmen of the new order would be merchants and free-thinkers to whom priests and theologians would now have to give place.[4]

The French Revolution and its aftermath in the Napoleonic occupation of the peninsula may also have created some doubts in the Argentine clergy about the wisdom of too close a dependence upon Spain. It is possible that for some of the clergy the

4. Rojas, *Obras,* Vol. 11, p. 744. "La vieja ciudad universitaria había plasmado su genio en oligarquía de fundadores hidalgos, quieta entre sus colinas del interior. Esta otra ciudad de comerciantes no muy escrupulosos, surgía por su propio esfuerzo mercantil a la vara de un río navegable y de una llanura pastora, inclinada al comercio y a la libertad."

Argentine Revolution was more of a Counter-Revolution, a re-action dedicated to holding back the spread of the French revolutionary spirit to the American continents.

These considerations help to explain the fierce and uncompromising zeal for national independence on the part of such priests as Castro Barros,[5] who aroused the people against the Spanish, but who found the incipient democracy quite distasteful. That these men were nationalist in outlook cannot be questioned. But after the tide of revolution had begun to run, their position was somewhat apart from the main trend. They wanted apparently a native authoritarianism which would undo the work of the rationalist tendencies which had set in with the creation of the vice-royalty.

These speculations, however, can explain only a part of Argentine clerical attitudes at the time of independence. And however useful clergy like Castro Barros may have been in breathing life into the new nation, they are not the most important clerics of their age. Infinitely more significant in the development of the new nation were those priests who struck out boldly for a new order—priests who were basically no less anti-rationalist than their fellows, but who saw the salvation of the country in terms of something different from a return to pre-1767 authoritarianism.

JUAN IGNACIO GORRITI

Of these priests the towering figure is Father Juan Ignacio Gorriti (1766–1842). Gorriti was of Basque ancestry and was born in the province of Jujuy, which he was elected to represent in the *Junta* of 1810.[6] He won degrees in theology and Canon Law at the University of Córdoba in 1790. He spent the next twenty years in pastoral work in his native province. From 1810 to 1831 he was a major political figure both in the independence movement and in the attempts to establish a national government. During this period he also held ecclesiastical posts in the diocese of Salta. According to his friend and disciple, Facundo Zuviría, Gorriti was also linked to the military operation of the independence movement in that he was a close collaborator with General Belgrano and served as a sort of Chaplain-General for Belgrano's

5. Rojas, *Obras,* Vol. 12, p. 190 *et seq.*
6. *Ibid.,* p. 86 *et seq.* offers an outline of Gorriti's life.

forces.[7] In 1831 the rising tide of *caudillismo* drove him into exile. From that year until his death he lived in Bolivia, doing pastoral work and writing.

Rojas, who makes plain that he disagrees with Gorriti's "theological principles," [8] laments none the less that for a long period Argentine historians neglected to accord to Gorriti his due measure.[9]

The measure, according to Rojas, is a very great one, and is to be found in two dimensions. There is first the Gorriti who is an active "founding father" of Argentina, organizing the independence movement and endeavoring to shape the policy of the new state. Secondly, Gorriti is the "major philosopher" of the Revolution,[10] who never deserted the cause, even when the Revolution had turned into a tragedy which threatened to crush him as well as the other surviving liberators.

Gorriti's significance for the political development of Argentine nationalism lies primarily in his early systematic espousal of federalism as the basis for the organization of the new commonwealth. As a North American historian has pointed out [11] the Revolution meant originally for Gorriti the end of Spanish centralism. He wanted to get rid of the old system because it was not compatible with his ideas of human freedom. At the same time Gorriti was aware that a native centralism could be as oppressive as any imported kind. To guard against it he sought a system which would do two things: (1) disperse authority through a multiplicity of centers, each with an inherent capacity to act on its own; (2) emphasize and protect the equality of the centers by restricting the over-all national authority and by preventing any *ad hoc* combinations of power among the larger and stronger

7. Facundo Zuviría, *Selección de Escritos y Discursos* (Buenos Aires, 1932), p. 32; see also Agustín Piaggio, *Influencia del Clero en la Independencia Argentina* (Barcelona, 1912), p. 138.
8. *Op. cit.*, Vol. 12, p. 90.
9. For treatment of the works of Gorriti which Rojas caused to be reissued in the twentieth century, see *ibid.*, p. 82 *et seq.*
10. The accolade is from Rojas, Vol. 11, p. 868. Though accurate in the sense that Gorriti spent a long intellectual life exploring the problems of the society that was coming into existence, this praise can hardly escape challenge from those who see in the Enlightened thinkers like Moreno the "philosophers" who sparked the Emancipation Movement.
11. Harry Bernstein, *Modern and Contemporary Latin America* (Philadelphia, 1952), p. 190.

units composing the system. Working for these points of view in 1810 and in the later Congresses, Gorriti was doomed to failure. Neither the early Federalism nor Rivadavian Unitarism respected very much the freedom and spontaneity of the *pueblos* of the hinterland of which Gorriti was the spokesman. Nor was it possible to prevent power combinations among the more populous and wealthy provinces.

If Gorriti's ideas met with practical failure in their day, they were none the less the valid expression of a political ideal which has become a permanent part of Argentina. Federalism, as noted above, has become the accepted form for the Argentine political system. Gorriti's unique contribution to this development must be evaluated in terms of a final end in his concept of the system. Other statesmen might argue cogently in behalf of federalism as the means to protect regional autonomy or to prevent an unworkable centralization of power. Gorriti would recognize the legitimacy of these ends, but for him the more important one was the personal freedom of the citizen for which he saw the best guarantee in the divided and autonomous powers of a federal state.

Gorriti's advocacy of federalism is then a plea on behalf of personal freedom. Recognizing the necessity for government, for law and order, he wanted at the same time to reserve as large an area as possible for the free operation of the human spirit. This is the tone which Gorriti sought to introduce into the nascent political organization between 1810 and 1830.

Research and investigation in the future may yet reveal why Gorriti reached this position, but to date there exists no clear explanation of why he did. Superficially at least, everything in his background and career could as readily have produced another authoritarian nationalist instead of the liberal democrat. He was a priest who under the *ancien régime* had reached full maturity before the revolutionary ferment set in. He was learned and widely read, but he had lived and worked in a quiet colonial backwater. Unlike the more worldly clerics of the major urban centers, Gorriti had not been exposed to the stimulation of intellectual company and ready access to the new ideas that were flowing in from Europe. After 1810, moreover, he must frequently have been at odds with his fellow democrats over the philosophical bases for the system of liberty that they were all trying to establish. He rejected Rousseau and the whole idea of the Social Contract along with all the literature of the Enlightenment which was so much esteemed by most of the early Argentine liberals. The latter also found inspiration in the lessons of the French Revolution, which Gorriti regarded with horror. In these fundamental differences with other liberals of his times it need not be assumed that Gorriti was fighting a losing battle. His belief was that a free society could be constructed on a Christian basis, when apparently large numbers of his collaborators believed that it was necessary to find a new basis. It could not be said that either side prepared the way for an ultimate victory, but Gorriti's views have never been totally rejected in the subsequent history of Argentine politics.[12]

One explanation of Gorriti's liberal views has been based on the fact that he entered the university of Córdoba after the expulsion of the Jesuits when the management of the institution had been turned over to the allegedly more liberal Franciscans.[13] This explanation, however, involves assumptions about the character of both the Jesuits and their successors that are more far-reaching than warranted. There is even evidence that Gorriti, far from finding inspiration in his own theological training, had a very low opinion of it.[14] He called theology the "most important science," but he considered that it had been taught very badly.

An anti-theological bias does not indicate the origin of Gorriti's liberal convictions, either. The criticism of his own pattern of studies was not meant to oppose theology but to improve the study of it. All in all the effective sources of Gorriti's democratic philosophy remain a mystery. What stands out most clearly, however, is that his democratic commitments were never shaken. These along with his deep religious commitments are shown in his final and best-known work, the so-called *Reflections*.[15]

The *Reflections* were written in Gorriti's extreme old age and after he had been driven into exile in Bolivia. The book shows him

12. Zuviría, *op. cit.*, p. 31. "En esa época en que por consecuencia de nuestra precedente ignorancia, las ideas de libertad se insinuaron mezcladas con las de irreligión, el Sr. Gorriti, tan austero en sus costumbres como en sus principios religiosos y políticos, sirvió de dique al torrente de impiedad que amenazaba arrastrar consigo la moral y fe de nuestros sencillos padres."
13. Rojas, Vol. 12, p. 88.
14. *Ibid.*, p. 96.
15. The full title is *Reflexiones sobre las causas morales de las convulsiones internas en los nuevos estados americanos y examen de los medios eficaces para reprimirlas* (Buenos Aires, 1916). It was originally published at Valparaíso in 1836.

to be still the preacher of the Gospel and the minister of salvation after a quarter-century's immersion in the turbulent stream of revolutionary politics. His interest remained focused in a plan of society where Christian doctrine would inspire a public and private morality which would make possible a broad range of individual and responsible freedom.

In Gorriti's later views the externals of the plan assumed less importance for him than the elements which would help to develop the conditions of freedom from within society. The key to this development was in his view universal popular education. He had come to see that no political system could of itself produce free citizens, but that instead an informed and educated citizenry was the only means to the freedom which a democratic system promised.

It is as the theorist of popular education that Gorriti completes his three-fold significance as a spokesman, perhaps as a prophet, of Argentine nationalism. He began as the exponent and defender of the freedom that was the implicit goal of the Argentine Revolution. As a Federalist he upheld the pattern toward which the structure of Argentine government has generally, if erratically, tended. Finally, as a propagandist on behalf of the instruction of the people, he takes his place in the vanguard of those national leaders who after 1853 sought to destroy *la barbarie* through universal education.

Gorriti's work went beyond a mere defense of the necessity of popular education. He also undertook to show how it could be achieved. One device on which he placed great reliance was the "prestige factor." He would give the teacher so high a place in society that all citizens would look up to him. As for the pupil as center of the educational process, Gorriti's appeal would be only to the pupil's own self-esteem. Physical coercion and other traditional inducements to learning he would throw away. He condemned them as productive of only fraud and hypocrisy.[16] In general Gorriti's approach to education coincided in many respects with what many years later would come to be labeled "progressive education."

These views of Gorriti's were the product of his old age and they were developed in an uncomfortable, Spartan-like exile.

16. See Rojas, Vol. 12, pp. 117–118.

He worked without books and without collaborators.[17] Gorriti's instinct for the valid elements in Argentine development must, however, have been very strong. For his isolation left scarcely any other connection to his homeland. Yet, as Rojas has pointed out, Gorriti became in this period the precursor of the work of "regeneration through science, industry and peace," [18] that in later years Echeverría, Sarmiento, Alberdi, and Mitre would carry forward. Rojas raises the question of whether these later figures were consciously influenced by Gorriti.[19] It is not known that any of them ever read his works, but Rojas notes that some of the ideas expressed in the *Dogma,* in Alberdi's *Bases,* and in Sarmiento's *Educación popular* are similar to those stated earlier by Gorriti.

Whether or not Gorriti influenced these individuals is, of course, secondary to the question of whether Gorriti had a genuine and abiding effect upon Argentina in general. The practical failures of Gorriti's career—rejection of his ideas by the *Juntas* and the Congresses, his final exile—have been noted above. It has also been suggested that his effect, if any, has received less than universal attention in the writing of Argentine history. At the same time the general consistency of his views with the long-range development of Argentine nationalism is apparent. Rojas seems to think that this latter feature of Gorriti's life is the important one and the one that ought to accord to Gorriti a high place in the history of Argentine thought. Writing with the hopeful optimism that seemed to be justified in the early part of the present century, Rojas characterizes the essential relationship between Gorriti and the development of the Argentine nation as follows:

> "We are carrying out his dream, although in divergence with many of his ideas. But Argentina, his country, has not discharged the debt of honor to him, as it has with other contemporaries of his, who served the country with less sacrifice or who enlightened it with less talent." [20]

A final question regarding Gorriti is appropriate for purposes of this study: Is there a conflict between Gorriti's democratic, liberal

17. Facundo Zuviría (see below, pp. 64–76) was in contact with him through this period, but he did not apparently influence Gorriti's final writings.
18. Vol. 12, p. 90.
19. *Ibid.,* p. 119; see also p. 116.
20. *Ibid.,* p. 120.

nationalism and the Catholicism of which Gorriti was an ordained minister? The question is not meant to suggest that Gorriti partook in any degree of the character of those liberal priests who in a moment of revolutionary fervor "hung up the cassock" and never put it back on. Questions on Gorriti's orthodoxy have, however, been raised. Rojas, his great admirer, suggests that Gorriti was somewhat less than a loyal Catholic. The evidence that he offers is meager: Gorriti had kind words for Protestants.[21] He also wrote and worked in the period when relations between the Holy See and Argentina were non-existent and when the organization of the Church had not been regularized. Therefore his work was "independent" and his attitude "more nationalist than Roman."[22]

Despite these and similar suggestions, the present writer is unconvinced that there is any serious reason to question the orthodoxy of Gorriti's Catholicism. Praise for specific features of Protestantism is far from unprecedented in Catholic circles. Beyond that, however, the "independence" of Gorriti's mind cannot be appraised exclusively in terms of the fact that for most of his public career there was no official communication with Rome. During such periods a cleric can act only in accordance with what his conscience dictates. If Gorriti's conscience had led him to champion a separatist course for the Argentine Church, if he had even taken a stand like that of the Brazilian priest Feijó a few years later,[23] then the "independence" of his position might loom as a larger factor in evaluating his work. Gorriti was, to be sure, no sectarian apologist. He was not concerned with defense of his Church against schism and heresy. He was, on the other hand, a defender of traditional Christianity against the challenge of the Enlightenment and the French Revolution. Moreover, this was his role at the very moment when he was most vigorous in upholding the right of the people to self-rule.

In Gorriti's background stands the factor of twenty years of pastoral work. Though there is no means of evaluating this factor, it is always present. It is probable that during the period he lived closely with the people and came to know them better than many of the other revolutionary leaders, the products of more com-

21. Rojas, *Obras*, Vol. 12, p. 88.
22. *Ibid.*, p. 114.
23. See Ch. I, p. 5.

fortable and detached circumstances, ever could know them. The roots of Gorriti's democratic faith are deep, and for a man as consequent in all things as he was, it is difficult to conceive that the two decades of pastoral work would fail to have a permanent effect upon his mind. Although there is yet no concrete evidence to support it, it is a logical speculation that the ultimate explanation of Gorriti's political and social outlook lies in his pastoral career.

Gorriti is the outstanding Catholic thinker of his generation, but he is not the only one. His work has been treated in some detail here because he is the most representative Argentine from the consciously Catholic ranks during the Revolutionary period. Of the Catholic laymen who shared his general orientation and whose careers overlapped with his, the most significant probably is the much younger Zuviría whose work will be examined later in this chapter. Gorriti's most important clerical contemporary is, of course, Dr. Gregorio Funes, Dean of Córdoba.[24] Less zealous as a democrat, although certainly no less significant than Gorriti in the politics of the Revolution, Funes too made an undeniable contribution to Argentine nationalism in his efforts to organize the country. Funes, however, presents problems which can more appropriately be handled in succeeding chapters, and further treatment of his work is reserved for later pages.

THE TYRANNY

The beginning of Gorriti's exile coincided with the triumph of the *caudillismo* that produced the disintegration of all that the liberators had sought to establish. With this triumph came the dominance of Juan Manuel de Rosas, whose ascendency dates from December 7, 1829, and who by March 1835 had established a dictatorship which was to prove one of the most savage that Latin America has ever known. The Rosas epoch represents the dark obverse side of the coin of Argentine nationalism. It is the triumph of the raw, primitive force that Sarmiento called *la barbarie.*

The validity of its appeal, however, is probably symbolized by the fact that for a long period the regime could be presented to

24. The work of other clergy in the independence struggle 1810–20 is treated in Piaggio, *op. cit.*

the people as the "Restoration," and Rosas himself as the "Restorer," although it is difficult to see that he restored anything. It seems more likely that the Rosas regime merely capitalized itself on the frustrations, deficiencies and failures that had characterized the preceding twenty years.[25] The close of the decade of the 1820's had coincided with a maximum frustration in the governance of the River Plate country. Rivadavia's centralism after 1824 had not produced the order and stability that it had promised. Nor had the federalism that had preceded it. Through the whole period since 1810 the new ideas set loose by the Revolution had not produced the good society, and many people were looking back with approval to the pre-revolutionary authoritarianism. This disillusionment and a yearning for order at any cost were factors in the rise of Rosas.

His regime put an end to the revolutionary spirit. It degraded and exiled all the leaders of the independence period who were still surviving. One of the claims of the regime was that it ended the trend toward centralism and restored the federal pattern. Supposedly, it took the country back to the Hispanic tradition as the vital principle of national organization by crushing the liberalism that had been tradition's most persistent challenger. The Restorer could also claim that he had succeeded in regularizing relations with the Holy See and in establishing a native Argentine hierarchy.

These characteristics and accomplishments of the Rosas regime have led certain historians and social scientists to see in the Restoration a triumph for Catholicism and to regard the Rosas dictatorship as identical with the Catholic state. Ingenieros, the noted critic and scholar, seems to tend toward this view, on the grounds that Rosas spelled the end of liberalism, and the Church too was anti-liberal. He also suggests that there was a kind of *Realpolitik* bargain between two reactionary forces which did not have a common philosophical basis, but which were united in opposition to a continuance of liberalism:

"Rosas was not a believer. He never had been before he needed religion as an instrument of his despotism. If not an atheist, he had been

25. For a defense of the Rosas regime at total variance with the view expressed above, see Carlos Smith, *Juan Manuel de Rosas ante la Posteridad* (Buenos Aires, 1936).

indifferent in the matter of religious beliefs. But his policy of reaction against revolutionary liberalism needed the mask of a fanatic which brought him as allies men of the colonial spirit." [26]

In an earlier volume of the same work Ingenieros indicates his general evaluation of the Church forces in the struggles of the nineteenth century. He asserts that there is an "international political party" at work throughout the century in those countries where the Catholic religion is the dominant creed and that this party operating under the guise of national interest pursues a single purpose: "to maintain the preeminence of the Holy See in all nations and under all regimes." [27] In this context the reference is not directed exclusively to the Rosas regime, but embraces the whole stream of Church-State relations in Argentina after 1810. It is nevertheless the general view of this author which is pertinent to his estimate of the Rosas period.

Rosas was the first Argentine ruler to come to a definite agreement with Rome, but Ingenieros probably has an exaggerated view of the international ties of Catholicism during the nineteenth century.[28] Yet many students of Argentine history who would hesitate to share Ingenieros' belief in a Catholic "international political party," would be in accord with his view of the Rosas regime as a Catholic restoration.

Evidence to support this view is of various sorts. The most important certainly is the fact that in 1837 the solution worked out by Rosas' *fiscal*, Pedro José Agrelo, settled the problem of relations with the Pope and resulted in the establishment of a national hierarchy. There is also the fact of Rosas' restoration of the Jesuits, a religious order which in the Latin American mind has been traditionally aligned with an allegiance to the Papacy in preference to any other. Rosas also had the loyalty and personal support of certain clerics who had turned the tide of *caudillismo* to their own advantage. Priests in Buenos Aires pulpits upheld the cause of *federalismo* in their sermons and used the same ecclesiastical precincts to join in demagogic denunciations of the

26. *La Evolución de las Ideas Argentinas,* Vol. IV, p. 102.
27. Vol. II, p. 49.
28. Recent historical treatment of the long reign of Pius IX, for example, E.E.Y. Hales, *Pio Nono* (New York, 1954), shows in how many different directions Catholic thought and action worked in that period, and how a superimposed unanimity of social thought was completely lacking—even after the *Syllabus!*

unitarios. Finally, there is the sacrilegious fact that portraits of Rosas were displayed on the altars of the churches.

All these developments bespeak the solid entrenchment of Rosas' power after 1835. It can be asked whether they also show a triumphant Catholicism, or whether the Church is merely yielding to a greater force, as in effect it had done during the unsettled first two decades. No entirely satisfactory answer can be given except that the Rosas settlement clearly was no triumph for the Catholic Church. A glance at that settlement as outlined above [29] shows that it did little more than perpetuate in legal form the *patronato* and all the regalism that had been the controversial inheritance from Spain. The native clergy had never been united in its favor, and the regalistic claims had for long been the major obstacle to regular relations with the Papacy. The fact that Agrelo's solution was later incorporated into the Constitution of 1853 [30] would seem to indicate that it is a solution which is consistent with Argentine nationalism as a whole, not merely with the reactionary manifestations of it, since both reactionaries and liberals have stood by it. It has been hailed as the "patriotic" solution by a wide variety of authorities including Ingenieros himself, Ricardo Rojas and the outstanding authority on the subject, Dalmacio Vélez Sarsfield.[31] The solution has, however, received only tacit acceptance in Rome and the Vatican has never confirmed it through a Concordat.

More significant probably for the actual situation of the Church under Rosas was the fact that the solution gave the regime the unquestioning loyalty of one bishop, Mariano Medrano, of Buenos Aires. The occupant of this see henceforth became the government's man and was in a poor position to resist the government, whatever the latter's political complexion might be. Nor does there seem to be evidence that Medrano, in frail health and with incipient blindness, was of a disposition to do so. On the other hand, Mariano José Escalada, who had a somewhat ambiguous status as auxiliary bishop to the same see, was apparently under constant suspicion of subversion. The regime regarded him as an-

29. Ch. I, pp. 20–21.
30. See Ingenieros, Vol. IV, p. 99.
31. Rojas, Vol. 14, p. 33. Vélez Sarsfield's views are contained in the notable work from his hand, *Derecho Público Eclesiástico* (Buenos Aires, 1871.)

other savage *unitario,* and while he was never imprisoned, he could not function freely in the diocese.[32]

Neither could it be claimed that the readmission of the Jesuits resulted in any great advantage to Catholicism. The Jesuits apparently returned to Argentina with the conviction that there would be a role for them in the new state which would be comparable with the one they had played in their days of glory at Córdoba. The majority of the Jesuits soon found, on the contrary, that they could not accept the lawlessness and baseness of the regime. They, too, came under suspicion, and their Superior, Father Berdugo, was forced to flee. His flight was preceded by evidence of a breakdown in the disciplinary unity which is characteristic of the Jesuit Society, when Berdugo's authority was challenged by Father Magestó, one of the company who remained loyal to Rosas.[33]

All in all it is difficult to see that there were any substantial gains for the Church in terms of its institutional interests during the Rosas period. If there were priests who obliged the dictator by taking the cues set for their sermons, it is more than likely that many of them were terrorized into these acts. Among the many things that the tyrant sought to restore was a high moral tone in the clergy—which had allegedly been lacking. This gave him and his unofficial police, the *mazorca,* the excuse to hurl wholesale accusations at any clergy who were suspected of resistance. Capital punishment in especially horrible forms was used against these clergy, as Félix Frías has described in detail.[34] This terrorism falling alike on clergy and laity was symbolized in the *cause célèbre* of Camila O'Gorman, whose name has ever since indicated the ultimate and inhuman degradation of the dictatorship.[35]

The result of all this was that both the Catholic spokesmen of

32. Ingenieros, Vol. IV, p. 52.
33. *Ibid.,* p. 187 *et seq.*
34. In his ironic article, *La gloria del tirano Rosas* (Buenos Aires, 1928).
35. Camila O'Gorman was executed while carrying an unborn child, whose father was allegedly a priest, who was also executed. The trial and conviction—a total farce conducted by a terrorized court, only one of whose members had the courage to defy the dictator—resulted supposedly from Rosas' desire to elevate standards of clerical behavior. Apart from the fact that the general condition of the clergy never justified measures of such extremity, the killing of the unborn child with the mother was regarded as an unprecedented brutality.

the previous generation like Father Gorriti, and those who were to make their mark on the succeeding generation like Félix Frías,[36] were driven into exile as the only possible circumstance which would permit them to resist the dictator. In this aspect the Catholics were like the rest of the large body of opponents of the tyranny, including those who had no fundamental commitment to the Church. Genuine resistance was possible only through flight and exile. On the other hand, the Catholics who stayed at home complied with the directives of the tyranny, or suffered the consequences of doing otherwise. In this respect it may be observed that the Catholics were not unlike the rest of the Argentines who found ways of living with the dictatorship, even though they did not like it. Dalmacio Vélez Sarsfield is a prime example of the latter.

The Rosas period in its totality sheds no luster on Argentine Catholicism any more than it reflects any credit on the Argentine nation as a whole. It is an inglorious epoch for everyone concerned. It happens to be the period when the permanent pattern of Church-State relations was established. The settlement was the work of an anti-liberal dictatorship, but it has been perpetuated by the liberal governments that followed Rosas and down to the present day it has not been fundamentally disturbed. Since both liberals and anti-liberals have firmly adhered to it, it becomes doubtful that the settlement itself justified the identification of the Rosas tyranny with the Catholic state. Of the secular scholars who have treated the question, Ricardo Rojas is most vigorous in rejecting this widely held view, when he condemns the "latter-day 'sociologists,' badly informed in national history," who "have certified that the dictatorship of Rosas was a Catholic reaction." [37]

Rosas, by virtue of the fact that he could rule for so long, represents something that is difficult for the whole Argentine nation to live down. And the Church has undoubtedly been used in some quarters to explain away the disgrace of the tyranny. The fact that this is not the most creditable chapter in the annals of the Argentine Church does not of itself make the explanation true.

36. Frías' Catholicism at the time of his exile has been questioned. See below, pp. 80–81.
37. Vol. 14, p. 30.

CATHOLICISM AFTER 1853

In the decades following Rosas' downfall the movement of Argentine nationalism reached full maturity, and the organization of the country was consolidated under the Constitution of 1853. Two obstacles stood in the path of effective conversion of the national spirit into a workable pattern of social organization. The first of these was the threatened survival of *caudillismo,* and the second was the separatist attitude and course of action that the province of Buenos Aires followed until 1861.

As has been indicated briefly above, the men who dedicated themselves to the task of organization have left a record of success, solid achievement, and even occasional heroism. Just as the long tyranny is a period in which hardly any group of Argentines can take pride, the organizing period is the time when all the exuberant claims of a glowing nationalistic patriotism may find justification.

In this period Catholic thought followed on the whole the general contemporary trends. It shared in the renewed and universal enthusiasm for personal freedom. Catholic thinkers made their contributions to the quest for balance between liberty and authority. Catholic leaders joined numerous others in seeking to marshal the resources which would make universal education a bulwark against the resurgence of any demagoguery. In short, Catholic thought shared the common attitudes of the day which were tending to spell out a system of ordered liberty, of freedom under law.

At the same time Catholic thought began to strike out on its own and to demonstrate a quality which it would not be entirely accurate to call dissident, but which certainly represents a distinctiveness that had not been present previously. In the Independence period Gorriti, Funes and the other Churchmen may not have shared the philosophical bases on which many of their fellow-revolutionists thought that national freedom should rest. This lack of a common basis, however, did not divide them as to goals. (There was, of course, division in the revolutionary ranks, but not of the sort to put the Catholics in one camp and rationalists in the other.) Similarly during the tyranny some Catholic leaders shared exile with free-thinkers, while other Catholics managed like other free-thinkers to weather the dictatorship at home and even to serve it. But after 1853 a distinctive Catholic school began to take shape, and before the end of the century it had established its own particular character and identity.

The Catholic group in this period was not marked by any solidarity of organization or by persistent unity of purpose. Rather its dominant characteristic was a general tone of conservatism. There were important exceptions to this conservative trend, and it may even be that the conservatism was more than anything else a surface phenomenon. Nevertheless, Catholic thought in this period was on the whole more concerned with moderation than with reform and was more avid in its search for the means to establish the equilibrium of society than it was in promoting rapid social progress.

In the Catholic school of the second half of the nineteenth century four names seem to be outstanding. The list starts with Facundo Zuviría (sometimes written Zubiría), the President of the Constitutional Convention of 1853. Félix Frías, the journalist-politician, has an important place in this company. The priest, Fray Mamerto Esquiú,[38] also belongs here, although he has a very different significance from that of the first two figures. A still greater difference separates the university professor, José Manuel Estrada, from the others. These men are not the exclusive representatives of Argentine Catholicism in the second half of the century, but they are, with the exception of Esquiú, the Catholics who left the most thoroughly documented record of their thought and activity. In the pages that follow, their work will be examined along with that of contemporaries who made lesser contributions to the Catholic school.

FACUNDO ZUVIRÍA

Of this group Zuviría (1796–1861) alone was old enough to have witnessed the wars of independence and to have participated in the initial organization of his native province, Salta.[39] An intellectual prodigy, Zuviría obtained the doctorate *in utroque jure*

38. Esquiú was a bishop. However, his long resistance to the reception of episcopal orders and the fact that he died soon after consecration have left him in history's eyes essentially the priest and friar.
39. See the introductory biographical article by Miguel Solá in *Escritos Y Discursos de Facundo Zuviría* (Buenos Aires, 1932); see also Rojas, Vol. 14, p. 864 *et seq.*

from Córdoba at the age of seventeen. He was elected President of the Salta legislature in 1822, after having played the main role in the drafting of the provincial constitution of 1821. In general Zuviría seems to have regarded himself as a law-maker rather than as an executive or popular leader. He refused the Governorship in 1822, and the most notable parts of his career consist of legislative work and presiding over law-making assemblies.

In the struggles of the 1820's Zuviría aligned himself firmly with the *unitarios*. It may be noted that this circumstance places him in the ranks led by Rivadavia and other reformers who were not especially acceptable to the Church. This relationship, however, does not of itself make Zuviría a dissident Catholic. The triumphant *federalismo* of the tyranny drove Zuviría into exile along with many other Unitarists. Like Frías, his much younger contemporary, Zuviría was a major Catholic figure of the exiled generation. But unlike many other *emigrados*, Zuviría did not use his exile to travel in various parts of the globe. Frías, Alberdi, and Sarmiento, to name but a few of the émigrés, scattered over a large part of Europe and America. Zuviría, however, established himself in Chuquisaca, Bolivia, close to his native Salta. In Bolivia he shared exile with Gorriti, to whom he always referred as his "best friend," and to whose family he was allied through marriage. In 1850 Zuviría judged it safe to return to his home in Salta, and he lived in obscurity, though apparently not in hiding, until the fall of Rosas in 1852.

Immediately afterward, Zuviría was elected to his old seat in the provincial legislature, of which he again became the presiding officer. The following year he went to the Constitutional Convention at Santa Fe as a delegate of Salta and was elected President of the "Sovereign Congress." In the immediately following years of Urquiza's presidency Zuviría had various cabinet posts, including the Ministry of Justice and Public Instruction and that of Foreign Affairs. While the Capital remained at Paraná, before the adherence of Buenos Aires to the federation, he was at various times a member of the Senate and the Chamber of Deputies.

Zuviría is frequently described as an "austere man." He had a deeply religious sense of life, which appears to have been inculcated into his character at a very early age. Like Estrada he shows in his writing a broad familiarity with Sacred Scripture, both Old and New Testaments, a knowledge which may not have been too common among laymen of his generation. Some of his briefer articles in exile demonstrate an influence of the Hebrew Prophets on his own style.[40]

A key to the understanding of Zuviría's religious commitment probably lies in his frequently expressed respect for suffering, trial and hardship as the tests which determine the true worth of man. Like the other exiles he resented the injustice of his own lot, but he also gloried in it. The hardships of the exiles were oppressive, but they had the merit of gathering the sufferers into a company of the morally "elect," for whom Zuviría had great veneration. This attitude is especially evident in the oration which he pronounced at Gorriti's funeral.[41] He paid tribute to Gorriti's accomplishments both as priest and political leader. He dwelt on Gorriti's virtues as a patriot and a statesman. But the high point of the oration is reached in the passages where Zuviría treats the figure of Gorriti in exile, the priest who has buried himself in obscurity after a quarter-century of prominence and who has abandoned comfort and honors for poverty and misery. While Zuviría deplores the injustice meted out to the priest, at the same time he finds in the harsh, final decade of Gorriti's life the true justification of the man.[42] It is as though a Providential dispensation had determined that Gorriti should fulfill a certain greatness, but the dispensation did not stop here. A conventional greatness was not enough: something superior was offered in the adversity and hardship of his old age.

What Zuviría's attitude shows more than anything else is a profound respect for the human spirit. He was a politician and a lawyer, whose public activity was a cautious search for the compromises which would unite people and build institutions. But at the basis of all his activity is a real interest in the human being who participates in social life not so much by creative contributions of effort as by endurance of the hard knocks and misfortunes

40. *El Emigrado* in *op. cit.*, beginning on p. 49; also *Deprecación, ibid.*, p. 36.
41. *Op. cit.*, p. 23, *et seq.* This oration was given at the request of the Archbishop of Sucre. The fact that Zuviría, a layman, was asked to fulfill this role at the funeral of a priest and in the presence of the local ordinary would seem to confirm the contemporary acknowledgment of his status as a leading Catholic.
42. *Ibid.*, pp. 84–85.

which, in Zuviría's view, are inevitable and many. It is this capacity to endure which determines the value of man. Moreover, one has a right to ask for the quality of endurance in men, because the human spirit is no finite thing, nor is its final destiny among the powers of this world which batter and oppress it. Therefore, in Zuviría's concept, if the spirit gives in to the powers of this world, it betrays itself. It can be true to itself only when it resists by enduring all things.

What Zuviría asks for in men is little short of heroism, but he promises no tangible rewards or future ease for heroes. Unlike many Catholic thinkers of a slightly later period in both America and Europe, Zuviría does not teach that a sound social organization holds out the promise of a better life in this world. Austerity, he seems to suggest, is the natural and proper condition of man. The most that can be asked of social organization is that it make this condition honorable.

It is against this general attitude that Zuviría's specific contributions to Argentine nationalism must be evaluated. His specific contributions are three in number. First, he used his various public positions after 1852 to try to turn into a concrete reality the general principles which Urquiza had promulgated after the battle of Caseros, namely, that the unity of the Argentine nation should mean that there were neither victors nor vanquished and that no reprisals would be taken against those who had followed Rosas. Secondly, he labored for the incorporation of the province of Buenos Aires as an indispensable part of the new federation. Finally, he sought to instill a doctrine of liberty under law which would take its form from the national character in giving due weight to both the *civilization* and the *barbarism* which had by this time been so clearly identified.

Zuviría's work on behalf of a national organization that would leave the past in a merciful oblivion was a special manifestation of his general role of law-maker. The legislative posts that he began to occupy immediately after the tyranny's collapse were used to further the cause of institutions which would be limited in power, but which would also be strong enough to prevent a resurgence of *caudillismo*. He was not interested in unraveling the tangled web of wrongs and misdeeds that had been the work of the tyranny. Taking his cue from Urquiza, he said in effect: Let us start anew and let us be mindful of our immediate past only to the extent that we guard against unwittingly recreating it.

The insights into the national character which brought him to this position were probably the result of his own experience. Zuviría had been an *unitario*, a member of the party which the *rosistas* had proscribed with immense popular approval. He had also been one of the intellectuals of the Rivadavian period against whom the common people seemed to feel they had a grievance. Zuviría never apologized for either part of his record, but in his old age he thought that he had come to discern the error of the early intellectuals. He publicly recognized that their capital sin had been to trust in imported and exotic systems and institutions while they failed to study the national character and circumstances.[43] At the same time, he admitted that the "instinct of the people" had been sound in rejecting what the intellectuals had tried to impose. While he clearly saw the need for a new national organization, he was fearful that those who were seeking the antithesis of Rosas might try to take the country back to the unsuccessful centralism of a previous generation.

The country had in his view not one past, but two: an intellectual, formalistic democracy and a massive, vital demagoguery. As a perpetrator of one and a victim of the other, he knew them both. In the final decade of his life he reached the point where he rejected both and strove to find national unity on a different basis.

His basis was in large part pragmatic, and his actions were characterized by extreme scrupulosity lest any element, however fragile but potentially capable of helping the cause of national unity under law, might be lost or wasted. This attitude is especially evident in Zuviría's forceful, impromptu address to the Salta legislature on the *Acuerdo de San Nicolás* in 1852. The *acuerdo*, as noted above, was the voluntary pact by which various governors bound themselves to the cause of national unity under Urquiza and called for a Constitutional Congress to be elected from the provinces. Zuviría was cognizant of the weaknesses of the pact, the greatest one being that Buenos Aires was not an adherent. He was ready to admit the dubious legality of the instrument, and he voiced what was probably a general resentment

43. *Escritos*, p. 128 *et seq.*

of the fact that the governors had themselves dictated a universal manner of electing the delegates to the *Constituyente,* thus denying provincial determination of the matter. In spite of all these objections Zuviría urged the legislature to accept the pact *in toto.* He even urged that the legislature amend existing laws where they ran counter to what the governors had agreed upon. He argued that the *acuerdo* offered the first real beginning of a possible national organization and that the only responsible thing that the law-making body could do would be to strengthen the *acuerdo* in every possible way. Above all he exhorted his colleagues not to search for legalistic obstacles to cooperation with the governors.

In this speech, and in others of the period, Zuviría was content to play the role of advocate of national unity and in this role he was sometimes more concerned with convincing his listeners than he was in making a strictly logical presentation. Thus he appealed to both those of Unitarist and Federalist sentiments with the relatively meaningless assurance that "centralization" of authority as foreshadowed in the San Nicolás document did not indicate "concentration" of authority, and that the new state would certainly have both "unity" and "federation." [44]

Zuviría, himself, may not entirely have abandoned his old Unitarist sentiments. He was not prepared to oppose Federalism, but he believed that the governors had usurped in advance a part of the function of the *Constituyente* when they announced that the coming constitution should be on a federal basis. In a note appended to the text of his speech, Zuviría recorded that he had desired to introduce a motion which would remind the governors of their error and restore the decision to the coming Congress. At the suggestion, however, that such a motion might jeopardize the tenuous appeal of the *acuerdo,* Zuviría immediately withdrew it. [45]

Zuviría believed in and worked for national unity, but he did not always take the obvious and seemingly popular channels to achieve it. As a result his conduct in the Constitutional Congress and in his role as President of that body is somewhat paradoxical. Palcos notes the initial paradox, namely, that Zuviría's ideas are much less liberal than those incorporated into the Constitution

44. *Ibid.,* p. 132.
45. *Ibid.,* pp. 145–146.

over whose making he presided.[46] In the same vein Rojas states that Zuviría was not regarded as a liberal by the liberal majority of the Congress, but that he had the majority's confidence and respect and for this reason was made presiding officer.[47] Zuviría confirms in a way both judgments with his statement at the end of the Congress that he had had no other part in the making of the Constitution than that of presiding over the assembly of delegates.[48]

The major paradox, however, consists of Zuviría's reluctance to accept the Constitution, once it had been drafted, in spite of his earnest efforts to achieve national unity through the Constitutional Congress. As the Congress came closer to the finishing of its task in April 1853, Zuviría urged that the adoption of any constitution be postponed.[49] He apparently was not greatly concerned to have the current draft rejected, but he opposed the adopting of any constitution at the time. The civil disturbances of the year had diminished the optimism with which Zuviría had come to the Congress, and he doubted that the country was ready to accept a constitution in the sense of a general willingness to make it work. Rather than let the 1853 document join the Latin American parade of unworkable paper constitutions, he counseled postponement.

It is quite clear that Zuviría, with his long experience in law-making, conceived of a constitution not as something from which a governmental system could spring but as something which would confirm and solidify a pre-existing unity and general agreement. He reminded his colleagues that their function was not merely in "knowing the principles of constitutional law and in applying them without regard to anything but their theoretical truth, but in combining these same principles with the nature and peculiarities of the country in which they are to be applied . . ."[50] He was of the opinion that the time had not arrived to make this combination and that there should be a year at least in which a provisional government under Urquiza's direction

46. *Loc. cit.*, p. 6.
47. *Obras*, Vol. 14, p. 864.
48. *Escritos*, pp. 221–222.
49. *Ibid.*, p. 183 *et seq.*
50. *Ibid.*, p. 118.

should try to promote internal peace before imposing the Constitution.[51]

In the background of this proposal is the second broad aspect of Zuviría's work, namely, his constant concern to bring the province of Buenos Aires into the new federation. Obstacles to incorporation of the province consisted of its own independent attitude, the failure of the pact of San Nicolás to provide for a proportional representation of the largest province in the Santa Fe Convention, and the attitudes of other provincial delegations who thought that their constituents had grievances against Buenos Aires. The specific grievances were in large part economic, Buenos Aires having taken full advantage of her river location to manipulate the trade and commerce of the inland provinces. There was also a general remembrance of the fact that the strength of the tyranny had been in Buenos Aires, whose governor had been Rosas.

With more objectivity than might have been expected of a non-citizen of Buenos Aires, Zuviría labored to overcome all these obstacles. His principal contention was that the country could not exist without the province. In August of 1852 he had expressed to the Salta legislature his chagrin over the fact that the San Nicolás document had accorded Buenos Aires only equal representation with all the other provinces. He doubted the wisdom of this arrangement, but conceded that he was in no position to challenge it.[52] In the first session of the Santa Fe *Constituyente,* replying to Urquiza's inaugural message, Zuviría dwelt on the national misfortune involved in Buenos Aires' absence from the meeting. He urged the other delegates to take a conciliatory attitude toward the dissident province in the hope of drawing her in. Directing his words to those who would place the guilt of the tyranny on the one large province, he argued not that the record was free of crime and terror, but that the crimes should be charged only against Rosas and his coterie, not against the people at large.[53] A short time later he was to ask Congress to negotiate

51. Recognizing the fact of provincial autonomy, Zuviría's proposal called for a council of one member from each province to oversee the work of the provisional government.
52. *Escritos,* p. 142.
53. *Ibid.,* p. 156.

directly with the provincial authorities in the hope of winning their adherence. This attitude smacked of a humility which was clearly unacceptable to the majority of the Congress. Negotiation was less in the air than the prospect of compelling Buenos Aires to join through use of force.

The prospect was abhorrent to Zuviría.[54] Buenos Aires was indispensable to a united Argentina, but he did not believe that a union achieved in this fashion would last. In the years after 1853 he constituted himself a kind of advocate for the interests of Buenos Aires. As a *salteño* he had no strong ties to the province, but his advocacy was directed toward the goal of national union.

A private letter written in 1855 displays an attitude toward the question of constitutionalism that is somewhat similar to Lincoln's at the outbreak of the North American Civil War. Zuviría in this letter [55] again urged that negotiations between Paraná and Buenos Aires should be undertaken. As a preliminary step he urged that the two governments, federal and provincial, send representatives to a joint assembly. To this assembly would be assigned the task of amending the Constitution in such a way that Buenos Aires would join the federation. He admitted that there was a legal technicality which stood in the way of this proposal. The obstacle was the provision of the Constitution itself which enjoined any amendment during the ten-year period ending in 1863. Zuviría acknowledged that there had been good reasons for establishing this prohibition in 1853, but like Lincoln a few years later, he argued that what was important was the spirit of the Constitution, not an individual clause. The end and aim of the Santa Fe instrument had been strong national union. It was therefore, Zuviría asserted, beyond reason that a provision of the Constitution itself should be invoked to defeat the larger purpose. Moreover, if the larger purpose could be achieved in the way he proposed, then a technical violation would be a small price to pay for it.

Here again Zuviría's counsel was rejected, and the practical turn of events would seem to invalidate the wisdom of his advice. It was the force of arms, not a deliberative body, that finally

54. His attitude is summarized in the phrase: "Con la *fuerza* se conquista, no se convence; se domina, no se gobierna." *Escritos*, p. 199.
55. *Ibid.*, p. 254 *et seq.*

united the province and the federation. Given the character of the man and his long political experience, it was impossible that he should have espoused any other course than he did. His whole development had been as a legislator, as a law-maker who drew on a vast fund of theoretical and legal knowledge, but who was more impressed with the concrete than with the abstract. It would be unfair to say that, compromiser though he was, Zuviría was ready to sacrifice principle. He was, however, afraid of formulas and doctrinaire positions, and he was not only ever ready to sacrifice these, but in his later years he was also predisposed to condemn them, no matter what their source. As the incident just related demonstrates, Zuviría was keenly aware that the "letter killeth," and he would never hesitate to sacrifice the letter in order to keep the spirit alive.

This attitude is thoroughly consistent with the third aspect of Zuviría's public career, listed above: his defense of a doctrine of liberty under law, which has generally been regarded as containing a severely restricted concept of liberty. This doctrine was a long time maturing, and it was probably the result of experience and observation more than it was of study and abstract development.

Its beginnings certainly lie in the Rivadavian period when as a young intellectual leader Zuviría was on the side of the expansive doctrine of individual liberty, then widely accepted in his circles. There is a strong suggestion, however, that even in this period he had some misgivings, to the extent that the new ideology seemed to conflict with the traditional view of man and his destiny that is contained in Christian teaching. Early in his exile Zuviría spoke of "our simple fathers" who in the Liberation period failed to understand that the new ideas of liberty were tainted with those of irreligion.[56]

After Zuviría's return from exile, the longer he studied his native society, the more he seemed to relegate to the background the philosophical content in his concept of liberty. He came to believe that any system providing for human freedom in his country would have to emerge from the Argentine character as nature and history had combined to form it.

What was Zuviría's view of the national character? Briefly, it

56. *Escritos,* p. 31.

was as follows.[57] Nature has made Argentina a land of abundance. Man has not only exploited this land of abundance to his own advantage, but also he has been tempted by its very richness to abuse it. He "abuses everything that abounds." The accusation is general, but if he had made it specific, his bill of particulars would probably have included the following: the lavish and careless disposal of rights to land, enriching a few, impoverishing most; the wasteful practices of the cattle-raisers who slaughtered animals by the thousands for hides alone and left the carcasses to rot on the plains; the fierce vitality of the plainsmen which could lead them to deeds of brutality as readily as to acts of heroism. Into this environment of abundance and abuse, Zuviría suggested, the eighteenth century ideas of liberty had been introduced. The ideas took on the general character of the environment. Superabundant liberty had spelled the end of authority and had produced anarchy. This in turn led to the abuses of the dictatorship.

To correct these abuses Zuviría wanted a government which would be strong enough to contain and restrain all the abundant forces and energies of the nation. More authority and less liberty were the means by which this could be achieved. It would be unfair to say that between the two Zuviría always chose authority, but he certainly looked upon authority as the element which needed to be expanded in the Argentine constitutional system. There is a Hamiltonian note in his contention that vigor and force in government are the "first guarantees of liberty." [58]

The central authority would arise, he seemed to trust, if the trend toward national organization that had originated in the *Acuerdo de San Nicolás* were allowed to develop fully. Meanwhile, it seemed important to him to prevent a misdirected liberty from thwarting this development. Accordingly, he was willing to place restrictions on the people in their participation in the affairs of the nation. The most obvious restriction and the one most consistent with his view of the national character was that of limiting the franchise (which in most provinces had hitherto been nominally universal). In addition, he was also willing to curb the freedom of speech and press.

57. It is contained in many speeches and papers, but the clearest statement is probably in the inaugural address to the Salta legislature in 1852. *Ibid.*, pp. 80–93.
58. *Ibid.*, p. 86.

His basic argument in favor of these restrictions is one that frequent conservative reiteration in the past century has made commonplace. It was simply that the masses, *"desnudos de toda propriedad y saber,"* [59] have no tangible interest in a stable society. Therefore they must not be permitted to participate in decisions affecting society as a whole. Such participation must be limited to those who can demonstrate three qualifications: property, education and morality.[60] Zuviría believed that the three were practically inseparable, and the demonstration of one of these qualifications implied the possession of the other two. It can be argued that he would give them a broad interpretation, since he specifically suggested that the concept of property was not limited to tangible assets, but also included such things as the skill of the artisan, who might be otherwise without property. Nevertheless, there is little doubt that Zuviría's purpose was to exclude from suffrage a vast proportion of the population. His proposal was aimed at the great masses of unattached and unsettled men who had given the *caudillos* their strength and who had helped to make *caudilllismo* the scourge of the nation.

Zuviría had no success with any of his restrictive proposals. They were vigorously opposed by the other new, and generally younger, leaders of the 1850's, who sometimes charged Zuviría with harboring anti-democratic sentiments.[61] There is little doubt that Zuviría was distrustful of the people in politics, but in his own defense he would probably plead two considerations. One is the purely legalistic concept voiced in the Salta legislature regarding the right of suffrage.[62] Here he distinguished between "individual rights" and "social and political rights." The former were sacrosanct, inhering in the human person and beyond the reach of government. The latter had their origin in society and its needs at any given period, and consequently could be granted or withheld as society operating through the state might determine. The

59. *Escritos*, p. 115.
60. *Ibid.*, pp. 103–124. Here the ideas are developed in connection with a provincial election bill, but they appear frequently in his later writing, especially the emphasis upon property as a qualification for responsible citizenship.
61. His position was not far afield from the one enunciated by the authors of the *Dogma* in 1839, but after 1853 not all of the members of the *Asociación de Mayo* continued to adhere to this position—if in fact they ever did as a majority group within the lodge. See below, Ch. V, pp. 133–134.
62. *Escritos*, p. 107.

right of suffrage fell in the second category, and consequently was always subject to political control. The weakness of this position is too obvious to require comment.

His second point is more convincing, but is colored by sentimentality. His view of the people was that they were "innocent and inert." [63] Bad and irresponsible leaders had frequently led the masses into deplorable deeds, for which, Zuviría always argued (with the people of Buenos Aires uppermost in his mind), they should not be held to account. But he recognized a prevailing disposition to blame the people for the excesses of the dictatorship and he thought that they would not have been blamed if they had not had a nominal suffrage which had been demagogically manipulated to support the tyranny. Therefore in his view universal manhood suffrage had saddled the people with a responsibility for misdeeds which they could not be asked to bear. Until the people reached the condition where they could reasonably be asked to bear this responsibility the suffrage should be withheld from them.

In many ways Zuviría did not belong to the times in which the most conspicuous parts of his career unfolded. He had been born in the eighteenth century, and he reached his position of national eminence when he was already an old man. The Rivadavian intellectual of the 1820's had turned conservative, but of the twin forces of Argentine nationalism he had facility for handling only one. Though he recognized the weakness of the tactics of the party of his youth in trying to impose civilization upon the country, he apparently never learned how to meet the forces of barbarism by any other means than repression. The men around him in his old age were cleverer and broader. He was out of step with his colleagues of the 1850's.

It is probably the thread of "austerity," however, running throughout Zuviría's life, which gives him a significant place in the development of Argentine nationalism. It is a symbol of the survival of the better side of the Argentine national character, a promise and a pledge of the moral strength which later in the century would bring Argentina into realization of her potentialities as a full-fledged and responsible nation.

63. *Ibid.*, p. 234.

FÉLIX FRÍAS

Like Zuviría, Félix Frías properly belongs in the ranks of nine-teenth century conservatism, although for a large part of his life Frías liked to classify himself as a liberal. He is a unique figure in the history of the Argentine republic, and is hardly less out-standing in the annals of Argentine Catholicism. Rojas sum-marizes his position by saying that Frías in the midst of a liberal generation defended the "ark of his religious faith against terrible adversaries," and he asserts that Frías stands in the tradition of Gorriti and bequeaths the same to José Manuel Estrada.[64] While this classification is fundamentally true, it will be apparent from what follows that Frías was more conservative than either Gorriti or Estrada. Also, more than any other contemporary spokesman for Catholicism, Frías urged a program of direct action in the political sphere to guard and advance the specific institutional interests of the Church.[65]

Frías was a politician and an extremely facile professional journalist. His perpetual interest in journalism was defense of the Church. His writing is varied and without system, although cer-tainly not without focus. If he had had any humor in his make-up —it appears to have been totally lacking—it would not be unfair to suggest a comparison between Frías and the twentieth cen-tury English writer, G. K. Chesterton. Both were talented, pro-fessional writers, imbued with a burning zeal for Catholicism, and the widest variety of circumstances, including both the common-place and the bizarre, could offer an occasion to either one for the exercise of his talents on behalf of the cause of Catholicism.

Frías was born in Buenos Aires in 1816. He attended the uni-versity there and established an early reputation for brilliance and erudition.[66] He began his journalistic career on *El Iniciador* in company with other names later to become famous in Argentine history, Cané, Juan María Gutiérrez, Mitre and Tejedor. While

64. Vol. 13, p. 628.
65. Estrada in his last years was also a promoter of political action on the part of Catholic groups, but this activity was not characteristic of the whole of his life and the larger part of it was spent in purely intellectual activities.
66. These biographical data follow the essay by Pedro Goyena which is in Vol. I of the four volume collected works of Frías: *Escritos y Discursos de Félix Frías* (Buenos Aires, 1884).

still in his twenties Frías entered the army of General Lavalle, who had called for an uprising against Rosas. He apparently worked closely with Lavalle and is generally believed to be the drafter of Lavalle's proclamation urging the people to rebel against Rosas. Lavalle met with defeat and was killed in 1841. Frías secretly smuggled the general's body into Bolivia to prevent its mutilation and exhibition according to the custom of the *rosistas*. Frías then remained in Bolivia, beginning an exile which was to last many years.

Later on he lived in Chile where he served as a consular officer for the Bolivian government. His major work in Chile, however, came to be that of a newspaperman for *El Mercurio* of Valparaíso. The *Mercurio* sent him to Europe as a correspondent, and there he was to witness and report on the turbulence of 1848 and the years immediately following. In France Frías came under the influence of the Catholic leaders Montalembert and Lacordaire. After Rosas' fall Frías did not return immediately to Argentina. He severed connections with *El Mercurio*, but remained in Europe as the correspondent of the new Catholic paper, *La Religión*, which was founded in 1853 by the priest Federico Aneiros (later Archbishop of Buenos Aires) and the Dominican Fray Olegario Correa.

Frías returned to Buenos Aires in 1855 and soon founded another newspaper, *El Orden.* Shortly afterward he was elected to the Buenos Aires Senate. After 1861, when Buenos Aires rejoined the Argentine federation, Frías was elected to the national Senate. In 1869 he went to Chile as Argentine minister. Goyena reports that in 1874 President Avellaneda recalled Frías from the Santiago post with the intention of making him Foreign Minister. Frías refused to accept the appointment and instead took a seat in the Chamber of Deputies. The reason for this choice, according to Goyena, was that the boundary question between Argentina and Chile was then in an acute stage and Frías judged that from a seat in Congress he would have greater freedom to defend Argentine interests than he would in the Foreign Ministry.

In 1880, fearing the threatened civil disturbance over the rival presidential candidacies of Roca and Tejedor, Frías sought to persuade both candidates to withdraw and to support *"un candidato de transacción,"* who might avoid civil war. His efforts were unsuccessful, and a brief outbreak of violence ended by assuring Roca of victory. Somewhat disillusioned by this course of events and in very poor health, Frías set out for Europe. He died in Paris on November 9, 1881.

The foregoing biographical outline gives prominence to the political posts in Frías' career, but his total work must be evaluated against the background of the professional journalist. It is no libel on that profession to say that a great deal of its output is worth reading only on the day that it is produced. In spite of the transitory significance of much of his writing, Frías did, however, leave some permanent contributions to the growth of the Argentine nation.

Before examining these contributions it may be well to note that Frías is in many ways the most *sectarian* in outlook of all the important nineteenth century Catholic writers in his country. Paradoxically, however, he finds the religion-inspired national societies that he wants the Argentines to imitate almost exclusively in the countries where Protestantism is the dominant religion. His highest praise is, with certain exceptions, reserved for Protestant leaders in England and the United States. Frías' life was spent entirely in the Catholic cultures of Latin America and southern Europe, but his admiration for both the United States and England is profound, and it rests solely on the fact that he believed that these were the two countries which had most thoroughly kept the Christian tradition as an active social influence.

Familiarity with Frías' tendency to take up the ready and easy argument on behalf of a cause he is defending may lead the casual reader of his works to misconstrue the paradoxical quality of the orthodox Catholic's admiration for Protestant cultures. Frías sought an audience that was really more interested in political and economic success than it was in religion. If he could show that the two countries whose names glowed brightest with the aura of success were also religious countries, would not his readers be inclined to admit religion to a more secure place in their own society? It might be argued that such was his intention, but the argument would probably not be sound. Frías did not portray either the United States or England as ideal countries, and he was quite specific about what he found wrong with them. He informed his readers that the condition of the industrial proletariat in Britain was inexcusable, and he deplored the existence of slavery in the United States up to the time when it was abolished. His recognition of what was good and what was bad in both societies can lead only to the conclusion that Frías' admiration for these countries was sincere in the sense that he did not hesitate to qualify it.

One other facet of Frías' history should be noted here, namely, the accusation that his commitment to Catholicism was opportunistic. The accusation has issued from some rather highly placed sources. Ingenieros asserts [67] that Frías was not a Catholic when he took up the struggle against the tyranny. The reasons given are that Frías joined the *Joven Argentina* in 1837 and that the lodge was anti-Catholic in character. Moreover, Ingenieros suggests in the same passage that all the avowed Catholics of the time were on the side of Rosas. The position of Gorriti and numerous other lesser clerical figures at the time makes the latter assertion extremely dubious. The secret nature of *La Joven Argentina* gives more validity to the first reason, since the antipathy of the Catholic Church to secret societies is well known. However, the *Joven Argentina* was not at any time a part of organized Freemasonry, and Ingenieros himself has to argue at some length in other passages to try to prove that the lodge had a definitely anti-Catholic character.[68] The argument is suggestive, but not conclusive. At the same time Ingenieros notes that while Echeverría, the principal author of the *Dogma* and the leader of the lodge, had strong anti-Catholic convictions, he went to some pains to conceal them lest they alienate his followers. What in the long run may be more significant, however, is the fact that while certain members of the *Asociación* could in later years qualify as nominal Catholics in the sense of Article 2 of the Constitution, Frías stands alone as the only major figure of Argentine Catholicism to emerge from the famous lodge of the 1830's.[69]

The opportunistic character of Frías' Catholicism is established by Ingenieros [70] on the basis of Frías' relations with the "*sociedad conservadora de Bolivia*" after his exile. Here and also in Chile,

67. *La Evolución de las Ideas Argentinas,* Vol. IV, p. 396.
68. *Ibid.,* pp. 273–275.
69. *Ibid.,* pp. 280–81.
70. *Ibid.,* p. 396.

it is suggested, Frías came under obligation to important Catholic families, and it was to his advantage to take on the role of champion of Catholicism.

Sarmiento, too, records a disbelief in the genuineness of Frías' early Catholicism. In the obituary tribute which he published in the *Diario* of Buenos Aires in 1881, Sarmiento says that *"ser católico en todas las consecuencias"* was true only of the last phase of Frías' life.[71] He asserts that when Frías first went to Chile in the 1840's he was not a practicing Catholic, but a "literary partisan" of religion.[72] The fierce apologist came later, he suggests, and shows the influence of Louis Veuillot. The implication is that Frías at best is only "moderately" Catholic.

From 1855 to 1880 Frías and Sarmiento had frequently been antagonists on the public scene. Yet they held many views in common, and they admired each other as men. Sarmiento wrote the above judgment immediately following his long-time opponent's death, which happened to coincide with the time in which the major battles between Catholics and laicists were shaping up.[73] It is quite clear that Sarmiento, the laicist, was trying to do what was in his mind a kindness to the memory of his friend by toning down the Catholicism that was in his reputation. This fact, taken together with Sarmiento's notorious tendency to generalize on the basis of insufficient data, diminishes the value of his judgment on this particular point in Frías' life.

It is probably impossible to establish beyond all doubt just what the degree of Frías' commitment to Catholicism was in his youth. Questioning the judgments cited above does not, of course, establish him as a Catholic in that period. Whatever his initial motives may have been for becoming the promoter of Catholic views among the exiles, his record contains nearly forty years of active apologetics. It is on the basis of these activities that his work must be judged.

If allowance is made for the fact that Frías' religious commitment separates him to a certain extent from some of the other leaders of his generation, his general significance in the development of the Argentine nation is largely identical with that of the

71. Sarmiento's article is reprinted in Vol. IV, p. 426 *et seq.* of Frías, *Escritos Y Discursos.*
72. *Ibid.,* p. 430.
73. See Ch. VI, pp. 186–204.

rest of *La Joven Argentina,* as it has been summarized in Chapter II. Frías partook of the realism which dominated political thought and action after 1853. As a *porteño* legislator up to 1861 he labored to overcome the separation between the province and the federation and to strengthen national unity. He also shared in the great enthusiasm for building a system of universal education.

His realistic outlook is demonstrated first by his attitude toward the fallen Rosas and his followers. Like the other exiles who were returning to occupy public offices in the 1850's, Frías had no reason to defend the tyrant and his system. But, he argued, the system had lasted for so many years and had so complicated the whole picture of social relations that reparation for all the injustice of the regime was impossible. Opposing a *"juicio de Rosas"* in the Buenos Aires Legislature in 1857, he reminded his fellow-members that: "When a country has lived for half a century in disorder, everybody has sinned a little; we can confess it without much modesty." [74] He was arguing that if the Legislature undertook reprisals against Rosas, it could unwittingly start a reign of terror which would eventually spare no one. Apart from his conviction that the wrongs of the past could never be righted, Frías thought that the future of the country demanded so much attention that time and energy would be wasted in looking at the past: "The enemy is not behind us, but in front of us. The enemy is the ignorance of the people in their state of demoralization; the enemy is the vast and unpeopled plain. Let us build schools, let us raise high the Cross on new towers so that the emigrant reaching the Plata's majestic waters may know that a vigorous civilization is rising here." [75]

The rhetoric does not cloud over the very practical ends which Frías sought. Like Alberdi he wanted to fill up the wide empty spaces of Argentina with European immigrants.[76] If the present sparse population of the country was to engage in a perpetual family fight, then no newcomers would be attracted. Though most of his liberal contemporaries would regard immigration as a sound program, the circumstances under which Frías offered these views

---

74. *Escritos,* Vol. III, p. 293.
75. *Ibid.,* pp. 315–316.
76. In 1849 Frías had presented to Victor Hugo the idea that South America would be a cure for Europe's economic and social ills, because the new world could absorb the old's excess population. *Ibid.,* Vol. I, p. 57.

involved him in the risk of being tagged a reactionary. For his attitude was expressed in debates over bills to expropriate some of the lands which had been privately acquired by legal swindle during the dictatorship.[77] Frías opposed expropriation, not out of love for the *rosistas*, but because he was afraid of where the precedents thus established might lead. Since the effect of Frías' efforts was to defend followers of the tyrant, these actions may have helped to give him the reputation of being a reactionary. The text of his discourses, however, shows that Frías was actually more fearful of a rising legislative tyranny than he was of the fallen despot. He told the legislators that the business they were engaged in was not properly theirs. It belonged to the courts, where specific questions of property rights are traditionally settled. If the legislature was to usurp this function of the judiciary, then it could begin to usurp others.[78]

A second aspect of Frías' realism is one held in common with most of the others in the generation of 1853. It is shown in the firm intention to eliminate doctrinaire and philosophical systems as the bases underlying political authority. Frías' disdain for and condemnation of the "philosophers" appear so strong in some passages that he could be described as anti-intellectual, if it were not for other passages which show a contrary quality. His characteristic lack of system, noted above, makes it almost impossible to fix his definite position.

The name Rivadavia was supposed to symbolize all the errors which the leaders of the 1850's attributed to the early intellectuals. Yet Frías, viewing Rivadavia in retrospect, found him admirable and praised him highly.[79] As a Catholic he could hardly eulogize Rivadavia's ecclesiastical policy, but Frías brushed this off as the product of the "errors of the age rather than of the man." Echeverría was another intellectual whose name was not especially acceptable in Catholic circles, although, as noted above in Chapter II, Echeverría had led a very different intellectual movement than had Rivadavia. For Echeverría, too, Frías expressed his admiration and approval.[80]

77. *Ibid.*, Vol. III, p. 284, "El juicio de Rosas," p. 285, "La Casa de Anchorena," p. 302, "La Ley de Tierras."
78. *Ibid.*, p. 305.
79. *Ibid.*, Vol. I, p. 330 *et seq.*
80. *Ibid.*, Vol. III, p. 302 *et seq.*

Frías' critical attitude toward the intellectuals was more likely to be general than specific. On occasion he condemned them *en masse,* but he rarely attacked individuals. Like Zuviría, Estrada, and other Catholic thinkers of the century, his distrust of the intellectuals centered in their role in the period between 1810 and 1830. Their "philosophy" had resulted in chaos, and the dictatorship had been the reaction of the people to the chaos. Now in the post-1853 period the masses were being blamed for the excesses of the tyranny, but Frías maintained that responsibility for the excesses could be traced to the *"sabios"* who had confused the people so much that they did not know what they were doing.[81] Frías recognized that the *civilization* which the new leaders were trying to secure would need the force of ideas as well as action, but he clearly never wanted the men of ideas to be exclusively the directing agents of the nation. A year before the fall of Rosas he had summarized his ideas in a letter to Alberdi; he wrote that a "true civilization" would be a "great capital of honor and virtue rather than of principles and ideas." [82] To support his views he pointed to France, the country of the intellectuals, in which, he said, admirable ideas flourished, but which was a poor thing in comparison with England and the United States where ideas were meager, but where actions produced "true civilization." The latter countries set the examples which Argentina should copy. He did not mean copying their constitutions—he was strongly opposed to that—but he did urge that the respect which Anglo-American institutions showed for tradition and custom made them worthy of imitation.

Moreover, copying this feature of the United States would be in his view the best guarantee that the southern republics would not fall prey to the expanding power of the United States. Doctrinaire liberalism, he argued in another article, was sapping the vitality of Latin America and western Europe. From this, he prophesied, anarchy would result. Anarchy would open the door to Russian dominance of Europe and to United States mastery of the western hemisphere.[83] Mexico had just lost Texas and California to the northern power. According to Frías' forecast—the

81. *Escritos,* Vol. III, pp. 247–248.
82. *Ibid.,* Vol. I, p. 20.
83. *Ibid.,* pp. 460–461.

date is 1854—Nueva Granada (Colombia) would soon find the United States taking over the Isthmus of Panama. Frías seemed to entertain no animosity toward the United States for acts of this sort, but he suggested that the growing nation in the north could not tolerate the threat to its own interests which the chaotic conditions of the republics to the south offered. And he put the responsibility for these conditions exclusively on Mexican and Colombian intellectual liberals. Historically, this is, of course, a vast oversimplification, and Frías' argument loses weight accordingly. It is, however, a demonstration of his basic antipathy to what he considered the influence of the doctrinaire in Latin American politics.

This antipathy was largely shared by Frías' coevals who had come out of the *Asociación de Mayo*. Their *Dogma* had rejected doctrinaire liberalism, and had put forth the "necessities of the country" as the criterion of political organization and action. Frías, however, included a specific grievance against the intellectuals which was not shared by the majority. This was the fact that he attributed to the vast body of them in the time of independence as well as in his own time a bias against religion.

In his treatment of this matter he alternates between two bases of argumentation and he uses one or the other depending upon which seems more likely to convince his audience of the moment. One is the concern with the social and civil effects of religion. It is related to his contention that everyone and every human society needs a final system of values that is above "capricious changes" and the reach of tyrants, and is "superior to human laws" with all their imperfections.[84] Only religion can offer this system. The "philosophers" who attack this system or who undermine the possibility of maintaining such a system by showing that human beings have only the knowledge of this world to guide them do an injustice to humanity. Therefore they are bad.

His other basis is more directly related to his own personal faith. He frequently felt that the intellectuals were challenging it, and he interpreted their challenge as one to his right to profess his own creed. Like most Argentines, Catholic and non-Catholic, Frías was not opposed to toleration of a diversity of creeds.[85] But he felt that *"libertad de cultos"* in the intellectuals' eyes was too

84. *Ibid.*, p. 33.
85. Religious toleration will be treated in Ch. V, pp. 153–158.

frequently a *"libertad contra los cultos."* [86] In the passages where this consideration is uppermost in his mind, he is much more the doctrinal apologist than in others.

Recognition of these two standards probably helps to clarify the apparent confusion between Frías' contradictory claims to be both a liberal and a conservative. He is in the long run entirely conservative, but there were many occasions in his life when he insisted that he was a liberal. These were generally the occasions when he was trying to demonstrate that a liberal society and a democratic government were entirely compatible with Catholic teaching. Thus in 1849 he wrote an article from Paris for publication in Chile in which he maintained that he was a Christian, because he was a liberal.[87] A few years later he wrote the Chilean Catholic leader Tocornal that "our first duty" is to demonstrate that Catholicism belongs in a new society dedicated to social progress.[88] On these and similar occasions Frías could profess liberalism, and there is not much reason to doubt that the profession was sincere. When, however, he met with what he considered a challenge to his right to hold his own religious belief and to have it protected with all the traditional safeguards of a Catholic culture, he immediately became what he called a conservative. In this vein he could tell Sarmiento in 1878, when the battles over laicization were beginning to shape up, that "my opinions were always conservative." [89]

Frías' liberal-conservative dichotomy is more apparent than real, and on many occasions it has no more validity than a mere journalistic convenience. Yet it cannot be ignored, because it shows Frías, the Catholic, responding to a variety of forces and trends in the 1853–1880 period. The Catholic liberal responded in one way, the Catholic conservative in another.

Frías' years in Europe had taught him, or so he thought, that it was possible for a Catholic to be a liberal. The men whom he followed and for whom he had a life-long admiration were Montalembert and Bishop Dupanloup of Orléans.[90] When he returned

86. *Escritos,* Vol. I, p. 53.
87. *Ibid.,* p. 6.
88. *Ibid.,* p. 236.
89. *Ibid.,* Vol. III, p. 216.
90. *Ibid.,* pp. 266, 270; *ibid.,* Vol. I, p. 52. A letter from Estrada to Frías in 1871 indicates, however, that Frías may have had some doubts about Montalembert's

to Buenos Aires, he found that the intellectual and social climate of the new state was favorable to both Catholicism and liberalism as he understood them. The new leaders, excepting a few, were not ardent Catholics. At the most the majority could claim only a nominal adherence to the creed. But they had decided that religion was a necessity for the people, and they had written into the Constitution what was on the surface at least a protection of religion. Frías found this atmosphere congenial, and to the extent that it was the condition that prevailed for most of the rest of his life, his Catholic liberalism is consistent with the national trends of the period.

In contrast, his conservatism is not typical of the age. It was stimulated by the laicizing movements which began in the provinces in the 1860's and reached their culmination on a national scale only after Frías' death.[91] The objective of the laicists, in which they were largely successful, was to remove certain functions from ecclesiastical jurisdiction and put them in the hands of the state. These included the keeping of vital statistics, regulation of marriage, burials and education. This change in jurisdiction was carried out without disturbing the pattern of Church-State relations which the Constitution had established and with no overt threat to the "official" position of the Church. Frías fought against the movement on two grounds. He attacked it first because it was a departure from tradition and, he declared, out of keeping with the spirit of the Constitution, though there was no violation of the letter. Secondly, while he did not oppose the right of the state to intervene in these matters to the extent of protecting public interest, he assailed the claim of exclusive jurisdiction which was being pushed in certain matters, e.g., marriage laws and records.

In these battles Frías upheld a minority position. The main current was running strongly against him, and by the end of the century laicization was largely complete. This part of his record was to lead future historians to categorize him as conservative

---

position after 1870. See Estrada, *La Iglesia Y El Estado* (Buenos Aires, 1930), p. 100.

91. Some examples of Frías' treatment of these movements are found in the following: his attack on the Governor of Santa Fe, *Escritos*, Vol. III, p. 9 *et seq.*; "Los Derechos de los Frailes," *ibid.*, p. 108 *et seq.*; his polemic with Sarmiento over public charity, *ibid.*, pp. 138–144; articles on the school question, *ibid.*, pp. 180, 389, 416.

and reactionary and out of step with the main developments of Argentine nationalism in the later years of his life. In reality there probably never was much change in Frías' outlook from the date of his exile down to his death. What changed was the spirit of the times. As a Catholic liberal he could join forces with the leading men of the first two decades after 1853. Later, however, these men and their successors moved further in the direction of the secular state than Frías was willing to go. Standing pat on the first position, the Catholic liberal found himself a conservative according to his own definition and according to his critics.

It has been suggested above that Frías was generally in accord with the prevailing ideas of his generation about the form of national government and the institutions which would build national unity. This means that he was a Federalist, even though like Zuviría he had some record of Unitarism in his early background. His work on behalf of national unity, however, was less general than Zuviría's in that it was directed almost exclusively to the task of bringing his own province into the federation through negotiation and compromise with the national authorities.

Some inconsistencies in his record ought to be noted in this connection. Frías did not, after returning to his country, join the Federalist forces at Paraná. Alberdi did, and so did some of the other one-time members of the *Joven Argentina*. Frías chose, rather, to remain in Buenos Aires and to accept a seat in the provincial legislature. In this his decision was like that of Mitre and Sarmiento, who also refused to support the federation until after Urquiza had been removed. The record does not show, however, that like Mitre and Sarmiento he was opposed to Urquiza, and Frías' claim that he used his legislative post only to further the work of union at all times is probably justified.

The claim is supported by the fact that although he was willing to hold a legislative office, he refused to take part in the executive structure of the Buenos Aires government. He refused to serve after being elected Vice-Governor.[92] While the explanation of his refusal is vague, probably deliberately so, it is likely that he could not in conscience accept even a relatively innocuous post in an administration which was headed by Mitre, who was the sworn enemy of Urquiza and—so long as Urquiza remained—the lead-

92. *Escritos*, Vol. III, pp. 224–225.

ing obstacle to provincial incorporation. To be allied with Mitre would have disqualified him for the task of negotiation which, he thought, was entirely consistent with his legislative office.

It is also possible that there was an opportunistic element in his action in that union of Buenos Aires with the rest of the provinces was bound to take place at some day, and Frías could have foreseen that on that day he would not want his name linked with any record of opposition. A few days before the battle of Pavón, which was to leave Mitre the victor over Urquiza, Frías wrote to Mitre urging him to avoid the bloodshed of another civil war and to try again to negotiate the differences between Buenos Aires and the central authority.[93] In this letter Frías bluntly told the Governor "we do not belong in the same ranks." Mitre replied with the dexterity which was to make him Argentina's most successful politician of the century, and assured Frías that they did belong in the same ranks.[94] Their differences were concerned only with the procedures to be employed in obtaining national union. Since the differences between them were those between war and peace, it may be argued that they were somewhat deeper than the merely procedural. Nevertheless, when Mitre's action did achieve national union, Frías did not oppose it, even though he had urged that it ought to be obtained in a different manner.

The emphasis on universal education has been noted as a dominant characteristic of the leaders of Frías' generation. Here again Frías' attitude may be said to be largely identical with that of the others. Like the other young men in exile in the 1840's, he had come to see *barbarism* as a threat to national development that could be met only through a system of education for all. He stressed this view in correspondence exchanged with Alberdi while both were émigrés.[95] He expressed it again in speeches and articles after his return.[96] Frías did not, however, make any original contributions to the development of an educational system.

After 1865 Frías' interest in education shifted from a general one to that of protecting what he called the "freedom of instruction." This involved him in another aspect of his fight against laicization. His concern was that the traditional role of the Church

93. *Ibid.*, p. 166.
94. *Ibid.*, p. 168.
95. *Ibid.*, Vol. I, p. 26.
96. *Ibid.*, Vol. III, p. 257.

in the educational process was being jeopardized by state control of the function. Here again it should be stressed that Frías was not opposed to state intervention *per se* so far as the state had a responsibility for the general welfare of the people. His quarrel with the laicists, however, rested on his belief that they were extending official control too far and also on the apparent fact that the laicist movement was leading up to elimination of religious instruction from the public school curriculum. (The latter was not accomplished until after Frías' death.) Frías' activities in connection with these matters raise questions which can more appropriately be treated in a later chapter.[97]

Frías' lack of system and the segmented, fragmentary character of most of his work make it extremely difficult to reach any definite conclusions about his place in Argentine history. He was the Catholic lay apologist *par excellence* of his generation. He was also a part of the full tide of Argentine nationalism in the years following 1853 when the force of *civilization* overflowed the country to submerge the *barbarism* that had been flourishing there. To say this much, however, still leaves his work and his position somewhat undefined. He was the outstanding religious apologist of his day, but he was hardly a "great" Catholic spokesman. He offered no systematic exposition and defense of the Catholic creed *in toto*. He realized that underlying his secularist adversaries' challenge was a total rejection of the validity of Christian doctrine as formulated by the Roman Catholic Church. But their overt challenge was piecemeal. They were content to leave the Church itself in a traditional, official position, while they attacked specific features, sometimes seemingly minor features, of its authority. Frías always chose to respond to the immediate, overt issue. He might have advanced his own cause more, had he directed himself to the larger underlying challenge. That he did not is probably best explained by the fact that he was a politician, not a philosopher. The immediate, tangible issue was the one that held his attention and he probably attacked it with so much zeal in the hope that the larger long-range problem need never come up.

There are limitations too on Frías' role as a spokesman for Argentine nationalism in the second half of the century. He had started out in full conformity with the spirit of his generation as

97. See Ch. V, pp. 155–156.

that spirit was manifested in the *Joven Argentina* and the *Dogma*. He was later one of the leaders who carried over that spirit into the forming of the nation. In his final years the conflicts with a rising secularism separated him to a certain extent from the majority of his generation. The conflicts separated him, but it would be too much to say that they isolated him from the over-all development of his nation. Though few of the men of 1853 had had any strong religious commitment, they had almost unanimously recognized a necessary place for religion in the new state. Their decision about its definite place may not have been the wisest one, and, as noted in Chapter I, Catholics and secularists alike have since attacked the decision. Whatever may be said in criticism, however, the decision to a large degree honors the traditional position of religion in a Catholic society. To the extent that Frías is a spokesman of this tradition, which has survived in the Argentine Constitution into the twentieth century, he has a valid status as an Argentine nationalist.

FRAY MAMERTO ESQUIÚ

As Frías was the most provocative Catholic layman of his generation, Fray Mamerto Esquiú was in almost exactly the same period the most universally revered Argentine cleric. Esquiú's life (1826–1883) runs parallel to that of Frías, and they both sought to serve substantially the same ends. But their careers and their characters offer more contrasts than similarities. The articulate, aggressive, verbose Frías was frequently a storm-center in his own day, and he has not yet ceased to be a subject of controversy. The retiring, ascetic Esquiú was sparing of his words, and hardly anyone has ever written or spoken of him except in terms of admiration and respect. Frías found his natural *milieu* in the polemics of the daily press and in the hurly-burly of legislative chambers where he traded arguments with unsparing opponents. Esquiú's early and lasting fame was as a pulpit orator who aroused in his listeners only a thoughtful and silent assent.

After a brief career of seminary teaching, Esquiú sprang into national prominence at the age of twenty-seven. The cause was his sermon, *Laetamur de vestra gloria,* preached on the occasion of the swearing of oaths to support the new Constitution in 1853. This was followed by another notable sermon on the inauguration of the new national administration.[98] The Urquiza government, looking upon these sermons as effective propaganda for national unity, had them printed and widely distributed. Public office was subsequently offered to Esquiú, but he refused it and continued to be a teacher of philosophy and theology. In later years President Sarmiento proposed Esquiú for the see of Buenos Aires, but the nomination was refused. In his middle years Esquiú spent a great deal of time away from Argentina. This included a long sojourn in Jerusalem, where he would have liked to remain indefinitely. He was, however, required to return to Argentina, and in the Avellaneda administration he was persuaded—after a long resistance—to become bishop of Córdoba. Soon afterward he died.

The universal veneration of Esquiú probably arises from the fact that he preached a patriotism that was bulwarked by Church doctrine and he gave to the developments of Argentine nationalism the sanction of religious approval. The chief formulations of his position are to be found in the sermon on the Constitution in 1853 and in the sermon given when Buenos Aires was established as the "federalized" capital in 1880. In these orations he expressed a concept of the Argentine nation and of the means by which it should be organized and governed. With this concept nearly all his listeners could agree, even though not all of them subscribed to his religious principles.

The first sermon was given in an atmosphere of enthusiasm and hope. The country had just emerged from a bloody tyranny. The task before it was to organize itself under the new constitution. Esquiú urged the people to apply themselves to the task, which, he maintained, was one that their religion imposed on them. "Religion and the Fatherland," he told them, "have identical interests, are born of the same principle, pursue . . . a common end . . ."[99] The end could be served only by stability in society and government, and the best hope for stability lay in popular acceptance of the Constitution.

His plea for acceptance of the Constitution appears to have been directed especially to two classes of persons. The first was

98. Rojas, Vol. 14, p. 277 *et seq.*, outlines Esquiú's biography; *"Laetamur de vestra gloria"* is the first article in Esquiú, *Sermones de un Patriota* (Buenos Aires, no date), *prólogo de* Mons. Miguel de Andrea. (This is Volume XVII in the second series of *Grandes Escritores Argentinos,* ed. Alberto Palcos.)
99. *Sermones,* p. 2.

made up of those who might entertain reservations out of the habits that forty years of chaos and dictatorship had engendered. They were primarily those citizens who had misinterpreted the doctrine of popular sovereignty, which had fraudulently but zealously been perpetuated by the dictatorship. The misinterpretation that Esquiú feared was the one which held that since all power resides in the people, the people might do anything they chose, including the rejection of constitutional government and the establishment of another dictatorship.

This view would, of course, be the justification of the barbarism that the new regime sought to eradicate and also an insurmountable obstacle to any kind of social stability. In trying to dispel this view Esquiú did not attack the concept of popular sovereignty, but he undertook to demonstrate its limitations. He affirmed that the "public law of modern society fixes sovereignty in the people." But he cited "religion" as the source which teaches that this is a sovereignty "of interests," not "of authority." [100] In part the distinction is only a rhetorical convenience, but in the same passage there is the citation of *Omnis potestas a Deo ordinata est.* Thereby Esquiú wanted to drive home to his audience the idea that no matter where ultimate power was located—in the people or in a monarch—it must be a responsible power. It must be accountable and must answer to a higher and more permanent standard than mere volition. He would acknowledge the right of the people to choose their own government, but he would first make them conscious of the limitations which a concept of moral responsibility imposed on their choice.

This qualified sympathy with the notion of government of and by the people continued to characterize Esquiú in his later years. In 1861 during the turmoil between Buenos Aires and the rest of the Republic he expressed it again. He noted that both Europe and America had been the scenes of revolutionary warfare to establish democratic institutions, but he confessed bafflement over the fact that the revolutions had been so similar in both hemispheres. He reasoned that they ought to be different. The European revolutions, he said, had been undertaken to do away with hereditary privilege and to attain civic equality for all. With these aims Esquiú was not unsympathetic, but he argued that they could

100. *Ibid.,* p. 12.

not justify revolution in America, because from the beginning of independence the American countries had proclaimed equality.[101]

If equality had not been honored in practice, if barbarism had all but suffocated law, he did not hesitate to say who should be blamed. Responsibility rested on "the people." It was the fashion of the times, he noted, to put the blame on the *caudillos*, but "some individual names cannot be the cause of our wars; it is not good logic to seek in little things the cause of the great things; a war of half a century throughout America is too vast a fact to be explained in terms of the caprices of *caudillos*." [102] The explanation lay rather in an impious and rebellious spirit which "agitates the hearts and hands of the American people so that they are in perpetual war with themselves."

These were harsh sentiments from a professed friend of the people. They may have been shared by others, but almost no one else at the time could have expressed them without sacrificing popular esteem.[103] Esquiú, however, did not have to consider this factor. What he wanted to establish was the logic of democratic responsibility: if the people rule—and in Argentina and on the whole American scene he could see no other possibility—let them take full responsibility. Do not, he said in effect, excuse their misdeeds as the acts of *caudillos* who have deceived the people. Right will replace wrong only when the people know that they bear the responsibility for both.

While all this is an extreme, and otherwise unformulated, expression of the views of the men who were trying to impose *civilization* on Argentina in the second half of the century, it is probably consistent with those views in the main. The spirit of the times could not fail to acknowledge the popular base of political and social institutions, but those who shared the spirit were also fearful that *barbarism* and popularity might again become identical. The aim of Esquiú's work was to destroy whatever identity existed between the two. For this reason his words were welcome wherever the fear persisted.

101. *Sermones*, p. 117.
102. *Ibid.*, p. 119.
103. The authors of the *Dogma* had had their doubts about "the people," but they had been careful not to expose them. They had limited the concept of popular sovereignty by denying universal suffrage and by establishing sovereignty in the abstract notion of the "reason of the people." *El Dogma Socialista*, p. 216.

The second class of persons to whom Esquiú's Constitution sermon was directed was composed of those Catholics who objected to the 1853 provisions governing Church-State relations. As noted elsewhere, these provisions perpetuated the regalistic arrangement for which Rosas had earlier succeeded in obtaining *de facto* acceptance. Their regalistic quality had alienated some Catholic sympathies, and it was feared that this factor might jeopardize effective acceptance of the Constitution.

Esquiú, in his sermon, confessed that he too found the provisions unattractive, but he urged all Catholics to accept them. The important consideration was, he asserted, not whether the provisions were ideally suitable, but that the Constitution be accepted as the supreme law. The major interest of religion lay in the stability which the new instrument had been designed to promote. To reject the Constitution would be equivalent to reawakening the spirit of rebellion and renewing the anarchy in which no purpose of religion would be served.[104]

The subordination of the matter of Church-State relations to what he regarded as the larger interests of religion and of the country did not mean that Esquiú had no concern for the subject. The concern, however, continued to be subordinate. Thus in later years he publicly lamented moral conditions that prevailed in the nominally Christian societies of Latin America, but indicated that the only possible cure for them lay in greater devotional practice on the part of individuals rather than in any institutional improvement of the position of the Church.[105]

A quarter century after his emergence as a national figure Esquiú preached his other most notable sermon on the day that the government was formally installed in the recently federalized capital of Buenos Aires. His audience included the President of the Republic and the other high officials of the nation. The occasion in a fundamental sense marked the completion of the process of national integration. The nation was united, the Constitution had survived for 27 years, and the large, rich city was now the capital of the land, no longer a powerful and divisive instrument to be used by provincial politicians in attempting to dominate the nation for the province's advantage.

104. *Sermones*, pp. 14–15.
105. *Ibid.*, pp. 179–180.

By a less independent-minded orator than Esquiú the occasion might have been hailed with the tone of joy and glory that had been in his *Laetamur de vestra gloria* of 1853. Esquiú specifically rejected this theme, however. He did not sound a note of gloom, but he refused to flatter his audience. In the time between the two great sermons had occurred many events that belied the hope he had expressed in the first. Buenos Aires had resisted the rest of the nation for nearly a decade, and the resistance had brought bloodshed. There had been other resorts to arms, including the incident recently passed when the city's population had briefly arisen to oppose federalization. These events had "frozen for all time my former words of congratulation." [106]

An obvious purpose of the sermon is to impress on the audience the fact that the history of the country even in the past three decades has been full of trouble, and Esquiú warned his listeners that no easy course could be expected in the immediate future. As in 1853, he stated that the main task was to win from the people acceptance of the idea that government must be by law, and on this later occasion he tied the concept of law more directly to a divine origin than he had before. In summary his exposition of the concept is the following:

The social state of man is the indispensable condition of the intellectual life of the individual. The individual man is the product of the "intervention of a creating and conserving God." But in creating the individual, God also creates a social being. If one accepts the individual man as a divinely created being, logic establishes then that there is a divine intervention in the creation of the societies in which man lives, since man without society would not be complete man. To this Esquiú added the claim that the divine authority had, through revelation and reason, not only instructed man in the abstract principles of social life, but had also established the concrete forms of domestic and civil society and of the "divers nations that cover the earth." [107] Law arises from the instruction and from the establishment of the concrete forms.

In part Esquiú's plea for recognition of divine intervention may

106. *Sermones*, p. 198.
107. *Ibid.*, pp. 202–203.

have been directed against the rise of laicism, which was to show its strength in the Roca administration, then new in office. But if it was that, it was also something more. Esquiú wanted to convince his listeners that Argentina, their nation, had enjoyed the dignity of divine origin and sanction. He therefore hoped to persuade them to treat their nation with the reverence which the origin merited. The sermon drew on the Bible and on the whole range of human history to demonstrate that the division of the human family into national units was the work of the Creator. While many in his audience were not of a mind to accept the authorities Esquiú cited, they could all subscribe to his purpose, which was to strengthen national unity through a recognition of the ultimate worth of the nation.

Speaking directly to the occasion, the establishment of the new capital, Esquiú proclaimed: "The Argentine nationality is the result of the law of history. Its republican, federal form is equally so. These two providential facts require as a condition of life and peace the definitive capitalization of Buenos Aires. Accept it then with submission not so much to men as to God Himself, to our supreme interests and those of all the Republic." [108]

When Esquiú spoke, the Argentine nation had been for a long time in the process of being created. It was a process which had attracted men of genius and imagination, and they had at long last, it was hoped, out of diverse and contradictory materials, welded a unity which gave the nation a definite being. In the tortuous and discordant course of Argentine nationalism, Esquiú had not been a front-line fighter or a major protagonist. He was rather the prophet or holy man commanding respect in all circles, whose function was to consecrate the work of hands less unblemished than his own. It is not too much to say that in the process Esquiú's was the function of innocence with all the peculiar strength that that quality provides. He was an Argentine who had nothing to share with his people except the best hopes of the nation and who had no interest to pursue except that of the well-being of his fellow-citizens. These features explain the esteem and veneration that the Argentine nation has always accorded to Esquiú.

108. *Ibid.*, p. 212.

José Manuel Estrada

José Manuel Estrada (1842–1894) was the intellectual heir to the other Catholic writers who have been discussed in the preceding pages. Though basically more liberal than Zuviría or Frías and no less so than Gorriti, he adhered rather closely to the paths that his predecessors had marked out.[109] He greatly extended those paths, however, and the basic theme which runs through Estrada's voluminous writings [110] has been identified as "Christian liberalism." [111] Important aspects of this theme make his work a more appropriate subject for the succeeding chapter. Nevertheless, Estrada's significance in the final stages of the development of Argentine nationalism should be noted here.

Estrada was a *porteño* by birth and by virtue of deep roots in the provincial history.[112] He was a great-grandson of Santiago [Jacques] de Liniers, Viceroy at the time of the English invasion. He was also related to Manuel de Sarratea, first Governor of Buenos Aires. In his youth Estrada was greatly influenced by a broad and learned teacher, Fray Buenaventura Hidalgo,[113] reputed to be a kinsman of the more famous Mexican priest of the same name. Hidalgo may have been the one who awakened the spirit of inquiry and who established the habits of system and order that were to characterize Estrada in later life.

Estrada began his public career serving as a journalist on the staff of *La Nación Argentina*, which in later years became the great Buenos Aires daily *La Nación*. In 1868 Estrada founded a periodical, *La Revista Argentina*, and he continued to write for

109. He disagreed with Frías over specific issues, but the disputes did not destroy the large area of common agreement between the two.
110. *Obras Completas de José Manuel Estrada*, 12 vols. (Buenos Aires, 1899). The title is somewhat misleading, as certain writings have been deliberately omitted.
111. Rojas, *op. cit.*, Vol. 14, p. 371.
112. The biographical sketch is based on the long introductory article by Juan M. Garro in Vol. I. of the *Obras*; on Francisco Tessi, *Vida y Obra de José Manuel Estrada* (Buenos Aires, 1929); Carlos de Patagones, *José Manuel Estrada* (Buenos Aires, 1938). Paul Groussac in his impressionistic essays, *Los Que Pasaban* (Buenos Aires, 1919), devotes a chapter to Estrada.
113. This is apparently the same Hidalgo whom Ingenieros, *op. cit.*, Vol. IV, pp. 61–62, identifies as a member of the *Junta* of "Citizens, theologians, canonists and jurists," who advised the government on the problems of the *Patronato* in 1833 and 1834. Ingenieros notes that Hidalgo dissented from the unqualified regalism offered in the majority report which was given to the government in 1834.

the press throughout his life. Journalism became, however, something of an avocation after Estrada had started on a teaching career which was to establish him as Argentina's first political scientist.[114] In this connection his first post of importance was the professorship of civic instruction in the Colegio Nacional, to which Sarmiento appointed him in 1869.[115] In 1875 he became Professor of Constitutional Law at the University of Buenos Aires. In the same year he was named Dean of the Faculty of Philosophy and Humanities, and in 1876 he was appointed Rector of the Colegio Nacional. Estrada simultaneously held these several posts until 1884. For brief periods he also combined these duties with those of an administrative officer in the public school system of the province.

Estrada's principal significance is as an educator, and his most notable writings are his university and college lectures. Like Sarmiento, however, Estrada the scholar was largely the result of an autodidactic process. He had been tutored in his childhood and early youth, but he had never attended a university or taken a degree. Hidalgo and the other tutors had started him on the road to scholarship, but his progress was almost entirely the result of his own reading and organized study.

In 1883 and 1884 the laicist trends of the Roca government aroused strong resistance from members of the Catholic hierarchy. An open conflict between Church and State followed, and Estrada became involved in the conflict. Certain bishops were threatened with criminal prosecution for the opposition to the government which had been voiced in their pastorals.[116] Estrada spoke out in defense of the bishops. His defense was directed not so much to the substance of what the bishops had written—though there is no reason to doubt that he was largely in agreement with them— but to the right of the bishops to speak freely to their followers. The government, however, took the view that the bishops were officers of the state and as such could not openly attack public policy that had been formulated by competent civil authority. A

114. Salvador Dana Montaño, *Las Ideas Políticas de José Manuel Estrada* (Santa Fe, 1944), p. 20.
115. The sources differ on the precise dates at which Estrada took up his various academic posts. The dates given above can be regarded as approximately accurate.
116. There were several distinct issues under controversy, but they centered chiefly in the school question which will be treated in Chapter VI.

professor was also an official of the state, and Estrada's participation in the conflict earned him quick dismissal from all his academic posts.

The last ten years of Estrada's life were spent in active politics. During the Roca and Juárez Celman administrations he sought to organize public opinion on behalf of ecclesiastical interests. He led in the formation of *La Unión Católica,* which later merged with other groups in *La Unión Cívica,* to become temporarily the major opposition party. He served in Congress as a Deputy from Buenos Aires during the same period. The acute differences over Church policy simmered down somewhat with the advent of Luis Sáenz Peña to the presidency in 1892. In the effort of the new administration to establish a spirit of reconciliation, Sáenz Peña offered Estrada a cabinet post in his government. Estrada's poor health led him to decline the offer, but he accepted the lesser appointment of Minister to Paraguay. He died in Asunción two years later.

Estrada's major significance in Argentine intellectual history is as a political philosopher whose basic pursuit was the demonstration of the validity of democratic principles in government and society. His democratic convictions go deeper and are subject to fewer qualifications than those of any other leading Catholic figure between him and Gorriti. The content of his theory will be examined in Chapter VI.

Here his democratic position is noted chiefly to identify the qualifications which distinguish his work slightly from the main trends of national development after 1853. Generally speaking, Estrada fully shared most of those trends at least until 1880. He was a slightly younger exponent of the *civilization* which the men of 1853 had sought to establish. Like them he rejected the doctrinaire and the abstract idea as bases of political organization. Estrada was, however, a systematic philosopher, even if a self-made one, and he could not avoid the abstractions which a systematic development of his subject entailed. His system and method were organized on an historical basis, and in 1863, in an early and rather immature piece, he set forth the large outline of his thought, as it was to remain more or less fixed throughout his life. He declared then that his studies had led him to see only three possible "social formulas" in the record of human history:

14019

(1) the "utilitarian law of the Pagans," (2) the "liberal law of Christianity," and (3) the "Utopias of the modern socialists." [117] Every thoughtful man must choose one of the three, and Estrada's choice was the second.

At the time he was probably too young to realize the primitive inadequacy of his categories, which are objectively not as rigid as he then believed them to be. In maturity, however, the polarization of his thought continued to be what is suggested in this passage. The forces at work on human societies were either Christian-liberal or utilitarian-utopian. From his university chair or in the Congressional Chamber he would expound on political and social issues in terms of a choice between the two.

For most of the time up to 1880 Estrada's attitude made him a welcome collaborator in the organizing work which the generation of 1853 was bringing to completion. The leaders of the day favored a liberal society, and if Estrada's liberalism was built on a more popular base than most of them were willing to accept, he was still essentially an academic figure with only indirect political effect. Moreover, he shared with the contemporary leaders the conviction that the real evil in Argentina's past had been the *caudillo*. His democratic commitments were of a sort which precluded his sharing the view of Esquiú, that the people were to blame for the acts of the *caudillos*.[118] With the leaders of the organization, especially Sarmiento, the eradication of the very notion of the *caudillo* was the *sine qua non* of the task for substituting *civilization* for *barbarism*. Estrada's mode of participating in this task was then entirely in keeping with the dominant spirit of the times.

In the final stages of Argentine nationalism, however, Estrada's chief work was as an educator. He sought and acquired a large audience. In the early 1860's he formed a society with other young men who conducted classes in reading and writing for workingmen and their families. In these classes he tried to instill in his pupils a sense of their nationality through elementary instruction in the history of Argentina. In 1866 he tried to make a wider and more literate audience conscious of the historical integrity of their

117. *Obras*, Vol. 2, p. 35.
118. Esquiú also differed somewhat from Estrada on the Church-State question in the 1870's; see Tessi, *op. cit.*, p. 196.

nation. The means he used were two volumes of historical lectures which he published that year and which covered the whole sweep of Argentine history from the colonization to his own times.[119] Rojas has pointed out that subsequently both Mitre and López wrote better histories of the River Plate region, but that Estrada's had the merit of being a pioneering venture.[120] As noted in Chapter II, Estrada was the first to see the importance of the *Dogma Socialista* as a primary source of the Argentine political system. He was the first to undertake an exposition of the *Dogma's* doctrine for the benefit of his students and the public at large. In this he emphasized the "Argentineness" of the *Dogma's* character and purpose.

In these and in many other historical works Estrada showed himself to be primarily a scholar, or, as he sometimes called himself, a "scientist." But at the same time he was a propagandist of Argentine nationalism. He sought to give instruction in the events which had culminated in the creation of Argentina, and he wanted the people to realize that they were an integrated people whose unity could be made the agent of their own destiny.

Estrada's story is one of success up to 1880, when it began to turn toward failure. He had been an eloquent exponent of the whole national development up till then, but as the laicist movement challenged the Christian half of his Christian-liberal synthesis, like Frías he found himself a member of a dissenting Catholic minority. Estrada might have avoided an open clash with the government at the time of the difficulty with the bishops. He could have done this by adhering to the strictly legalistic view, supported by the Constitution, that the bishops were officials of the state.[121] Had he done so, the clash would only have been postponed for a year or two, and the consequences would not have been different for Estrada.

The laicist challenge was directed to more than mere accusations of misconduct on the part of certain bishops, and for Estrada it raised fundamental questions of conscience which he

119. *Obras*, Vols. 2, 3.
120. *Obras de Ricardo Rojas*, Vol. 14, pp. 368–369.
121. As noted in Chapter I, Estrada had in 1871 opposed continuance of the traditional pattern of Church-State relations and had argued for "freeing" the Church through "separation." Whether or not he continued to hold these views in his later years is a subject of controversy.

could not have resolved in any other way than through the sacrifice of his academic career. He believed in the right of every man to make his own decisions, and this is the root of his liberal democratic philosophy. But if the decisions were to be good and reasonable, their maker must be free to draw on a source of moral instruction. Estrada saw in traditional Christian doctrine the only source of moral instruction that had been widely accepted in his society. He would impose the doctrine on no one, but just as he would leave everyone free to accept it or reject it, so too he would maintain that the source of the doctrine must be allowed to operate without restraint. He saw in laicism an attempt to restrict the source which he believed must be left free, and the restrictions took the concrete form of limiting the institutional functions of the Church.

The laicists saw the matter in a quite different light. For them "birth [baptism], education, matrimony and death," were "four acts through which the priesthood of a foreign cult could tyrannize a conscience." [122] To transfer jurisdiction over these "acts" to the state was for the laicists a triumphant liberation of the Argentine conscience and the supreme expression of the new moral force of the nation.

In Estrada's view, however, the movement enjoined the impact of religion from the four most decisive stages in the life of the individual and thereby became the equivalent of initiating the curtailment of Christian doctrine as a source of moral instruction. The state, he thought, would eventually replace the Church in this general function, and with the shifting stands of the state a kind of Caesaro-Papism would succeed to the Christian religion. This view, that a combination of politics and religion under a single direction, or an eclipse between civil and religious society to the advantage of one and the detriment of the other, would produce a totalitarian social structure, was not a new one for Estrada in the 1880's. He had voiced it years before in the criticism he had leveled at the Jesuits in their management of the Paraguayan Missions.[123] There, however, his criticism had fallen on Churchmen, not politicians, and his words had caused no turmoil because they dealt innocuously with a situation two centuries past.

122. Rojas, Vol. 14, pp. 50–51.
123. "Los Comuneros de Paraguay," *Obras*, Vol. I, p. 235 *et seq.*

Estrada's attack in the eighties originally provoked astonishment and surprise in both Catholic and laicist circles. Some in the former had entertained doubts about his orthodoxy through a misinterpretation of his liberalism, while many laicists had thought that Estrada's nationalist liberalism necessarily put him in their camp. Neither side had any real reason to be surprised. Estrada was a liberal and he was a nationalist with a boundless enthusiasm for human freedom and for the well-being and progress of his nation. But he was also a philosopher, and his philosophic system rested on the "liberal law of Christianity." The dire potentialities that he saw in the laicist movement never fully materialized—perhaps the counter-action that he helped to stimulate was one of the reasons why they did not. He saw them, however, as a threat to the basis of his system, and his reaction could not have been otherwise than it was.

NATIONALISM AND CATHOLICISM

In Argentina the status of the Church has not offered persistent problems, nor has it often given rise to acute conflicts between civil and religious authorities, as it has in many other Latin American countries. Zealous Catholics have from time to time deplored the regalism on which the status rests, and convinced liberals have often found the official support of the Church incongruous. Yet neither group has to date done anything serious to make the situation more to its liking.

The relative harmony between Church and State has meant, among other things, that as the Argentine nation-state developed there was no strong force of doctrinal or credal origin to pull Catholic thought and sentiment away from the main trends of that development. Spokesmen for the Catholic position have deviated only slightly from the prevalent nationalist line, and one of the principal reasons for this state of affairs has undoubtedly been the general lack of institutional conflict.

This is not to suggest that a distinctively Catholic pattern of social thought necessarily requires conflict to thrive on in the modern world. But the almost monotonous conformity of Catholic thought in Argentina with the dominant trends of national development, to say nothing of its insufficient originality, raises the questions of just what its claim to distinctiveness may be and whether it has been a conscious, contributory factor in the growth of the nation. Gorriti has a brilliant originality and stands in the forefront of his times. So too does Estrada at a later date. Zuviría and Frías march at a more pedestrian pace in the realm of the intellectual. But in the supposedly Catholic culture of Argentina all of them are equaled or surpassed in effectiveness by secularist leaders, with whom, despite underlying differences, they were in general agreement on programs of action. Gorriti, even with allowance for the "historical neglect" which Rojas has lamented, is seen as being outshone in his own day first by Moreno and then by Rivadavia. The secularly inspired Alberdi, Mitre and Sarmiento head the movements which Zuviría and Frías support and which Esquiú blesses, but this support does not give the movements a Catholic character. Estrada, for all his talents, does not win a permanent political following. A logical development from his doctrine would have been the emergence of a Christian Democratic political party. Argentina did not see such a development until 1955 and then in a wavering and uncertain form with only a tenuous connection to Estrada's doctrines. In contrast, his no less talented Chilean kinsman, the anti-Catholic leader Francisco Bilbao, is frequently acclaimed as the intellectual ancestor of the very substantial and long-established Radical parties in both of the southern republics.

With full allowance for the merits which Catholic thinkers have demonstrated, one is still tempted to take a somewhat unflattering view of Argentine Catholic thought. One may be led to believe that it is at best imitative and at worst mediocre. It produces largely *agreement* with secularist trends, even though the agreement is offered on a different basis. When it is in *disagreement*, it generally fails to turn aside the specific trends which it opposes and at the same time generally fails to protect the specific Catholic practice which is menaced. Meanwhile the basically harmonious pattern of ecclesiastical-civil relations persists, in spite of occasional discord, from Rosas to Aramburu. It persists, however, one is tempted to believe, because secularists and laicists want it that way, not because Catholics are in a position to keep it that way.

Admittedly the temptation to make these judgments is strong, but they would have only a superficial validity. Such judgments could result from a narrow concentration on one aspect of Argentine development, but they would ignore the rest of the factors that enter into the complex. Viewed in the totality of Argentine experience, Catholic thought can be assessed in a more positive way.

Its position can be evaluated in terms of the interplay of the forces that have caused Argentine national existence. At its inception the new nation was, with the exception of a few urban centers, a primitive, crude thing. The men of vision who tore the region loose from its imperial ties foresaw gigantic tasks ahead of them. They saw a wilderness to be opened up and populated and organized in the name of modern civilization. There was also the idea in the minds of many that in the society to be created the human being should have both a greater measure of individual freedom and a voice in determining who should direct and rule society as well as how it should be ruled.

In attaining these goals Argentina has no record of unqualified success. Oligarchies have sometimes betrayed the democratic implications of the goals. Other times have seen tyrants and dictators perverting them. Yet the goals remain, and in the long run they have been served. Their persistence as goals, as well as progress toward their attainment, is the justification of the Argentine nation.

Particularly in the period considered in the foregoing pages, these goals establish for Argentina a character that calls up the adjectives, *new, bold, experimental, venturesome, revolutionary*. In the same period national development draws on the fund of common experience of Western Civilization, but it is not bound by precedent. Tradition has in part been consciously rejected, in part, proven inapplicable.

The quality of primitive newness in the nation stands in vivid contrast to the ancient creed which is professed by the vast majority of the people and which is under the tutelage of a tradition-laden, authoritarian Church. The contrast between the New Nation and the Old Church could have been made into the cause of major social disruption and perpetual conflict. It was in several other Latin American republics. In Argentina it was not.

Where conflict has occurred, however, it has not usually been the simple result of the contrast between the new and the old, but rather the consequence of a distortion of the contrast by one side or the other. Catholic spokesmen have seen in the liberal standards of the new societies a total menace to religion with which no compromise is possible. (On occasion they have been encouraged in this view by parties who have had a vested interest in the survival of certain features of the *ancien régime*.) On the other hand, liberal secularists have seen in the authoritarian base of the Catholic religion an obstacle to freedom and a threat to national independence in the universal Church's ties of loyalty to Rome. (On occasion they have been encouraged in this view by parties who sought a personal advantage in a redistribution of Church properties.) Both these views are oversimplifications, yet both have been applied with disastrous results.

The work of the Catholic social thinkers in Argentina has been a large factor in sparing their country the unfortunate consequences of such distortions. To acknowledge this is not to deny credit to Argentine secularists who have also labored to prevent a distortion of the contrast between civil and religious traditions. On behalf of the major Catholic writers, however, it must be made clear that they have not merely followed and imitated the secularists. They saw not only that there was nothing in the promise of a free society that denied any essential of religion but also that the new nation-state offered an attractive theatre of action for Christian principles. They carried this idea to the people. Whether with the boldness of a Gorriti or with the caution of a Zuviría, their contribution was a creative one. They did not hold back the people from the task of nation-building, but rather offered them their particular form of encouragement in the task. Viewed in this light their work was not imitative, but distinctive and necessary to the development of Argentine nationalism. It was subtle rather than mediocre.

CHAPTER IV

The Argentine Search for Democracy

IT IS necessary at this point to pause briefly in our examination of Argentine Catholic thought to consider another most important factor in the background against which Catholic thought has developed. This is the search for democracy as the system which makes possible the rule of the people. The search may be regarded in many respects as the inseparable twin of the movement of nationalism. The history of this movement has indeed its dark pages where the emphasis which nationalism places on *the people* produces as its political manifestation a massive demagoguery rather than an ordered democracy. But the promise of Argentine nationalism is the rule of the people as the guardians of a system which through law seeks the balance between order and liberty, which in turn makes for freedom of the individual and accountability of those who hold political office.

The preceding chapter shows that there is a general endorsement of the content of this promise on the part of the nineteenth-century Catholic writers. As the quest for democracy became a more conscious search for the forms, procedures and standards that would be consistent with that promise, these writers and those who came after them in the present century had to attempt to solve problems of evaluation within the framework of this general endorsement. Some of their solutions lined them up with the main trends of Argentine development. Others questioned and opposed the prevailing trends, sometimes to the point where Catholics were judged anti-democratic. Chapters V and VI will deal with Catholic attitudes toward various problems which the search for democracy has involved.

Before approaching this subject, however, it will be useful to devote the present chapter to a short consideration of the national search for effective democracy and particularly to the obstacles which the search has encountered. Catholic positions in the later chapters will then stand out in somewhat clearer relief against the background.[1] This account does not undertake to evaluate the whole range of the democratic effort, its success, and its failures. It is in large part merely an acknowledgment of some chief obstacles to democratic growth, obstacles which in themselves indicate the reality of the search.

A general problem of achieving a working balance among the three branches of government has long plagued Argentine democracy. Though the Constitution of 1853 makes the legislative, executive and judicial branches theoretically co-equal, it does not maintain a genuine division and balance among them. The powers of the executive, especially that of "intervention," [2] are so extensive that they make the President a dominant figure in whose shadow the other two branches must work. This is not to suggest that the Argentine President is necessarily a tyrant, but the powers at his command are enormous and they are not always checked by corresponding powers in the legislature and judiciary.

Related to this situation are two other obstacles which have impeded the march of democracy from time to time. The first of these is the inadequacy of the electoral process as a sanction for the accountability of officials to the people. The other is in the threat of military intervention in the political processes. The treatment of the electoral question which is offered below is focused on the Electoral Reform of 1911–13. In this account President Roque Sáenz Peña serves as the symbol of the forces seeking to surmount this particular obstacle in the path of effective democracy, but it must be understood that in the background of the Sáenz Peña reform there is a broad-based social movement exerting tremendous pressure for popular democracy, and threatening revolution if no other channel for the popular will is opened up.[3] In succeeding pages attention is given to the problem of

1. Treatment of the problem of Argentine democracy is found in many works by both Argentine and foreign authors. Among the latter Ysabel F. Rennie, *The Argentine Republic* (New York, 1945), gives a good general history. Some penetrating evaluation and criticism may be found in Arthur P. Whitaker, *The United States and Argentina* (Cambridge, 1954).
2. Intervention is treated in terms of concrete examples below, p. 119.
3. See Whitaker, *op. cit.*, pp. 56–60.

military intervention in terms of its three significant manifestations since 1930.

THE ELECTORAL FACTOR

A good part of the history of constitutionalism in Western society can be written in terms of the evolution of guarantees of accountability of the governors to the governed. But the guarantees of constitutionalism are largely, though not exclusively, those of structure or framework. They can give democracy a vertebrate character, but they cannot create the organic vitality in which the democracy must manifest its being. This vitality must spring from both the tissues of society itself and from the processes of their sustenance and development.

The efficiency of any process is a relative matter, and all structures are marked by imperfections. Nevertheless, in a political system where both structure and process are sufficiently effective to make government by the people a reasonable and attainable possibility, a claim may be made for the existence of democracy. The claim cannot often be in absolute terms. The relative efficiency of the processes will almost certainly make that impossible.

The student of democracy in Argentina is confronted with a great temptation to dispose of the case by saying that the structure has been excellent, but that the processes adequate to a working democracy have never taken hold. Though this may be superficially convincing, it is a judgment that could be made only at the cost of reducing a most complex situation to unjustifiably simple terms.

In the constitutional history of Argentina one can readily detect a respect for the people as the source of power and authority. It is reflected in the 1853 instrument of government in various ways. The provision for periodical elections and the prohibition against successive terms for the Chief Executive are steps in the direction of enabling the electorate to make free choices in selecting and changing their officials. Under Perón the prohibition against successive presidential terms was done away with, but as long as the article stood it was honored, in spite of the disproportionate power of the President.

In contrast, however, the electoral process has rarely, perhaps only once or twice in a century, enabled the electorate to make a free choice in an open election between rival candidates for the Presidency. Too often the voters have been confronted with one candidate who could not lose. The articulate spokesmen for the various interests in the dynamic society of Argentina after 1860 learned early and thoroughly the value of quiet compromise and behind-the-scenes deals. They were also sometimes afraid— and this may be to their credit—that open contests might provoke bloodshed. Consequently, in the heyday of the "oligarchy" rivalries were often dissolved well in advance of elections by finding a *"candidato de transacción,"* whom no conspicuous or powerful group would challenge. These men faced nominal opponents, but the victory was never in doubt. In office they displayed more often than not statesmanlike abilities, but they were aware that they were not the free choice of the electorate.

The emergence of more completely organized political parties early in the twentieth century, with the Radicals (*Unión Cívica Radical*) assuming the role of the "opposition," promised to change this situation. The rise of the Radicals together with the electoral reforms sponsored by President Roque Sáenz Peña in 1912 [4] gave grounds for hope that contesting parties might in the future be able to bid openly for majority support and that out of these contests would emerge governments headed by men who had learned the lessons of democratic accountability. Three successive Radical victories between 1916 and 1928 did not prove that the hope was well grounded. In the 1930's the *Concordancia*, representing an agreement between Conservatives and right-wing Radicals, took charge, repeating the compromises characteristic of the later nineteenth century.

Sáenz Peña's reforms were, it should be noted, designed to accomplish something more than the emergence of parties with definite platforms and sets of principles. His electoral law sought to establish the "secret and obligatory" ballot and thereby to end a fraud which had been notorious. The statute also promised an assured legislative representation to what Sáenz Peña called the minority. To accomplish the first aim voting was tied to the system of military conscription. Each adult male was required to register for military service. His registration certificate, kept in

4. Law No. 8871, promulgated February 13, 1913.

the enrollee's possession, then became his ticket of admission to the voting booth. The certificate, presented and stamped each time the holder exercised the right of suffrage, became the key instrument in a plan to prevent illegal multiple voting, the stealing of votes, etc. Minority representation in the Chamber of Deputies was guaranteed by the device known as the "incomplete list." Under this arrangement the majority party in each province obtained two-thirds of the provincial delegation to the lower house of the Federal Congress, while the party with the second largest number of votes received the remaining one-third.

President Sáenz Peña was able to secure passage of his bill in spite of strong opposition. Criticism of the measure continued for more than a generation after its enactment. It undoubtedly was a far from perfect statute.[5] It represented, however, the first serious and concerted attack on the problem of making the government more truly responsive to popular control. It was also—at least in part—a successful attack. For these reasons it is appropriate to dwell briefly on its origins and the environment in which it developed.

A part of its origin must lie in the personal character of Roque Sáenz Peña himself. In this respect he furnishes the appealing spectacle of the right-wing Conservative and romantic aristocrat who, paradoxically, sought to open the doors to popular participation in public affairs. Sáenz Peña's stand as a tribune of the people was genuine enough beyond all question, but there is no doubt that he had been helped to reach this position by a personal experience in the early 1890's. He himself had felt the heavy hand of the oligarchy's "caucus," which had maneuvered him out of a presidential candidacy in 1892.

5. Contemporary criticism was voiced even by those who upheld the President's position. For example, the statesman-educator, Joaquín V. Gonzáles, *Obras Completas* (Buenos Aires, 1925), Vol. XI, p. 117, voices doubts about the wisdom of tying the voters' registry to military enrollment because of the remote danger of military influence on voting; the same author, *ibid.*, p. 135, questions the value of the obligatory vote. A generally favorable treatment is given by Rudolfo Rivarola, *El Presidente Sáenz Peña y la Moralidad Política Argentina* (Buenos Aires, 1914). (This was originally published in *La Revista Argentina de Ciencias Políticas*, Año IV, Tomo IX, número 49.) A severely critical analysis is offered by Roberto Kurtz, *Votar No Es Elegir, ensayo crítico de la ley Sáenz Peña* (Buenos Aires, 1931). Kurtz asserts, p. 101, that the "caucus" had governed the country well since 1860, and the reform movement refused to acknowledge this fact, emphasizing only its errors and refusing to credit its merits.

At that time Sáenz Peña was just past forty years of age, but he had already established himself as a political figure of great promise. Ex-Presidents Mitre and Roca, finding his candidacy unacceptable but too strong to be openly opposed within Conservative circles, killed it with a weapon against which the younger man was utterly defenseless. They persuaded Sáenz Peña's father, Luis Sáenz Peña, to accept nomination for the office. The senior Sáenz Peña had already reached the age of seventy, and after being elected he found the burdens of office excessive for his years. He resigned long before his term was up. In 1892, however, the manipulations of the political bosses were successful in eliminating the younger Sáenz Peña. He could not campaign against his own father, and he was forced into a withdrawal, which, as he himself characterized it, was not a "political act, but a moral duty." [6] Furthermore, during the father's tenure of office the son felt himself obliged to detach himself entirely from the political scene.

Two decades later Roque Sáenz Peña reached the presidency. His 1910 candidacy was popular with the masses, but it lacked the spontaneous approval that he had enjoyed on the earlier occasion. He was a candidate now much more in the way that his father had been than in his own early and independent manner. Moreover, he had no illusions about the honesty of the election. He was the official candidate, and he could not lose. He was sixty years old and suffering an impairment of health which was to prove fatal before he had finished his term. It is then reasonable to speculate that Sáenz Peña's vigorous action on behalf of electoral reform was the action of a man who had long been thwarted in his desire to act on the basis of his own honestly-felt convictions, and who was conscious of the fact that this was his "last chance."

Another factor that helped to bring about the electoral reform was the fact that Sáenz Peña and his followers could recognize the legitimacy, and indeed the necessity, of opposition. They could understand, as few or none of their predecessors in power had been able to, that unless there was a feasible alternative party to the one in office, then it was a sham to say that the one in

6. Fermín V. Arenas Luque, *Roque Sáenz Peña, El Presidente del Sufragio Libre*, *prólogo de* María Raquel Adler (Buenos Aires, 1951), p. 96.

office had been democratically selected. The chief benefactors of this attitude were Sáenz Peña's opponents, the Radicals.

The Radical party had emerged out of the dissatisfaction which was widely felt in the final decade of the nineteenth century. The Radical strength was in the urban middle and lower-middle classes, unhappy with a public policy designed largely in accordance with the needs of the great agricultural interests. The first recognized party leader was Leandro Alem, upon whose death the mantle of leadership descended on the famous Hipólito Irigoyen, nephew of Alem.

So much has been written in criticism of Irigoyen that it seems unnecessary to repeat here the long list of inadequacies for leadership with which he has been customarily charged. Let it simply be admitted that Irigoyen showed his weak points as party leader and subsequently as President. They certainly did not include, however, a lack of persistence, even when persistence became an almost irrational stubbornness. Nor could one deny that Irigoyen actually enjoyed a genuine popularity among the people, equaled by no other leader before him.

President Figueroa Alcorta, Sáenz Peña's immediate predecessor in office, looked upon Irigoyen as a revolutionary and on the Radicals as organized subversion. In the 1910 elections the Radicals had charged that fraud would determine the outcome for the government's candidate, and they withdrew their own candidates, ordering the party members to abstain from voting. The government sensed revolution in the air, and the press was reporting threats of revolution from the Radical side as late as two days before Sáenz Peña's inauguration in October.

One account [7] has it that the outgoing President decided that the only way to assure Sáenz Peña's inauguration was to arrest Irigoyen. Sáenz Peña was at the moment returning from a European trip, and President Figueroa Alcorta sent an emissary to meet his ship at Montevideo and determine whether he would approve of Irigoyen's arrest. Sáenz Peña's reply is reported to have been, in effect, to leave Irigoyen alone. He gave the not entirely apposite but still compelling reason for his decision in these terms: 1910 is the centennial anniversary of the May

7. Juan Antonio Yantorno, *Males de la Política Argentina* (Buenos Aires, 1950), p. 128.

Revolution which put Argentina on the road to national in-dependence. It would be a shame to spoil the celebration of a century of freedom with the imprisonment of a political leader. If this was Sáenz Peña's habitual romanticism speaking, it also proved to be a shrewd political stroke.

The same source and at least one other writer report that after his arrival in Buenos Aires Sáenz Peña did in fact hold a secret meeting with Irigoyen to allay the immediate difficulties and to dispose of future ones.[8] Irigoyen, supposedly, presented the President-elect with a face-to-face threat of revolution unless the election law was reformed. He argued that his party sought only to obey the constitution and to attain office through legal means. However, the government party was, he insisted, guilty of violat-ing the constitution by perpetuating the tradition of fraudulent elections. Therefore, it would be no more subversive for the Radicals to achieve power by the extra-constitutional means of revolution than it was for the government to hold on by the equally unauthorized means of fraud. Sáenz Peña did not bother to defend his party from these charges. He offered rather the pledge that his administration would seek reforms which would guarantee honest elections. If he could obtain the guarantees, he would see that they were enforced. Irigoyen then withdrew his revolutionary threats, and it is reported that this meeting was the occasion when the military enrollment certificate first was discussed as a technical means for securing honest registration.

Yantorno further reports that the two leaders then determined to have drawn up a document in which their agreement could be specifically formulated. They would sign the document and release it to the public. Legal advisers, whom they individually consulted, however, later counseled each man that he could not sign such an agreement. In Sáenz Peña's case the advice was that he could not pledge as President what ultimately depended upon Congress and that while he was at liberty to lead and encourage

8. *Ibid.*, pp. 128–130; Arenas Luque, *op. cit.*, pp. 235–236. Yantorno attributes his account to the personal reminiscences of Dr. Ramón Cárcano, a deputy in Congress at the time and a friend of Manuel Paz in whose house the two leaders allegedly met. Arenas Luque's sources are somewhat more obscure. The material has been presented here because the actions described are entirely consistent with Roque Sáenz Peña's character and because the material also tends to explain the disappearance of Radical intransigeance early in the Sáenz Peña administration.

Congress he could not obligate it to a course of action through a solemn promise given to the opposition leader. On the other side, it was advised that Irigoyen, in the absence of a specific mandate from the party, could not bind his followers to a single course of action. The agreement therefore became entirely tacit, but the events of the next two years suggest that it was effective.

When Sáenz Peña had to present and defend his program in the Congress and before the people he frequently relied upon oversimplifications and clichés. These devices clearly demonstrated the intent of his proposals, but they did not suggest the difficulties that had to be resolved or the obstacles that had to be overcome before the program could be effective. Probably this tactic was necessary; the task was to convince a Congress largely hostile to his ideas, although nominally allied to him in its major partisan divisions.[9] The tactic is illustrated in Sáenz Peña's defense of two vital points in his program, minority representation and compulsory voting.

His argument on the first was quite likely to be reduced to repetition of the formula which he had used in his Presidential inauguration address, where he said: "It is beyond doubt that majorities ought to govern, but it is no less certain that minorities must be listened to . . ." [10] The guarantee that the minority would be heard consisted of giving it a determined place in the legislature. It is difficult to imagine that this astute and experienced politician did not realize the perils that the incomplete list opened the way to: the opportunities for inter-party deals, the possibility of serious distortion of the true majority, the invitation to torpidity in the leadership of a party with a guaranteed representation, etc. Sáenz Peña's greater concern, however, was to bring party organization to a higher stage of development, and the incomplete list was an encouragement in that direction.

The plea for compulsory voting was presented in simplified theoretical terms. It is the collectivity which "arms the citizen with the right to vote." The collectivity, or State, does this, because the welfare of the community requires the citizen's participation in the electoral process. Therefore the State can de-

9. For a good discussion of Sáenz Peña's relations with Congress see Rivarola, op. cit., pp. 16–20.
10. Roque Sáenz Peña, Escritos Y Discursos (2 vols.) (Buenos Aires, 1914–15), Vol. II, p. 48.

mand this participation.[11] At the same time Sáenz Peña was willing to recognize a limit on the power of the State to enforce the demand. As a practical matter non-voting could not be made a crime. Widespread resistance could make law enforcement an absurdity, and it was wiser to recognize this than to attach stiff penalties to the failure to vote. Nevertheless, the State had a right to demand, and the citizen had an obligation to comply.

In reality Sáenz Peña's desire for the compulsory vote seems to lie deeper than these superficial, theoretical considerations indicate. In private he maintained that it was the immigration factor that made obligatory suffrage necessary. At least 45 percent of the population was foreign-born, and the percentage was increasing with the daily arrival of new immigrants. He estimated that the percentage would shortly reach the figure of sixty or seventy. Like all Argentine statesmen Sáenz Peña was friendly to the idea of mass immigration, but he saw in the uprootedness of the foreign-born potential dangers both for themselves and for the society which they had recently entered, but of which they were not yet an integrated part. Some kind of civic roots must be put down as quickly as possible, he believed, both by the older elements in the population and by the new arrivals as soon as they became naturalized. The vote was a means of rooting the individual in the organized body politic, and this circumstance justified making the vote a civic obligation.[12]

Though Sáenz Peña would impose this obligation on all citizens, it must be understood that he was no Führer seeking to arm the populace with a vote which would merely provide the opportunity for endorsement of his programs through meaningless plebiscites. He truly believed that out of the mass of votes and the representation of varied interests could come policies that would articulate the needs and desires of the people. The terms of a democratic life for Argentina were, in his own words, "a people which votes and a government which administers." [13]

Sáenz Peña was, moreover, willing to face the logical consequences of his reforms, namely, the possibility of an opposition victory and the defeat of his own party. Never anything but a

11. *Ibid.*, p. 104.
12. *Ibid.*, p. 77.
13. *Ibid.*, p. 435.

Conservative in spirit and inclination,[14] he did not find terrifying
—as many Conservatives did—the prospect of a Radical or even
Socialist majority, so long as the majority had been attained by
constitutional procedures. In the 1913 Congressional elections
the new law benefited the Radicals and brought a few Socialists
into Congress. In the eyes of many Conservatives these gains were
as dangerous as inviting an enemy party into a besieged fortress
in time of war. The Radicals were revolutionaries and the Socialists even more so. Sáenz Peña argued in his annual message to
Congress that such a view was unfounded. The Radicals and
Socialists were "parties which operate in order and in liberty with
their doctrines and their standards protected by the Constitution.
By the very fact of voting they are not revolutionary parties. . . ."[15] Sáenz Peña's faith in the rationalizing effect of the
ballot was profound.

His two successors were apparently of less strong faith. Sáenz
Peña died on August 9, 1914. He had been on leave from office for
some time previous. Vice President de la Plaza, who finished out
the term, took a heavily qualified view of the recent electoral reform. In his first message to Congress de la Plaza expressed his
concern that the law might operate to give all advantage to
the "partidos avanzados" and to penalize the "partidos tra-
diconales."[16] That he did not allow this concern to disturb the
fundamental operation of the law, however, is best proved by the
fact that in 1916 the Radicals won the Presidency with Irigoyen
as their candidate.

14. Sáenz Peña's conservatism deserves more analysis than is possible within the
scope of the present study. He belonged to a class of hereditary wealth and power.
He was a friend of the people, but no egalitarian. He was a strong traditionalist.
The great glories of the Spain of the past had a special appeal for him, and he
was a firm Hispanophile. During the Spanish-American War he was an apologist
for the Spanish side and a bitter critic of the United States, toward which his
attitude was expressed in the words: "La felicidad de los Estados Unidos es la
institución más onerosa que pesa sobre el mundo," Derecho Público Americano
(Buenos Aires, 1905), p. 203. Sáenz Peña's traditional conservatism, however,
apparently did not blind him to the necessity for social change and for acts of
public authority to meet the needs of modern urbanized society. Dr. Carlos
Ibarguren, who held a ministry in the Sáenz Peña cabinet, has stressed in recent
years that Sáenz Peña was prepared with social legislation proposals which were to
follow his electoral reform. These had little chance of success, however, because of
the President's poor health and the uncomprehending attitude of his Congress. For
Ibarguren's views see Arenas Luque, op. cit., p. 233.
15. Escritos Y Discursos, Vol. II, p. 435.
16. Rivarola, op. cit., pp. 50–53.

Irigoyen obtained a clear majority of the votes, but he nearly lost the prize in the Electoral College. Though the choice was eventually in his favor, the outcome remained in doubt for some time after election. Whether the hair-breadth nature of Irigoyen's victory explains his subsequent conduct in office or whether the explanation lies elsewhere, Irigoyen as President certainly did not display the ultimate faith and confidence in the people that Sáenz Peña had. Or it may be that Irigoyen, backed by a very genuine majority sentiment, merely distrusted the system by which the people expressed their choice. At all events his term was marked by a definite trend toward gathering into his own hands control over the nation and over his party. He used the device of intervention [17] freely to assure that the provinces had governors who would be amenable to his direction. He could not succeed himself, but he engineered the party's selection of Marcelo T. Alvear as the candidate in 1922. In 1928 Irigoyen insisted, against strong opposition within the Radical ranks, on running again for the Presidency. He was unbeatable, but his second term was brief. The inability of his regime to deal with critical economic problems in 1930 brought on the Army revolt which toppled him from the Presidency.

From 1913 to 1930 democracy in the electoral sense was more strictly honored in Argentina than at any previous time. After 1930 there was no immediate move to repeal the Sáenz Peña law, but the open inter-party contests which had gone on were no longer characteristic of Argentine politics. A schism had already occurred within the *Unión Cívica Radical,* largely as a reaction to Irigoyen's one-man dominance of the party, the dissident Radicals having organized themselves under the banner of *"Anti-personalismo."* The brief military government under General José Félix Uriburu further demoralized the parties. Civilian government was restored in 1932 with Agustín P. Justo as President. Justo, an Anti-Personalist Radical, had won with the backing of his own group and the Conservatives, the two being united

17. Under Article 6 of the Constitution of 1853 intervention was widely used by the Federal authorities. The article provided: "The Federal Government intervenes in the provinces to guarantee the republican form of government, or repel foreign invasion, and, at the requests of their constituted authorities, to sustain or re-establish them, if they have been deposed by sedition or by invasion from another province."

in the *"Concordancia"* through which the traditional Conservatives dominated the government until 1943.

Justo's victory may also be explained in terms of the organized fraud in the 1931 elections, which Uriburu's government tolerated or helped. The successful renewal of fraud showed that the Sáenz Peña Law could be nullified by simpler and easier means than repeal. Roberto Ortiz, also an Anti-Personalist, succeeded Justo in 1938. Ortiz too had the benefit of Conservative backing and one-sided administration of the electoral law. His poor health, however, forced him to transfer the Presidency to his Conservative running-mate, Ramón Castillo, who headed the government at the time of the military uprising of June 4, 1943.

The events of June 4 produced eventually the Perón revolution with consequences so far-reaching that the electoral question by itself pales into relative insignificance. It suffices to note here that Perón seems to have accorded at least a superficial adherence to the norms of the law and to have expanded—again superficially—the scope of the electoral process in the law of woman suffrage.

From the foregoing brief résumé of the operation of the electoral process in modern Argentine history there is probably only one chief conclusion to be drawn. It is the unfortunate and negative conclusion that the Argentines have yet to learn how to install permanently in their system a mechanism which will effectively translate the forces of public opinion into valid and recognizable mandates from the people, mandates which will both determine the composition of the government and which will identify a course of public policy.

A second and entirely tentative conclusion might also be drawn from the results during the years 1913–1930, namely, that free and unhampered elections tend to give a majority to the left-center parties. The Radical ascendancy during the period and the Socialist growth would seem to support this, and generally speaking a left-center show of strength is not untypical of heavily urbanized political communities. The conclusion, however, probably has to be qualified by at least two considerations. One is the influence of Irigoyen's enigmatic but powerful personality on the voters during the period. The other is the probability that the Radical majorities during the time contained a basic element of protest votes. Political errors and misdeeds of the pre-1913 period could be made the subject of wholesale and unqualified presentation as the sins of the Conservatives, since no non-Conservative had been able to head the government. Whatever advantage this situation may once have afforded the left-center parties, it is an advantage which no longer exists.

THE MILITARY IN POLITICS

Three times within a single generation the Argentine military forces have turned a constitutional government out of office, and imposed their own kind of regime in its place. In 1930 they removed a Radical President, in 1943 a Conservative, and in 1955 they drove from power a President whose regime rested on revolutionary social doctrines with totalitarian overtones. Nor have the military objectives been limited to governments with constitutional foundations. In October, 1945, a substantial group of the Army officers participated in an unsuccessful counter-revolution against the Farrell-Perón Revolutionary Government, and military influence seems to have been an important factor in removing Provisional President Lonardi in November, 1955, and in substituting General Aramburu in his place.

One of the most noteworthy features of this series of interventions is that it is contrary to tradition and is entirely the innovation of a single generation. Prior to 1930 the military did not play a political role. The nineteenth century had its politico-military *caudillos*, and various Presidents, Mitre and Roca among them, had significant military experience in their backgrounds. But before 1930 the military did not engage in making such drastic political decisions as those involved in the removal of the Constitutional executive or in suspending a duly-elected Congress. Instead, the military on the whole regarded themselves as subordinate to the civilian organs of government.

A second general feature which should be noted is that these military *coups* have not had the unanimous support of all the armed forces. Important sectors within the forces have been able on each occasion to impose their will on the nation, but they have always encountered resistance within the military establishment itself. In 1930 General Agustín P. Justo refused to support General Uriburu's dictatorship and later helped to restore constitutional government.[18] In 1945 and in 1955 some of the officers abstained from or actively opposed the uprisings.

Except for the revolution against Perón, these ventures have been carried out through tactical maneuvers which have met with little resistance and which have produced practically no bloodshed. While it may be pleaded in defense of the military forces that this circumstance in itself shows the existence of a kind of popular consent to their actions, the fact remains that decisive military intervention is not a means of keeping public authority accountable to the people. It cannot support democracy, because it is a contravention of its basic principles. The military record poses at least three fundamental problems of evaluation which it seems impossible to resolve in terms that offer any genuine promise that military intervention can be entirely eliminated from the Argentine system of political dynamics.

First of all, one of the more obvious characteristics of military intervention may be noted. On the face of the record it might be claimed that the military carefully refrain from attacking constitutional governments that are functioning with reasonable success in the management of the affairs of the nation. In 1930 General José Félix Uriburu directed a revolution against a government which was already crumbling into disintegration. The aged Irigoyen had returned to the Presidency two years earlier. His irresponsible followers were taking advantage of the President's senility to turn positions of public trust into means of private gain.[19] By the time Uriburu took over on September 6, the executive branch of government was a shambles. Grave deterioration of competence in the executive was again the invitation to the military venture of June 4, 1943. President Castillo was perhaps not to be compared personally with Irigoyen, but by 1943 his regime had shown that it could do little better than to hold Argentine domestic policy to a dangerously erratic course, while in the foreign policy field his government floundered in the quest for national security in the midst of a world war.

The 1955 revolution against Perón is admittedly a different matter. Perón had not reached the end of his rope in the manner of Irigoyen or Castillo. The Peronist government, however, was

18. Whitaker, *op. cit.,* p. 61.
19. Rennie, *op. cit.,* pp. 222–223.

one which could hold on only through repression. The armed forces—or an important sector of them—brought about its downfall.[20]

To say that it is characteristic of the military to bring down only the incompetent constitutional regimes is not, however, very much of a consolation, if the characteristic is very deeply examined. For it would appear that the practice is for the armed services leaders themselves to decide when a given government is so weak that it must be removed. Every one of the toppled regimes faced criticism in important sectors of the civilian population. This criticism, however, was unavailing to induce reform that might have preserved the government or made for an extraordinary, but still constitutional, transition of power. Yet in each case, after a certain point of deterioration was reached, the military were able to take the decisive action which brought about the ouster. While the record suggests that the military leaders recognize that there are limitations to their scope of action, a pattern of politics which leaves this ultimately decisive role in their hands is clearly inadequate to assure a steady continuance of democratic rule.

A second problem in evaluation of the military role in politics arises from another characteristic which superficially again displays a concept of self-limitation on the military's part. This is in the fact that the military do not hold supreme power indefinitely, and eventually they offer the means of returning the government to a civilian form. General Uriburu gave way to the *Concordancia* in 1931. The revolutionary regime which came into power in 1943 gave way within three years to the government which Perón headed as President. The present Aramburu government has signified its intention of withdrawing from power as soon as the constitutional machinery can be put in working order.

While the military may perhaps be praised for recognizing that theirs is the job of defending the nation, not of running it, it is still obvious that even in the decision to restore constitutional government there is on the military's part an element of finality in that decision which is not consistent with genuine democratic responsibility.

20. Whitaker, *Argentine Upheaval* (New York, 1956), analyzes the background of both the June 16 uprising and the later successful revolution which began on September 16. In connection with the latter, he notes, p. 28, "it was essentially the work of the armed forces."

Finally, there is the related problem of the possible combinations of power that the military may construct in conjunction with other forces. Thus it seems quite certain that General Uriburu's regime worked closely with certain sectors of the Conservative party and helped to return that party to a strong position after 1931. During the 1944–46 period Perón's appeal was to new forces of the left and while his maneuvering was resisted and challenged in important spheres of the military establishment, the ultimate victory of the labor forces in the Perón regime did not spell the end of military cooperation in the maintenance of the regime. The possibility then seems to exist that in the transition from a revolutionary government to one of constitutional regularity the military may again play a limited but basically self-selected role, which need not cease to be important when the constitutional form is restored.

All these are, as previously stated, problems in evaluation. It is not proposed to offer solutions for them here. While it may be granted that there is much in the picture which offers hope for the evolution of a more effective democracy in Argentina, it is still apparent that progress toward the goal of democratic accountability will to a certain extent depend upon the degree of success with which the Argentine people can come to master the elements which create these problems.

This chapter has been principally concerned with two of the pathological aspects of Argentine democracy, the record of inadequacy in the electoral process and the record of military intervention. While these have so far not been fatal symptoms, they have certainly marred the features of a system which theoretically rests on the authority of the people. They have not destroyed entirely the bright promises for a society of free men that are implicit in the history of Argentine national development, but it must be presumed that they have helped to prevent the reaching of the full maturity of those promises. Recognizing that Argentine democracy has its deficiencies, we may now turn in the next two chapters to the study of those Catholic positions and attitudes which have been formulated under the stimulus of the national search for an effective democracy.

CHAPTER V

Democratic Trends and Catholicism

IT IS clear that the Argentine search for democracy has produced no record of unqualified success. To acknowledge this, however, is not to call the quest a failure. The Argentines have not been able to perfect a permanent electoral system to guarantee the free choice of the people in open elections. On the other hand, down to Perón, Argentina was an open society where even the dominant "oligarchy" could rule only within limits of tolerance which depended chiefly upon the degree of disintegration on the part of the opposition at any given time. In spite of military *coups* the Constitution long survived intact, and the personal guarantees contained in it were honored in courts and in custom. Perón was undoubtedly a twentieth-century style dictator, and there may well have been, as his opponents have charged, an element of totalitarianism in his regime. With this exception, however, modern Argentina has not been a land of dictators. "Personalism" may never have been entirely extirpated, but the tyrant is not a familiar figure in the history of the past century. The history may be, and has been, interpreted in many ways, but no realistic interpretation can gainsay a hitherto inextinguishable spirit that struggles toward a system of just government by the consent of the governed.

This spirit has had no easy existence, but it has been sustained and nourished from a variety of sources. The material to be presented in this chapter is offered to support the thesis that some of these sustaining sources can be identified as Catholic. Obviously, this is not a claim that all the sources are Catholic. Nor does it imply that all Catholic social and political influences necessarily support a democratic development.

As parts of Chapter III may have already suggested to the

reader, there is a considerable body of Catholic thought and action which has, from the beginning, generally favored the trends that bespeak the national search for effective democracy. At the same time, however, it is well-known that in connection with certain periods of Argentine history, notably the two long dictatorships of Rosas and Perón, there have been allegations that Catholic influences have been exerted in a contrary direction. These contradictory entries in the bookkeeping of Argentine Catholicism do not cancel each other out. If they lead to the question, which is Argentine Catholicism's position, pro- or anti-democratic, there can be no absolute answer. Or, to put it differently, an absolute answer could be given, if at all, only in terms of a more narrowly defined concept of Catholicism than is generally used.

What has happened is that specific trends in the development of the country have evoked a variety of responses from individuals and groups. Where these responses reflect or are conditioned by a commitment to Catholicism, they may be called Catholic. In certain, though not many, cases the responses have come from the authoritative voice of the hierarchy, which puts their Catholic quality beyond discussion. In almost all other cases, however, the door to discussion of just "how Catholic" the response may be is, of course, open. Discussion, to be sure, can rarely deny some Catholic quality, if the response rests on a commitment which is consciously consistent with Catholic doctrine. (It goes without saying that an individual might claim a commitment to Catholicism in the face of specific disapprobation of his position by Church authorities. An extreme example of this has been offered in recent years by the so-called Feeneyite group in the United States. The problem created by this sort of aberration is not, however, of much importance in terms of the present study.)

This chapter, then, will undertake to treat those Catholic positions which have been generally regarded as favorable to democratic trends, as the latter have manifested themselves in Argentine political development. Treatment of Catholic positions which have been described as obstacles to this development—either because they opposed a dominant public policy or because they were in opposition to positions held by other groups that considered their own the democratic position—will be reserved for Chapter VI.

Over the course of a century and a half the Catholic positions supporting democratic trends have expressed what may be regarded as three basic concerns or fields of interest: (1) What is the basis for the rule of the people, and how is it made effective? (2) What is the nature of the personal liberty, or liberties, that popular government must respect and foster? (3) What is the moral component of a system of government of the people and by the people that will make for both order and liberty?

Obviously these categories of interest do not embrace the whole field of basic questions regarding democracy. Most Catholic opinion, however, falls within the rather ample range which they delimit. It should also be noted at the beginning that only a few of the Catholic positions represent any involved theoretical or philosophical construction. Most of them have emerged as philosophically grounded but still largely practical judgments in the face of specific issues.

THE RULE OF THE PEOPLE

Some kind of historical focus may be introduced in the treatment of this question by taking as a point of departure the work of Dr. Gregorio Funes (1749–1829), Dean of the Cathedral of Córdoba. Funes is certainly the best known clerical figure of the independence period, and for the decade beginning with 1810 his name is prominently associated with the central direction of the emerging national movement. He is not normally thought of as an apostle of democracy, and he is one of the most controversial historical subjects that the period offers. Controversy has turned less on the question of whether Funes was villain or hero than it has on how bad a character his alleged intrigues should have earned him.

In Ricardo Rojas' judgment, Funes could be nothing but the "representative of the theocratic oligarchy which governed the colony." [1] He was elected a Deputy from Córdoba in 1810 and immediately took part in the formation of the Revolutionary government. This fact "has given some of his panegyrists the illusion that he entered into glory by the same door as Moreno or Gorriti." [2] Funes was active enough in the creation of the new state,

1. *Obras,* Vol. XII, p. 125.
2. *Ibid.,* p. 122.

but according to Rojas' theme, his effort was to work a counter-revolution rather than carry out the democratic movement just set in process.

Ingenieros takes an even less flattering view of the Dean. He will not even allow Funes a religious orthodoxy. He further asserts that a salary from the public treasury, assigned to him by Riva-davia, bought and paid for Funes' "complicity" in the ecclesi-astical reform of 1820.[3] Reflection on the history of the Rivadavian reform has never left serious Catholics very happy about it. Yet, as noted in Chapter I,[4] few, if any, of them have ever regarded the reform as anti-religious in purpose or as representing a con-scious departure from orthodoxy. It may also be appropriate to state at this point that Ingenieros, for all of his breadth of talents, was not the best qualified judge of what constitutes religious orthodoxy.

It does appear that Funes after 1810 was much more of a po-litical figure than he was a Churchman. He held many public offices, beginning in the 1810 *Junta* and including the Presidency of the 1819 constituent assembly. He was constantly in the thick of political activity, his participation being welcomed by some, detested by others. He was ambitious, energetic, literate and fre-quently involved in a game of give-and-take, which has been called intrigue, and which, no matter what name is given to it, certainly gives him much in common with most of the other fig-ures of consequence in nineteenth century Argentina. In his last years Funes was not apparently a very successful politician. This may in part have been due to his advanced age, for he himself declined the presidency of the 1825 Congress with the statement that the long course of "my years has robbed me not only of part of my powers but also of my senses."[5] In any event he was de-cidedly out of things in this period, and his formal connections to Church office appear to have been rather tenuous. To alleviate his poor economic situation he tried to take up the practice of law.

In spite of a generally adverse atmosphere surrounding the name of Gregorio Funes, historians have in the main accorded to

3. *La Evolución de las Ideas Argentinas,* Vol. I, p. 244. Mecham, *Church and State in Latin America,* p. 278, notes Funes' defense of Rivadavia's measures.
4. Above, pp. 19–20.
5. Mariano de Vedia y Mitre, *El Deán Funes en la Historia Argentina* (Buenos Aires, 1910), pp. 170–171.

him an important place in the origins of Argentine federalism. In this connection it has been asserted that he also originated the practice of universal suffrage.[6] To the extent that this is true, it is explained by the following. When in 1810–11 the Buenos Aires *Junta* sought some kind of organic connection with the provinces which would both assure its own central authority and provide some recognized liaison units in the hinterland, the solution to this problem was provided largely by Funes. He proposed that a *junta* be set up in each province. The *junta's* members were to be chosen by electors. The electors in turn were to be chosen by popular vote which was not to be restricted. The *Junta* decreed as Funes had recommended.

If this is the first official appearance of universal suffrage in the River Plate region and if Dean Funes is its principal originator, some credit is, of course, due him. Probably not too much, however, should be made of it. Funes was not without ideological commitment to popular government, in spite of what Rojas and Ingenieros testify, but it is unlikely that he was following any principle of popular rule here. Rather his aim clearly was to tie the people together with a new sense of national coherence. As a shrewd politician he recognized that any systematic tie must begin with a link between the individual and some representative of authority. In his plan the linking progressed from the individual to the elector and from there to the provincial *junta* and to the central *Junta*. In this way the individual who would be called upon to supply the energy and resources of the Revolution would come to regard the new national authority not as something alien and distant, but as something to which he had a clear connection.

All this is not to deny the promise for popular government that is contained in Funes' plan. Nor should it be overlooked that in many nations the practical politician, unencumbered by any precise ideology, has frequently been no less important in making democratic rule effective than the theorist or philosopher. The pragmatic element in Funes' action should, in fact, be emphasized, just as the same element characterized many of his other important acts in this period. So far as his position here demonstrates a Catholic attitude or influence, its importance is in a certain sense negative. What it shows is that an important Church-

6. *Ibid.*, pp. 48–49.

man, who in his late maturity became an important politician, found no reason in his theological or ecclesiastical background to oppose universal suffrage. Probably, however, it does not show that the suffrage proposal itself has its origin in that background.

Regarding the last statement, some doubt might be raised by a general assertion from the modern Catholic writer Juan Casiello. He says that a part of the native clergy at the time of independence were readers of Mariana, Suárez and Bellarmine.[7] These theological writers of much earlier centuries placed essential political power with the people. Hence their readers among the early nineteenth century clergy in Argentina were already indoctrinated in democracy and welcomed the Revolution for the democratic opportunities it offered. Casiello's statement is general, and it opens up interesting possibilities for research and exploration. Casiello makes no specific application to Funes, although as one of the more learned clerics of his times Funes can hardly have escaped some acquaintance with the theological writers cited, if other clergy were reading them. Even if these writings are in his background, there is no reflection of them in Funes' suffrage proposal.

Funes throughout most of his public career was a part of a new power structure that was rising somewhat clumsily but steadily in the midst of revolution. His major concern was to keep the structure in balance, and he was not unconcerned about keeping a place for himself in it. If he sought popular sanction and support for the new authorities, he was never unmindful of the practical value of such support.

The difference between a Churchman's attitude that found no wrong in democracy and one which was affirmatively on democracy's side is best represented by the difference between Funes and Gorriti. Gorriti's pro-democratic position has been described in connection with the development of Argentine nationalism.[8] It is needless to restate it here, but it may be noted that from the start there was in Argentina a strong, systematic espousal of democracy within the ranks of the Catholic clergy.

Catholics of a later period who were willing to follow Gorriti in principle, however, thought that they had found in the long

7. *Iglesia Y Estado en la Argentina*, p. 68.
8. Above, Ch. III, p. 50 *et seq.*

history of the Rosas tyranny a practical dilemma for the sponsor of democracy. Attempts to escape the dilemma are seen in Zuviría's conservatism leading to his desire to limit the suffrage.[9] Frías, increasingly conservative over the years, but never quite willing to abandon his liberal title, stated the dilemma again and again. His commitment to democracy was in terms of an ideal, and the dilemma arose where the ideal and the real were conspicuously different.

Frías' vision of democracy called for a society composed of individuals of proven worth and attainment. Each of them would possess the trained intelligence and the sense of responsibility which would make him the moral guardian of his own interests and which would effectively guide him in his relations with his fellows and with the community. Men of this sort could know no tyranny or other systematic oppression, and the wise rule of all would leave each free to develop his own potentialities. Frías recognized that this was an ideal, never entirely attainable, but it was proper for men to work toward it at all times. It was what he had in mind when he called democracy the "highest concept of civilization." [10]

But the Rosas regime had proven to him that the rule of all could also be the rule of the mob. Rosas, backed by and manipulating the masses, could claim to head a popular government, but the regime was constituted by a "single will and many hangmen." [11] The dilemma existed, then, for Frías because he could not abandon his vision of the ideal, but he did not think that it was strong enough to deny an historical reality. Democracy contained two possibilities, either civilization's "highest concept" or the tyranny of the mob.

For the dire possibility, already concretized in Argentine history, Frías would not hold Rosas exclusively responsible. Part of the blame was traced to the colonial regime which had not prepared the people to take the initiative, but only to obey. What was worse, the blind obedience had been not to "constitutional authorities, but to despotic authorities." After centuries of submission "we made in one day the violent transition from slave to

9. See above, p. 75.
10. *Escritos Y Discursos*, Vol. IV, p. 79.
11. *Ibid.*, p. 80.

sovereign." [12] Then the inexperienced and unprepared people had behaved as the worst of sovereigns by an irresponsible act of abdication of their power into the hands of the tyrant.

In large part Frías was airing a characteristic Catholic antagonism to whatever voluntarist elements could be found in the prevailing concept of the sovereignty of the people. He thought that in the years following independence the people had been given a false notion of the supremacy of their will. A will whose supremacy was demonstrated in self-annihilation or self-surrender was no will. Democracy resting on such a concept could not be other than a shadow. This antipathy combined with Frías' own personal experience to make him cautious and even somewhat grudging in his final attitude toward popular government.

In spite of his caution Frías never could abandon entirely the pursuit of his democratic ideal. His good society remained always one that was ruled by the people. Neither could he work his way out of the dilemma that the first forty years of his nation's history had constructed for him. In strictly democratic terms he never found an escape from it. Escape came eventually, as it generally did for Frías in any dilemma, and as we shall see below, through the invocation of a moral force which rested on the doctrines of his creed.

The Catholic who saw the same dilemma but who was ready to deal with it in terms of his own broad concept of democracy was Estrada. His most systematic presentation of a theory of democracy is found in the course of lectures published under the title, *La Política Liberal Bajo la Tiranía de Rosas.*[13] Here he drew together and built upon ideas that he had expressed in scattered articles during the late 1860's. The same philosophy also runs through the Constitutional Law Lectures at the University of Buenos Aires.[14] Estrada's theory seeks to demonstrate that "democracy is the only legitimate form of government," and that universal suffrage [15] is its only guarantee.

A voluntarist base for democracy was as abhorrent to Estrada

12. *Ibid.,* p. 100.
13. Originally published at Buenos Aires in 1873. The most recent edition is Vol. 8 of the series *Grandes Escritores Argentinos,* ed. Alberto Palcos (Buenos Aires, no date), *prólogo de* Pedro Goyena; it is also found in Vol. IV of the *Obras.* References here are to the Palcos edition.
14. *Obras,* Vols. VI and VII.
15. For Estrada this is universal *male* suffrage.

as it had been to Frías. Rousseau, Locke, Hobbes were all condemned in his writings because they offered a "conventional" theory of the origin of government. Human society, he insisted, was not the work of a convention or of any other kind of agreement. Society was the work of nature, a part of the divinely ordered cosmos. Government is, he posited, indispensable to society. Therefore the existence of one implies the existence of the other.[16] But the essence of society is "The People." Government is only "accessory." [17] If the essence of society is the people, then the people have not a right but a duty to direct it. Their direction establishes the sovereignty of the people. This sovereignty resides in the *reason* of the people, since social relations are determined rationally. Sovereignty should not be confused with *authority,* which sovereignty establishes and which is dependent upon it. The only way to exercise sovereignty is through the universal participation of the people in the selection of authorities. Estrada was most specific in rejecting the idea that the electoral process was on a par with the functions of government. The latter were functions of authority, but the expression of the people's choice through elections was anterior to any authority.

Estrada was not much concerned with refuting the theories of non-democrats. What perturbed him, however, was the inclination of self-professed democrats to urge limitation of the suffrage. In this respect he was critical of the famous document issued by the *Asociación de Mayo* of which Frías had been a member. The *Dogma Socialista* had, like Estrada, based sovereignty on the *reason* of the people. But the *Dogma* had deduced from this term a selective effect upon the exercise of the suffrage. It had declared that universal suffrage was an "absurdity." [18] Suffrage must be limited to those whose "reasonableness" has been demonstrated. But who, Estrada asked, will certify the titles to reasonableness? The people? If so, then the people are reasonable, and they cannot count themselves out. If someone else is to certify then the regime is not of the people. Their sovereignty is denied, and authority issues from privilege. This is a stand which democrats cannot logically take. All their arguments to limit suffrage move in a

16. Estrada recognized that there was a difference between *government* and *society,* but dismissed it as not important. See *La Política Liberal,* pp. 180–181.
17. *Obras,* Vol. XII, p. 89.
18. *Dogma Socialista* (Palcos ed.), p. 216.

"vicious circle." [19] Reason, Estrada argued, is in human nature not because individual men cultivate it, but because God put it there. Its reliability therefore is not something that human selectiveness establishes. It is rather the one certain factor to be depended upon and appealed to in any system of social relations.

The dilemma that oppressed Frías in his maturity and which earlier had similarly weighed down upon his youthful contemporaries of the *Asociación de Mayo* was resolved by Estrada in this fashion. He recognized that the fact of the Rosas regime could be cited to refute arguments in behalf of popular rule. Let it be conceded, he said, that Rosas did have majority backing for much of his tenure. But to use this fact as an argument against democracy is a distortion which springs from equating majority rule with sovereignty of the people. Majority rule is not, he asserted, democracy. The majority can construct a "multiform Caesarism," [20] as oppressive as any single tyrant, but the majority has of itself no right to govern. That right issues from society's "simple organic unity" [21] which is part of nature's order and in no way dependent upon majority rule. The electoral majority is merely a device which provides an authority, or authorities, to operate on behalf of this unity. Neither the majority nor the elected officials may, however, do anything that disturbs the "organic unity." They may work only to conserve and promote it. This does not mean that all must be harmony within the democratic state. Estrada saw nothing wrong in discord and dispute over policy so long as they did not disrupt the republic.

How could Estrada be sure that the majority and their selectees in authority would respect the limits of their functions? He had already admitted the historical reality of majority "Caesarism." What would prevent its recurrence? To answer this it is necessary to go back to the premise contained in the "reason of the people." God has made men reasonable, and if this fact is respected in such a way that each man is left free to use his reason he will not seek to disturb the social unity of which he is a part.

19. *La Política Liberal*, p. 177.
20. *Ibid.*, p. 27.
21. Vol. IX, p. 562. This concept of the organic unity of society as distinct from mere majority will became extremely important in a practical context for Estrada and other Catholics in the 1880's in their fight against the innovations in public policy regarding education and marriage. See below, Ch. VI, pp. 190–193, 201–203.

What then guarantees the freedom in which the faculty of reason is used? The guarantee is free and open elections where each and every voter may express a choice with no sense of exterior coercion.

Shifting to historical ground, Estrada argued that the Argentine people never had been free. In the background were the centuries of colonial oppression. Independence had brought chaos, which had eventually produced the dictatorship. It was absurd, he reasoned, to argue from these facts that the people could not be trusted. It would be more logical to say that the absence of freedom would necessarily lead the people into evil ways. Let the people be free to exercise their God-given attributes, his theme ran, and we shall at least avoid the horrors of the past when freedom did not exist.

It should be stressed that however much Estrada pays tribute to human dignity there is nothing utopian in his view of man and society. The democracy based on the universal suffrage which he preached would not produce any perfect society. For him "all human life is a series of struggles and incidents," but "for my part I fear less the people than those who claim themselves born to govern them." "Between the dangers of freedom and the dangers of authoritarianism," he was certain that he could best tolerate those of freedom.[22]

All Estrada's work is marked by strong egalitarian tendencies. These did not lead him to disregard natural differences of ability and talents in men, but he was certain that the importance of those differences had been exaggerated. Many in both his own and the preceding generation had argued that while all men were *in posse* reasonable, only those with a certain situation in society could be trusted to be politically reasonable. The man of property or learning had a stake in society, as the poor and the ignorant did not. Only those with a demonstrated interest in society should be granted the suffrage.[23]

Estrada assailed the assumptions underlying this attitude. Who, he inquired, has said that the prosperous and the wise have a greater interest in society than the poor and the ignorant? We have only heard from the rich and wise on this matter. Has anyone

22. *La Política Liberal*, pp. 44–45.
23. This view was not absent from Catholic circles. See above, Ch. III, pp. 75–76.

ever consulted the poor? Are the unlettered masses spared the sufferings and evils that go with social upheaval? The record of Argentine history shows that they are not. How then can it be assumed that they have no interest in the peace and stability of an orderly society? Does not the record suggest something quite different and more certainly ominous? It is the rich and wise who command peculiar advantages for disturbing society and for antisocial exploitation. This is what Argentines must be on guard against, not the ephemeral threat of the masses. And what better protection can be devised than the free and effective vote of all?

Estrada's first complete presentation of these ideas came in the early 1870's, a full decade before he was to break away from the liberal-progressive ranks where he had long enjoyed a congenial place. The writings indicate, however, at least a subconscious presage of the break. For as Argentine society began to enjoy a material prosperity, progressive thought found an increasing satisfaction in the improved economic situation of the country. The prosperous and educated citizen became more and more the central interest of the progressives. Estrada endorsed the trends which produced constantly larger numbers of such citizens. But the ranks of the propertyless were still the more numerous, and Estrada feared that they were being neglected. The situation of the country made it possible for a surprising number to pass from being poor to being moderately well-to-do or even rich. This happy transition delighted men of progressive thought, including Estrada. His concern, however, was for those who could not escape from poverty and who were in danger of becoming the forgotten men of Argentine politics. They were, he pleaded, just as important as their more fortunate contemporaries, and in terms of the political they merited the same respect. No progressive would consciously deny this to them, as Estrada well knew. His worry was that the progressives were so beguiled with the transition that they would find in it the justification of their society while a large part of the population languished in economic misery and political oblivion.

Estrada is clearly the Argentine Catholic with the strongest intellectual commitment to the right of the people to rule. It is a commitment without hedging or limitation. It may even be said that it contains an element of the daring. For he knew his country well enough to be aware that the democratic form could be abused and turned into a mask for tyranny. Catholic writers who in later years shared his commitment did not improve upon his theory. In fact, Catholic interest in this problem in the late nineteenth century shifted largely from the theoretical to the practical. This trend has continued into the present century.

Catholics following Estrada's line of "Christian liberalism" have not been so concerned with demonstrating the right of the people to rule as they have been in creating the conditions for the most effective exercise of the right. They have recognized that poverty, disease and illiteracy are perils that jeopardize responsible citizenship. They have urged that society must seek the means to alleviate the danger, and, if possible, to eliminate it. In other words it is the welfare politics of the modern state that has held their interest.

Social and economic democracy had relatively little accomplishment to show down to the advent of Peronism. Catholic thought and action on behalf of social democracy have not been notably out of proportion to the general trend. While there has been a core of self-conscious "social Catholicism," which has been dedicated to improved welfare legislation and has sought to better the condition of labor through sponsorship of unionism, it has produced no spectacular results. This is not said to belittle the honest efforts of good men, but merely to emphasize that the political environment in which social Catholicism operated, prior to 1943, was not greatly favorable to social gains through legislation or other means at the command of public authority. Nevertheless, because the economic and social well-being of the people has been a concern of Catholic thinkers from the beginning of Argentine history, the scattered manifestations of social Catholicism deserves some attention.

The remote ancestor of this development is probably the priest Saturnino Segurola (1776–1854), who was also a practicing physician. Segurola's political understanding does not appear to have been profound, but he was acutely aware that a major hazard to the material welfare of the people originated in disease and epidemic. His efforts to arouse the people to their dangers and to encourage them to avail themselves of whatever preventive measures they could, made of him an early, probably the earliest, exponent of a systematic program of public health. Segurola's scientific curiosity, and his eagerness to utilize all the known methods of a science still comparatively primitive, seem to have caused him to range widely in his activities and in his correspondence with physicians in other countries. Rojas reports that the Royal Jenner Institute of London accorded Segurola honorary membership for his work of introducing vaccination into both Argentina and Chile.[24]

A short while later the prolific journalist Frías, still in his early manhood, sounded a note which is strikingly in harmony with the ideas of social and economic planning as they have been treated in more recent social thinking. In 1845, while he was working for the Bolivian government, Frías recommended a program of economic development in which immediate and obvious economic advantages are drastically subordinated to long-range goals of social welfare.[25] As an economic plan his proposal is lacking in detail. Its purpose, however, is clear. Frías sought to persuade the Bolivian government to give up its reliance on mining as a major economic basis for the national society. Mining, he conceded, produces wealth, but it is wealth in the form of great fortunes. Great fortunes create a small privileged class and leave the bulk of the population in misery. The dire poverty with which a mining economy afflicts every nation where it dominates is sufficient to show that it should not be encouraged. The Spanish colonization, he argued, was too closely tied to the mining industry, and he charged somewhat glibly that this explains why it was so generally disastrous.

The Bolivian government, Frías urged, in abandoning its reliance on this form of economic development should turn to measures which will promote the "material welfare" of the people. Frías did not pause to specify what these might be, but seemed to trust that once the emphasis on mineral wealth had been given up, devising the measures would be easy enough. To emancipate the people from poverty was the first duty of the government, and this could not be done until public policy was reformed in its basic economic aspects.

24. Vol. XI, p. 785 *et seq.* Rojas also notes Segurola's place as one of the basic historians of Argentina, since he collaborated with Funes in collecting the manuscripts and other documents of the colonial and Liberation periods.
25. Vol. IV, pp. 5–6.

A similar concern for the material welfare of the people was not voiced by Frías in his more mature years. It would not be proper to say that his interest in the matter vanished, but it became an oblique interest and quite secondary to his preoccupation with the moral aspects of democratic government which will be discussed below. Estrada and the other young men who took up the instruction of workingmen's groups in the sixties offer the next, and rather imprecise, step in the development of social Catholicism.[26]

After 1880 aroused Catholic opinion became acutely and almost exclusively political in its intent. Social welfare considerations were submerged for the rest of the century in the organized Catholic resistance to the educational and matrimonial reforms of the period. This stage of Argentine Catholicism's history will be examined in detail in Chapter VI. It need only be noted here that the resistance produced the first large scale Catholic lay organizations which sought to exert pressure in public affairs.

Out of these groups came at the end of World War I the episcopally authorized lay institution, *Unión Popular Católica*. Paradoxically, in view of its antecedents, UPC did not engage in direct political activity. Rather, its program was closer to the social Catholic movements of contemporary Western Europe with major reliance placed upon the modern social thought of the Papacy. In one part UPC sought to improve the conditions of the working classes through indoctrination of the employers and other "directing groups" in society. In another part it encouraged labor organization, and some of its members were active in the formation of unions. UPC will receive further attention in the following chapter.

From the World War I period to the present day the most eloquent spokesman of social Catholicism has been Dr. Miguel de Andrea, Titular Bishop of Temnos. Bishop Andrea has been a public figure in Argentina for very nearly half a century,[27] and his activities have been so numerous that it is impossible to summarize them all here. Three of them, however, must be noted in

26. See above, Ch. III, p. 101.
27. His sermon given in the Buenos Aires Cathedral on the occasion of the national centenary seems to be the earliest event to mark him as a conspicuous Catholic leader. The sermon was published under the title, *Oración Patriótica de Acción de Gracias por el Éxito de las Fiestas del Centenario* (Buenos Aires, 1910).

connection with any mention of Catholic efforts on behalf of effective democracy.

First, he was for many years the leader in a welfare program which sought not so much to influence public policy as to organize under Catholic auspices a voluntary effort to relieve the poverty of the urban working classes. Much of this was undertaken through the *Unión Popular Católica* in which Andrea was the chief clerical figure. The most dramatic activities of the group led by Andrea came about as a result of the so-called *Semana Trágica* (tragic week) of 1919. The term is used to indicate a brief outbreak of terror in that year, which was a product of the worldwide hysteria with which the collapse of the old order in Europe and the rise of Bolshevism had infected many parts of the world in the years after the close of World War I. Argentina was as distant from the real scene of the post-war upheaval as any nation could be. Yet it was not spared a share of the universal hysteria.[28] The trouble began apparently with a labor dispute in a single factory. This set off a series of strikes, riots and mob-actions, largely aggravated by the inept and ruthless tactics of suppression employed by the Irigoyen government. Some Argentines were convinced that a Soviet-inspired revolution was under way. Hardly anyone in authority behaved reasonably. Mobs looted stores and pillaged churches. All transportation came to a halt. The slaughter of civilians, many of them innocent bystanders, brought tragedy into many homes.

Andrea, as his subsequent writings and activities show, saw two great deficiencies which had contributed as causes of the *Semana Trágica*. One was that the workers had, with few exceptions, no respected, articulate means of bringing their point of view to the attention of the authorities or the public. They lacked any voice that they could have confidence would be heard, and what they thought was a critical threat to their interest had turned them to violence. Complementary to this was the Government's own lack of communication with the urban workers. Governments had for so long depended upon the professional party politicians that, in Andrea's view, the politicians had become a kind of select guild. Within the guild enormous and bitter differ-

28. Rennie, *The Argentine Republic*, pp. 214–219, gives a graphic account of the week.

ences existed, but the professionals had techniques for resolving these among themselves. When issues arose, however, which were beyond the reach of their professional competence or craftsman- ship—simply because most politicians had enjoyed a comfortable isolation from the rising social issues—the politicians failed. The result of this failure was violence on the part of those whose real problems were outside the normal scope of decision of the po- litical guild. To overcome these deficiencies became one of Bishop Andrea's major purposes from 1919 onward.

Immediately following the Tragic Week he and his group pro- moted a national voluntary raising of funds to be spent on welfare programs. This was known as the *Gran Colecta Nacional,* appar- ently undertaken with episcopal approbation. A part of the funds collected were used to establish two institutes. The *Instituto Técnico Feminino* was created to promote the interests of work- ing-women. *El Ateneo de la Juventud* was established as a social- work center for working-class youth and children. Another part of the program was the construction of low-cost housing. Four housing projects were built in the following year.[29]

The low-cost housing feature would appear to have been the most promising part of a long-range social program, but it did not progress beyond the original four projects. The present writer has been unable to ascertain the causes for the halt in this activity, but it is a reasonable assumption that lack of capital was the prin- cipal factor. The money had come from voluntary offerings, prob- ably stimulated by the recollection of the 1919 tragedy. As the passage of time made the recollections less vivid, the stimulus to contribute may have diminished accordingly.[30]

From this activity it was a natural step for Andrea to move into the field of labor organization and to counsel and sponsor in the creation of new syndicates. The area of sponsorship that he marked out for himself was that of the women-workers, especially

29. Bishop Andrea summarizes these activities in *El Catolicismo Social Y Su Aplicación* (Buenos Aires, 1941), p. 23 *et seq.*
30. During the 1955 crisis a Peronist author dealing with the 1919 events charged that in reality the Catholics at that time had only been strike-breakers. One feature of his treatment, however, is puzzling—at least to foreigners. This is that he goes to some pains to exculpate Andrea from any responsibility for strike- breaking. This is an unexpected consideration from quarters where Andrea had been intensely disliked and vilified for more than a decade. See *Hechos E Ideas,* Año XVI, Tomo XXVII (June–July, 1955), p. 489.

those in the needle trades and on piece-work rates at home.[31] It will immediately be noted that this choice kept the Bishop from entering the heavy industry field where he might face some ideological competition from Socialists who were already active. It can also be said that he chose a group whose members, by reason of their sex, were traditionally believed to be most responsive to Church direction. These comments do not, however, suggest that the Bishop chose an easy course.

Women workers were paid the most miserable wages. Even when they were skilled, as in the needle trades, the labor market seldom permitted them to exploit their skill with real success. Their unions could not even have the minor political influence that those of male workers might have, because at the time women did not vote. Andrea had chosen the field where there was least prospect of tangible success for a labor movement. In later years he made clear the reasons for his choice. Here was a group of workers who had no advantages to use in any kind of collective bargaining to improve their livelihood. Their trade gave them no social cohesion, because working in their homes they were kept in isolation from each other. There were so many of them that the employer had the most unlimited choice in hiring and firing.

To change these conditions, Andrea had to make the women workers conscious of their common interest and make the public acknowledge the legitimacy of their interest. The first step, accordingly, was the creation of the women's syndicates. The second was to stimulate public pressure to bring about improvements through legislation. The Bishop was frank in indicating that to arouse public sentiment he saw no other course than an appeal on a religious basis. He thought it fortunate that there was a body of Catholic social teaching which he and his associates could use as propaganda in their efforts. For their efforts he claimed a modest success in the *Ley del Trabajo a Domicilio,* which he said could never have been enacted if it had not been for the Catholic pressures that he led.[32]

31. *El Catolicismo Social,* p. 26 *et seq.* See also Carlos R. Desmarás, *Ley Del Trabajo a Domicilio, prólogo del* Dr. Alfredo L. Palacios; *nota preliminar de* Monseñor Miguel de Andrea (Buenos Aires, 1942), p. xvii. (This linking of the Catholic Bishop's name with that of the Socialist intellectual and politician Palacios sounds an unusual irenic note.)
32. The law is the subject of Desmarás' volume cited in the preceding note.

If labor interests required special channels of action to influence public policy, this necessity arose, in Andrea's opinion, not only from the anti-labor attitude that a *laissez-faire* capitalism had engendered, but also from the fact that politics had become too narrow a specialization. "The great deficiency of our democracy is that it has become exclusively political," when it ought to become "economic and social." [33] This brings us to the third of Andrea's activities for strengthening the democratic base, which is his espousal of a "democratic Corporatism."

Corporatism was a major theme for the Bishop throughout the period between 1930 and 1943.[34] He argued that labor, business, industry, agriculture, the professions, the intellectuals all worked in isolation from each other. The development of one group's interests was undertaken with little concern for the others' interests. Politics made no efforts to harmonize these interests or to bring them organically into political life. The results were division and discord, economic unbalance and social instability. To overcome these divisions and to give society something closer to an integrated character Andrea urged that the policy-making organs of the state be revised to include representatives of all the economic and social groups. *Democracia corporativa* would seal this wholeness and the harmony within it would come from a common acceptance of Christian principles.

Throughout this period Andrea insisted that his Corporative democracy in no way resembled the Corporative State, as it existed in Europe. His basic belief was that democracy, which the Corporative State denied, was the best of all possible forms of government. An unbridled capitalism had weakened democracy and had sown the seeds of grave social disturbance. It had made democracy "sick" in many parts of the world, but, he argued, one administers medicine to a patient only to rehabilitate him, not to kill him. The Corporative State is medicine that kills. Corporative democracy is medicine that cures.

Andrea's claims are made in *Causas Que Favorecen la Difusión del Comunismo* (Buenos Aires, 1937), p. 11.

33. *El Catolicismo Social,* p. 21.

34. It is expounded in *El Catolicismo Social* and in *Las Causas Que Favorecen la Difusión del Comunismo,* previously cited; also in *Justicia Social* (Buenos Aires, 1943), *Conferencias* (Buenos Aires, 1939). These are almost all reprints in individual or collective form of sermons and public addresses.

Andrea could have strengthened his case if he had been more specific about the details of his proposed reform. He seemed to consider, however, that his task was to make the people and their leaders conscious of the problem. From them would then come the concrete work of reform. This left him in a somewhat weak position because, in spite of his disclaimer, he was sometimes charged with being an advocate of the Corporative State.

What is probably a more important weakness, however, is that of Catholic Corporatism in general. Andrea's approach was neither unique nor personal. Catholics in Western Europe and in England had in the twenties and thirties turned to something they too called Corporatism. They were conscious of the social perils of *laissez-faire* capitalism. They saw in Marxism and in the rise of the Soviets a critical challenge not only to capitalism but to Christianity. In the thirties their preoccupations were aggravated by the world depression. From this concatenation of dangers they sought escape in a Corporatism whose political form was to give a realistic recognition to the revolutionary impact of technology on human society, but which would preserve the traditional basic values through an organization imbued with the spirit of the Christian Gospel. Corporatism as a route of escape proved to be a blind alley, largely through the failure of its advocates to comprehend the genuine primacy of the political in any large-scale organization.

Criticism of Bishop Andrea causes this writer no little anguish, but the Bishop, too, seems to have gone down this blind alley. To his credit it can be said that he quite accurately saw the lack of social content in the Argentine democracy between the wars. It might also be speculated that he had more cause to plead a case for Corporatism than those in England and the other northern countries. His own land was linked to Spain by culture and inheritance. Immigration had created strong ties with Italy. In both these countries democracy had died, and the apparent success of the new regimes was winning the plaudits of misled admirers in Argentina. It is possible that to combat an incipient anti-democratic force of this sort Andrea devised his remedy for Argentina in terms of the very elements which fascists and would-be fascists could plead on behalf of their own position. If he was stealing their thunder, it was to save the democracy to whose destruction they might become committed.

One more brief comment on Bishop Andrea's work is appropriate here. As a supremely irenic figure, representing Catholicism but honored in many non-Catholic circles, he has sometimes been underrated as a Churchman. He has been portrayed as an exotic offshoot of Argentine Catholicism, untypical and in constant disagreement with the main trends of his Church. An important qualification of his ecclesiastical office will be noted below,[35] but it must be stressed here that this portrayal is inaccurate. Andrea's essential priestliness is evident throughout his writings and discourses. His mission is to preach the Gospel, and he invokes all the dogma and doctrine of his Church in his work. In his advocacy of social reform and of democratic government there is a clear belief that these are means that are not only good in themselves but also means that will serve the ends of Christianity itself. Again and again he repeats that Catholicism has nothing to fear from the rule of the people. The problem is to assure that the government that is called democratic truly represents popular rule. The people have no enmity with the Church but are its natural allies.

He does not deny that in some parts of the world the people have drawn away from the Church. This he explains by saying that in the non-democratic social systems of the past there were numerous abuses of the people on the part of the rulers. When the people found leaders to bring about a change in these systems and to abolish the abuses, some of the leaders mistakenly believed that the Church was linked to the old system and that it too must be abolished. For their mistake Andrea has only pity, and he will pronounce no anathema against them.[36] Wherever these leaders are genuine advocates of the people, let them be convinced, he urges, that Catholicism too is of the people and desires their welfare no less than they. The gain for Catholicism will be the reincorporation of the leaders and the people into the Church.

35. See Ch. VI, p. 205 *et seq.*
36. *Las Causas Que Favorecen la Difusión del Comunismo*, pp. 15–16, vigorously reproaches those who "in the name of Catholicism claim that to save a civilization

Few bishops in the Iberian or Ibero-American countries have voiced so irenic a plea. In this respect Andrea stands out as unusual. It must not be assumed, however, that this distinction sets him at odds, as some persons seem to have assumed, from the rest of the Church in terms of its doctrine or mission.

PERSONAL LIBERTY IN A DEMOCRACY

Most of the Argentine Catholics who can be counted as exponents of democracy have looked upon it as the system which best protects the integrity of the human person in the exercise of his freedom and rights. *Liberty* and *right* are obviously not identical terms, but the Argentine writers whose opinions will be examined here have linked the existence of the one so closely to the other that for practical purposes our examination may be directed to liberty as a central question. Estrada, as might be expected, provides the most schematic treatment of the question. We shall first consider the general nature of his position, and then examine certain Catholic views concerning concrete claims to specific liberties and rights.

Estrada opened his constitutional law course with the assertion that "All the science of politics is contained in the idea of liberty." [37] He immediately made it plain, however, that not all the idea of liberty was relative to political or social studies. Liberty is fundamentally *psychological* or *moral*.[38] *Political* liberty is a consequence arising from the psychological base. Psychological liberty is defined as "the faculty, companion to the intelligence, by virtue of which man acts without experiencing the influence of any interior coaction." [39] It can be considered only in connection with man as an integral and "isolated force." But man is not only an isolated force. He is also "naturally sympathetic and social." Political liberty as an idea arises from the application of the psychological liberty of the isolated man to the naturally sympathetic and social man.[40] The idea presents liberty in a less ab-

we ought to take all means and reach all extremes, even that of exterminating our adversaries."

37. *Obras,* Vol. VI, p. 1.
38. The adjectives are used interchangeably, although it does not appear that Estrada looked upon them as identical. They appear to indicate rather two largely overlapping concepts.
39. Vol. VI, p. 1.
40. *Ibid.,* p. 3.

solute quality because the possibility of social coaction is never entirely absent.

Political liberty does not depend upon the state. It is in the divinely created order of nature, although, Estrada contended, this was never recognized until Christianity came into the world. All other systems of antiquity and modernity, since they are not based on the Gospel, must look to a *social medium* for both the origin of liberty and its sanction. Christianity rejected a concept of liberty tied to the collectivity and made it entirely dependent upon the individual. Christianity did not, of course, reject the concept of collectivity or deny man's social qualities. It "entrusted everything to the individual" by giving him a concept of "moral duty" to God, which was absolutely independent of social or political obligation. Liberty rests in this moral duty, whose ultimate sanction is not in society but in eternity.[41]

Man, however, must live in society, and the liberty which Christianity continually creates becomes significant as man performs acts which affect society and as society in turn affects man. This inter-action between man and society must be in terms of a "social liberty" of which political liberty is only one half. The other half Estrada called *civil* liberty. Civil liberty is found in the "absence of all exterior hindrance that can interfere with the fulfillment of moral duty on the part of the individual." [42] It is the liberty which society must respect not passively, but actively. Political liberty then springs into sharper relief than indicated in the earlier idea as the "exercise of all the forces whose retention and activity are necessary to protect the responsibility" of the individual in the pursuit of his moral duty. Here the active role rests with man, not society.

Civil liberty is the business of the state; political liberty, the province of the individual. Politically free man claims specific *civil rights* which are "guarantees that the community is obliged to establish for everyone's benefit" to assure that no obstacle "interferes with the observance of moral duty." Estrada's examples of moral duties and corresponding civil rights started with the duty to worship God, for which the corresponding civil right is freedom of religion. The obligation to care for and educate chil-

41. *Obras*, Vol. VI, pp. 14–16.
42. *Ibid.*, p. 17. The citations immediately following are from the same passage.

dren established the autonomy of the family as a matter of civil right. The duty to work gives rise to the rights of property; that of sharing knowledge to the freedom to teach, the rights of free association, and the freedom of the press.

It may be suggested that Estrada assigned a narrow role to the state and that he left all possible initiative with the individual. Estrada himself would cheerfully agree that this is true, but he would insist that the narrow role was no denial of the necessity of the state or of man's social nature. Man must live in society, but his destiny is not there. Man must be regarded in terms of his final end which the Gospel promises and which he can reach only by fulfilling his moral duty. Man's social life imposes certain necessities, but these must be accommodated to his ultimate end.

Estrada, moreover, was not talking in a vacuum. His exposition was theoretical, but the actual state of Argentina was never far from his mind. He thought that the first forty years of his nation's history showed that liberty had never been widely or completely understood. Liberty was thought of at one time as virtual abdication of the state; later, as the power of the misled masses to do Rosas' bidding. Neither the necessity of the state nor the limitation which true liberty places upon it had ever been generally comprehended. Estrada sought to lay down a theory which would provide for both. Beyond offering a theory, however, he also wanted to demonstrate that the positive law could in no way create liberty, grant it or withhold it, although it could guarantee it. He wanted to challenge the uncritical Argentine reliance, as he saw it, upon the positive law.

Estrada's contemporaries and successors in the ranks of Argentine Catholicism have not all followed explicitly his theory of liberty, although most of them have shared certain of its features. On the other hand, with socially active Catholics his teaching has never been totally rejected. Other important Catholic thought has tended to be less concerned with a broad synthesis of liberty than with *ad hoc* treatment of rights and liberties as the latter have been involved in the public issues of the day.

For example, the right of property, which Estrada identified as a civil right, was not, at least before Perón, subject to serious ideological assault. Property rights as public issues were more likely to be connected with the simple question of *who* was the proprietor of certain real or personal goods than with more complex issues. As seen in Chapter III, Frías had something to say on this question with two general implications of some importance.[43] He doubted that public policy was in any way served by having the political organs of the state examine and re-examine titles to land. Secondly, he urged that if such examination had to be made it belonged to the Courts as the arbiters of the law. While these opinions may indicate a traditional concept of property, they obviously are not philosophically profound. Frías also had his doubts that property could be used entirely at the will of its possessor. Business and industry affected the general welfare with what they produced and offered for sale. To protect the public, he suggested, there would have to be state regulation of production and sales which would inevitably restrict, even though it did not abolish, certain aspects of property rights.[44] Frías did not carry this idea very far beyond the stage of suggestion, however, and he has left no indication of how far his concept of regulatory power would reach.

In more recent times Bishop Andrea has made some inconclusive statements regarding property rights. He is, as one might expect, firmly committed to the right of private property. Yet at the same time he condemns modern capitalism as resting on a distortion and exaggeration of that right. He is also convinced that the modern state has given a protection to property rights at the sacrifice of similar protection for other equally important rights.[45] His criticism, however, could not be called radical, and he does not propose any revolutionary changes for Argentine law and policy. Undoubtedly his labor and welfare activities have shown the hope for a gradual modification to eliminate the worst abuses.

With regard to freedom of expression, especially in the form of freedom of the press, Catholic opinion seems to have been somewhat sharper, although not entirely unified. Funes appears to have been the first Catholic and the first Argentine official to espouse freedom of the press. His proposal to lift censorship was made in April, 1811, and a few months later the *Junta* offered a decree in terms that followed his proposal.[46] Prior to this the new

43. Above, pp. 82–83.
44. *Escritos Y Discursos*, Vol. II, p. 79.
45. *Causas Que Favorecen la Difusión del Comunismo*, pp. 5–6.
46. Vedia y Mitre, *El Deán Funes*, pp. 61–72.

government had adhered to the colonial custom of submitting all printed matter to a censor before it could be distributed to the people. Funes' biographer calls his work the opening of the "era of true liberty of thought in the Río de la Plata." [47] Funes' argument was that the "tribunal of public opinion must always be open so that the general will may be known." When the general will is not known, governments are necessarily incompetent because they cannot do what the people want.[48] They will not know how to interpret from day to day the *social contract!* (Though this last term smacks of Rousseau, its writer was a priest and an official of the Córdoba diocese.) The affirmative aspects of the freedom of the press were his concern, not the negative. He was not much bothered by questions of what the state could tolerate in the way of such strain and discord as a free press might offer, but rather with the press as a contributory and conciliatory factor in promoting public stability.

It should be noted, however, that both the Dean and the *Junta* as a whole made one conspicuous exception to the freedom of the press. This was in the retention of previous censorship for all material dealing with religion and religious questions. Does this suggest that in their departure from the restrictive colonial standards the new rulers retained only that part of the tradition which was Catholic? The Catholic Church, as is well-known, insists on previous censorship of publications dealing with religion. Is this survival then evidence of the influence of the Church? It is not easy to separate out the elements which indicate the *Junta's* concern for the orthodoxy of religion *per se* from those of a quite practical and political nature. Funes' basic regard was, as noted, for the stability of society. Would it be served by unrestrained religious writings? Hyper-orthodoxy no less than heresy might stir up bitter controversies. Moreover, at this time the *Junta* was confronted with the early stages of the long insoluble problem of the relation of the Argentine Church to Rome and the accompanying problem of the survival of the *patronato*. Did the members want religious writings to complicate these delicate matters?

One seldom-noted fact of Argentine history suggests that the *Junta's* decision reflected both political and religious considera-

47. *El Deán Funes*, p. 62.
48. *Ibid.*, pp. 68–69.

tions. This fact is Moreno's plan for use of Rousseau's *Social Contract* as a text for popular education. Moreno, the man of the Enlightenment, not normally considered representative of Catholic orthodoxy, organized the distribution to the people of the translation of the work into Spanish. He thought of it as a means of instructing the people in the principles of democracy. The translation, however, was ordered by Moreno to be expurgated of all passages dealing with the Catholic religion because, he said, "the author had the misfortune to talk nonsense in religious matters." [49] Recent Catholic writers have interpreted this statement to mean that the most "enlightened" of the founders of Argentina had so much respect for the religion of the populace that he would not allow even the "Bible of democracy" to offend their beliefs. Whatever Moreno's motivation may have been, his action is clearly in line with the *Junta's* decision in this respect. What these two decisions suggest, however, is that neither the enlightened liberal nor the Catholic priest, both of whom wanted freedom of the press, thought that the freedom extended to religious matters.

After the middle of the century Frías, the leading Catholic journalist of his day, took a somewhat ambivalent position on the issue of freedom of the press. Immediately after his return from exile he made a long plea for tolerance of diversity of opinion.[50] His argument reflected a line of thought similar in part to that of Funes. Writers for the press, he declared, as well as officials of the government all desire one thing and bend their talents toward serving it: the welfare of the country. None of them, however, is infallible. If any of them were infallible, they would long since have agreed upon a single common outlook, the people would have become convinced by this one prevailing opinion, and there would no longer be any divisions of opinion in either the people or their representatives. Since this has not happened, it will not happen, and all persons must be free to speak and write in accordance with their convictions. "Liberty, authority, order, progress, democracy are things that can be—that are—in every society interpreted in various ways." Since this diversity cannot be abolished, the welfare of the country will be advanced if each man

49. Casiello, *op. cit.*, p. 326.
50. *Escritos*, Vol. II, p. 51 *et seq.*

will respect the right of others to hold a contrary opinion, and if all can speak and write freely.

These sentiments may indicate as much as anything else the enthusiasm of the happy and hopeful man returning from a long exile. At this point Frías seemed to be convinced that all those who ventured an opinion were motivated solely by the desire to construct a sane and wholesome society in a land still littered with the ruins of the long tyranny. He was at the time the editor of a new Catholic paper, one of whose stated purposes was to combat the free thinking secularism of other new journals. He manifested a respect for his opponents, and he asked only that they accord him the same, confident apparently that both parties were free to oblige.

In the next decade, however, Frías became less certain that all the press was dedicated to the welfare of the country. Part of it, he thought, was pleading special interests with complete disregard for objectively ascertainable truth. The diversity of opinion that he had championed, he was afraid, had turned into an uncivilized brawl. He was particularly exercised over the tendency toward character assassination in some quarters of the press of Buenos Aires. He recognized that the persons on whom calumnies fell were not without means of defense. There was the protection of a law of libel. Rival journals could defend those whom others attacked. But Frías did not regard these as adequate means of defense. The power of the press was so great that, in his opinion, what was once printed never lost its entire effect. Even though it was later proven false, it was still part of a record which could not be erased. A new kind of *Mazhorqueros* (Rosas' secret and terrible police) had arisen to destroy innocent men with the pen where their predecessors had despatched them with a dagger.[51]

Though Frías had begun to have doubts about freedom of the press, he remained solidly opposed to official censorship. It was not within the competence of public authority to cure these abuses; it would probably render the situation worse. Was there a cure? The only one that Frías could see was to permeate the press with a knowledge of Christian doctrine in the hope that moral restraint would bring about improvement. This was not,

51. *Escritos*, Vol. I, p. 232.

for its times, a very realistic proposal, and undoubtedly Frías knew that it was not. His final position then is one of cautious and grudging acceptance *faute de mieux* of the freedom of the press and opinion.

This is the general norm which later Catholics, particularly in the laicist crises at the end of the century, will adhere to. Few of them will acclaim the freedom as a "civil right" in Estrada's sense of the term, but few of them will support any restraints which take the form of state control. Two factors which have made for continued Catholic adherence and which have little to do with any theoretical approach to the question may also be noted. One is that freedom of the spoken and written word is a part of the national tradition. It was formulated in the second year of national existence, and, despite the Rosas blackout, it is a tradition allied to the very being of the nation. No sustained Catholic activity has ever run counter to a firm national tradition—even the *patronato*, which as a political tradition has never been entirely acceptable to Catholic thought, has rarely been treated with other than soft-pedal complaints. A second influence has been that a free press has offered advantages and opportunities to Catholics, and they have not wanted censorship to interfere with their exploitation of these opportunities. While these considerations have nothing to do with the merits of a free press *per se,* they are a part of the picture which cannot be overlooked.

In theory the thorniest intellectual problem that a democratic system could be expected to offer Catholics would arise in the field of freedom of religion. At least an hypothesis resting on Catholicism's dogmatic unity and its denial of validity to other creeds might be constructed to demonstrate that this is so. In practice, however, no great problem seems to have arisen here, although, as will shortly be apparent, Catholics have involved themselves in controversies over just what the freedom of religion means. Chapter I has covered the unique situation of Catholicism in Argentina as well as the constitutional sanction of the long tradition of freedom of belief and worship, and it is unnecessary to reconsider this material here. If freedom of religion is an historical fact in this Catholic country, is it because Catholics want it that way, or is it because factors beyond their control have forced them to accept it?

Affirmative answers to the latter part of the question have emphasized the influence of free-thinkers like Alberdi in giving this freedom the protection of the basic laws. Catholics, in reply, will point to Funes' definitive work in the earlier constitutional undertakings. While critics of Catholicism are frequently disposed to dismiss Funes as a double-dealer, Catholics will insist on the fact that he was a priest and will point out that other priests who played public roles during the early history of the country went right along with the Dean. With regard to the 1853 renewal of the constitutional sanction, Catholics will wonder whether credit for the renewal belongs so exclusively to Alberdi and if it does not in part rest with the relatively obscure priest Benjamin Lavaisse, who was a delegate to the Santa Fe Convention. The proposed draft of an article on the freedom of religion was the subject of a long discussion in the convention. In an attempt to settle the Catholic element involved in the question, Lavaisse announced that his vote would be for the freedom of worship, which was a "precept of Evangelical charity in which is contained the duty that we owe to our neighbor." He emphasized that he was speaking as a "Deputy of the Nation," and that as a priest he would continue to preach the "Gospel and the truth of religion" with the same ardor and conscientiousness that he had always experienced.[52] Lavaisse did not see any incompatibility between his religious beliefs, which recognize no other valid religion, and the principle of freedom of worship for all creeds. In general this has been the attitude of nearly all Catholic thinkers in Argentina. If a secularist minority can claim some credit for the incorporation of this freedom into Argentine law, large credit cannot be denied to the Catholic majority who have supported it from the beginning.

A practical consideration that may take a bit of the shine off both the haloes is that as Argentines all of them were concerned with the promotion of European immigration, and neither secularist nor Catholic wished to place any obstacles in the way of the hoped for movement of new population across the Atlantic. They wanted to assure both Catholics and Protestants in Europe that they could count on free exercise of their religion in the new land of Argentina.

52. Casiello, *op. cit.*, p. 115.

While Catholics have not found in their own creed the basis to deny this freedom, there have been a few minor expressions of dissatisfaction with the constitutional arrangements. As has been suggested in Chapter I, the voice most often raised in protest here has been that of Frías. First of all, Frías wanted an official state religion. Article 2 was not enough for him, and as we have seen,[53] he sought unsuccessfully to have it amended in 1860. At this time, as well as in his attack many years later on Estrada's Church-State position he pleaded that a *religión del estado* was a natural and proper attribute of any society characterized by essential credal unity, as Argentina was.[54] Running through his usual list of favorite (and nearly all Protestant) countries, he contended that they all had their own state religion except for the United States, which could not have one because of its genuine religious diversity. In nearly all of them, he emphasized, religious liberty suffered no infringement as a result of the existence of the official religion. (The only country where he could see a logical basis for disestablishing the state religion was Ireland, where the official religion was not the Church of the people.) He would like to put Argentina on this list, but he protested with unquestionable sincerity that he would not permit the official Church to become an obstacle to religious freedom.

Though Frías would interfere with no cult and though he was dissatisfied with the constitutional arrangement, there is no doubt he counted on the provisions of Article 2 to give special protection to Catholicism, even if it was not the religion of the state. The focus of his demands for special treatment of Catholicism is in the school question, and writings of his in the 1860's form a portent of a major Catholic crisis which was to set in in 1880 and to continue for many decades.[55] Various examples of Frías' treatment of the question of freedom of religion in its special relation to the public school system show thought of a contradictory quality, sometimes casual and shallow, other times profound. In one article he denounced the recently established practice of permitting non-Catholics to become public school teachers.[56]

53. Above, Ch. I, p. 14.
54. Vol. IV, p. 224.
55. See below, Chap. VI, pp. 190–193.
56. Vol. III, pp. 180–181. The liberal Sarmiento had been hardly more tolerant in practice, but without Frías' zeal for religious orthodoxy. See below, Ch. VI, p. 189.

Teachers had to work closely with parish priests, and they should not be of a different faith than the priest, or the two would work at cross-purposes. What would Frías do with the fact that the schools were open to all, and some of the pupils might not be Catholics? If some of the pupils were non-Catholics why should there be no non-Catholic teachers, especially in a society where no one could be compelled to profess any creed? No one wanted to interfere with the beliefs of non-Catholics, Frías said, but they were so small a minority that they could not affect the problem.

In a more serious and more considerate view Frías showed that he was not concerned over the possibility that persons of Protestant faith might become teachers. It was the non-believer in the public school system who aroused his opposition. The non-religious teacher was, Frías believed, a tool of secularism, and the tool would be used against religion in the name of freedom of religion. Secularists had to oppose religion and above all the Catholic religion. To justify their position they had to deny Original Sin, the Redemption, the Divinity of Christ, and the authority of an *Ecclesia Docens*. Manifestation of these denials, either obliquely or directly, in the schoolroom could not be eliminated, and the religious instruction which was then a part of the curriculum would suffer from mockery or frontal attack.

Would Frías then, in the light of this particular expression of his attitude, refuse to give non-believers the full benefit of the right of freedom of religion? Subject to certain qualifications the answer is *yes*. Frías' qualified refusal identifies a continuing problem which serious Catholics of his times and later have had to face and for which they have not yet produced a practical solution. Their position starts with an affirmation of the right to freedom of religion and of conscience as the Constitution guarantees these rights. At the same time they maintain that the Constitution, though it has not established a Catholic state, has an *orientación católica*.[57] Between the freedom of religion and the Catholic orientation they see no contradiction. The one is no threat to the other, and Catholics will insist that history supports their contention that Argentine Catholics have not opposed the existence of a diversity of creeds. But, they argue, the Catholic content of the Constitution is as valid as the freedom of religion provisions.

57. Casiello, *op. cit.*, p. 78.

Whatever threatens to disturb the Catholic orientation is as much to be rejected as a threat to freedom of religion. They see a threat in secularist movements like the laicizing trends of the late nineteenth century. Laicists defend their position by an appeal to freedom of religion. Catholics reject the appeal as spurious and insist that freedom of religion is not at issue. The real issue is the survival of the Catholic orientation.

These two positions have clashed most dramatically in the school and marriage laws which will be discussed in Chapter VI. In these conflicts Catholics have generally been on the losing side. Their opponents contend that since the Catholic loss of the battles has not disturbed the religious provisions of the Constitution or brought about "separation" of Church and State, then the Catholics are mistaken in their judgment. From this secularists deduce that the laicist trends have not been anti-religious. They have been steps toward assuring freedom of conscience, and the Catholic antagonism amounts to a denial of the principle of this freedom. Catholics, naturally, will not agree. They say that the goal of secularist thought is "indifferentism" on the part of the state. By this term they understand a public policy which is unconcerned with religion in any way and which by denying religion any importance undermines it to the point of collapse. It is one thing, they contend, to say that a man may worship in any Church of his choice. But it is something quite different to say that religion does not matter.

Do Argentine Catholics then deny a right to religious unbelief? They would argue that they do not, and especially in recent times they would fall back on the statement in Leo XIII's *Immortale Dei* that men cannot believe otherwise than of their own free will. No one can be coerced into faith, but neither, they insist, does respect for this fact mean that public advantage must be given to unbelief. This advantage results whenever the *orientación católica* is restricted or denied by public policy, because secularism faces no other important antagonist in Argentina than the Catholic Church.

These conflicts have gone on in Argentina for nearly eight decades. They are likely to continue far into the future. The rare victory for the Catholic view does not appear, on close examination, to be a denial of freedom of religion, although it is frequently characterized as such.[58] The most appropriate comment for a North American to make on this still quite unsettled situation is that there is little or nothing in the experience of the United States and its citizens to provide any instinctive appreciation of this factor in Argentine history. The guarantees in the United States Constitution on behalf of the freedom of religion have been given special meaning by the existence of a genuine diversity of creeds. In Argentina this kind of diversity has never matured. The United States scene has been one of undeniable religious freedom, but it has also been one from which significant inter-faith tensions have rarely been absent. It is a mistake to transfer North American concepts of inter-credal antagonism and competition to the Argentine scene where the important tensions have existed between Catholic and secularist forces. That these tensions create a fundamental and still unsolved political problem for Argentina cannot be denied. Whether they constitute a problem in freedom of religion, however, is at best an open question.

THE MORAL COMPONENT

Catholic writers who have dealt with the moral aspects of democracy have in general followed a line of thought which is largely consistent with the position on freedom of religion noted in the foregoing section. Little of this thought has been marked by any startling originality. Yet because their adherence to a traditional position has brought most of them to a solidly pro-democratic commitment, the principal trends in their thought must be noted here.

The most fundamentally traditional element which is common to all of them is their view of the problem of good and evil in the social order. The problem, they attest, exists primarily in man, not society. In this respect they run counter, in typical Catholic fashion, to many modern currents of thought which make the problem of good and evil essentially one of social organization, and which see man's moral conduct as determined by the society in which he lives. In the present century Bishop Andrea has lamented the influence of Rousseau on democratic thought. Rous-

58. See below, Ch. VI, pp. 197–198.

seau "could not deny the magnitude of evil nor admit that God was its author." [59] Therefore he attributed a natural goodness to man, who was corrupted by social institutions. A century earlier Frías had written that liberty is the "sinner's sad attribute." [60]

Though man is a sinner, not naturally good, he has a potentiality for good. Most of the Catholics who have been cited in the preceding pages offer views which in synthesis seem to hold that the prime object of social organization is to provide the opportunity in which each man can on his own initiative most fully develop his potentiality for good. This also seems to include by implication a concept of a common good which is distinct from individual good and which society must also protect, though the concept of the common good does not receive any very thorough development. Three special emphases in the general line of Catholic thought can be discerned.

There is first of all that originally voiced by Frías in his oft-repeated insistence on *"buenas costumbres"* (good customs). Man is by nature free, but the price of his freedom is his capacity to sin. In society then man is free to obey or disobey the authority that society established.[61] This authority ought to be a just and righteous one, but even if it is, it cannot constantly compel obedience through institutions that intrude deeply into man's life. Part of this inability comes from sheer physical limitation, but another and more important reason is that the state has no right to intrude into man's private life, and if it does it is guilty of an infringement on man's natural freedom. The only successful means that Frías can see to obtain desirable compliance with the needs and the authority of society is *custom*. By this he means habits of conduct which have their sanction in a commonly accepted morality. This morality cannot be imposed by authority. Rather the people must be indoctrinated in it. The doctrine to be taught must be linked to religion, because religion shows man the ultimate destiny which he must reach through exercise of his own free will. In pursuit of his destiny the individual must live in society, but society can make no claim upon him, which is not consistent with both his final end and his own freedom and choice

59. *Conferencias*, p. 47.
60. *Escritos*, Vol. I, p. 401.
61. *Ibid.*, pp. 402–403.

of means to obtain it. Therefore it is in the interior convictions that religion gives to the individual man that society will find the best guarantees of good conduct.

A society which grounded its morality in this principle would, of course, be a democratic society. The people would be automatically prepared for self-government, because, in Frías' view, the man who had the means to govern himself was thereby qualified to partake in the government of the community.[62]

As would be expected, Frías has only the most minimal faith in the formal institutions of government. He nowhere denies their necessity, but he is convinced that too many Argentines have believed that social transformations could be brought about by institutional changes. Effective and desirable changes, he asserts, must be obtained not through institutions, nor through the masses of men, but through an appeal to the individual. He considers that the unhappiest parts of his country's history have been the result of a blind faith in institutions and a failure to understand human nature. Whether that nature was regarded as essentially good by the philosophers or essentially corrupt by the caudillos, on both views had been built institutions which were doomed from the beginning.[63]

Some contrast in emphasis is offered by the modern Catholic authority, Andrea. He is no less concerned than Frías with "good customs" and the maintenance of a moral climate which will allow the individual to develop his potentialities for good. But he is more generous to institutions in his view of how they may affect the environment in which moral principles must operate. In one sense it may be said that the bishop discerns two kinds of institutions which are important to man in society in pursuit of his ultimate goal. The institutions are of either divine or human origin.[64] Among those of divine origin are community, family and property. Since these institutions have by divine authority been placed in the order of nature, it is the business of the state to pro-

62. *Escritos,* Vol. I, pp. 98–99.
63. Pedro Goyena, Frías' collaborator and posthumous editor, stresses in his introduction to the collected works that this was a basic and enduring distrust on Frías' part. See Vol. I, p. xiii.
64. The institutions of divine origin are noted in many places. Their relation to Christian morality is summarized in *Conferencias,* p. 31.

tect them. While it does not appear that the bishop would deny the state competence to regulate in the fields where these institutions function, it is a rather narrow competence that he accords it. It is limited primarily by the consideration that the state can never do anything which infringes on or denies their divine origin and purpose. It would appear that in present-day terms the major emphasis is on the integrity of the family. With property the Bishop is at no time unconcerned, but his views must be understood in terms of his previously noted attitude toward capitalism and the welfare state.

Bishop Andrea's quarrel with much of modern thought, especially socialist thought, is that it denies a divine sanction to these institutions and would bring them within the power of the state to continue or abolish as circumstances might dictate. Thus the possibility would always be present that the individual in his pilgrimage through the world would lack the institutions which sustain his moral character. With these views Frías and the other nineteenth century writers would have been in complete agreement.

Andrea goes far beyond them, however, in giving an importance to purely human institutions in the maintenance of moral standards and practice. For, he insists, twentieth century life has made purely material factors of enormous importance in providing the opportunities for man's development of his potentiality for the good. He would not, of course, deny the primacy of the spiritual in human nature, but he emphatically rejects any notion that this primacy means that the material can be neglected. "One reaches the soul only through the body. The promoters of material welfare do not cease thereby to foster morality. Quite to the contrary, they contribute extraordinarily to moral development, since a certain degree of material well-being is absolutely indispensable for the practice of virtue." [65]

Thus the purely human institutions which make for material well-being receive full approval from this episcopal source. In addition it would appear that since many of these institutions depend upon the state for their creation and support, Bishop Andrea would allow a much wider latitude to the state in the

65. *El Catolicismo Social*, p. 17.

formulation and execution of social policy than would most of the earlier Catholic writers. The story of the bishop's own career which, as noted above, contains several chapters devoted to organizing pressures to bring about legislative action in the welfare field, suggests that he takes a most positive view of the role of the state in modern society.

He expects, of course, that public authority must look outside the structure of the state for the inspiration and guidance which will lead to the construction of the needed institutions. Primarily, he urges, the state must look to the Catholic religion as its principal guide. The reasons that he offers are that the problems of the modern state are those of social balance and solidarity and that Catholicism is the comprehensive source of all teaching and all other means on which human solidarity can be achieved. In this connection his concern is not one of evangelization as such. Though he would unquestionably welcome it if the idea of human confraternity produced universal agreement in a single religious creed, this is not his immediate purpose in urging Catholicism's role as a social guide. It is rather that Catholic ideas and Catholic experience in producing social harmony can affect the "practical life of man and the people." For the time being he asks only that this practical influence be allowed to function.[66]

Though Andrea's recognition of the role of institutions in moral matters is not at fundamental variance with Frías' reliance upon "good customs," it does give a very different emphasis. Both these positions have had wide acceptance among Argentine Catholics, Frías' in his own times and afterward as well, Bishop Andrea's down to the present day. A third position, held by Estrada, stands somewhat apart from both of these, in spite of a large element of common agreement. Estrada's moral stress is upon the role of an individualism which is neither dependent upon custom nor necessarily linked to institutions.

His concept is traditional in the sense that as a Catholic he believes in the Fall and the Redemption and finds his point of departure in this belief. He is, moreover, convinced that the Gospel alone contains the true basis of social organization. But, especially as a young man, he was not entirely certain that Chris-

66. *Conferencias*, p. 21.

tian doctrine had ever been fully accepted as a social force. "History shows us the paths we must avoid, but not those we must follow." [67] This is not a note of despair. The Gospel has been fully accepted in countless individual lives; the task is to get it accepted by society as a whole.

To secure this acceptance, however, it is necessary for each individual to expand the concept of his own place in society and in nature through a keener realization of his own ultimate worth. When man is genuinely aware of, or "awake to," the realities of social life, his first care must be to "emancipate his person." [68] Emancipation will come not only from "controlling passions" and "correcting instincts," but in recognizing that the human being has "noble faculties to develop." To develop the noble faculties is the individual's first duty, a duty imposed not by society but by God. Never denying or discounting the propensity to evil that is the consequence of Original Sin, Estrada made of his morality chiefly an affirmative and creative force, rather than a negative and restraining one. Man must seek the good through his own individual faculties. He must also avoid evil, not simply by rejecting it but by concentrating all his efforts on the good.

Man's moral duty to the state and to society is to exert every possible effort to see that the state not only does not interfere with the exercise of the noble faculties, but also provides the best possible conditions for their development. How can this be achieved? By "moralizing the people." Moralizing the people means that each individual must be made profoundly aware of his rights and no less so of his duty to safeguard these rights.[69] This in turn means that each individual must play an active political role in the community. Here as in many other instances Estrada comes back to universal suffrage as the ultimate and only reliable promise of a decent relation between man and society. It is probably needless to point out that Estrada does not think of this device as a creator of morality. For him morality rests on a basis which Christian doctrine has established. It is the business of the Church to proclaim this doctrine and teach this morality. But

67. *Obras*, Vol. XII, p. 66.
68. *Ibid.*, Vol. IX, p. 76.
69. *Ibid.*, p. 88.

the teacher is not the guarantor of the acceptance of the moral doctrine. This role must reside in the people, since moral doctrine is meaningful only as individuals adhere to it.

THE DEMOCRACY OF ARGENTINE CATHOLICS

Generally speaking, democracy has created few or no problems for serious Catholic thinkers so far as its acceptance as a political form is concerned. They have not, to be sure, been able to share an identical concept of "sovereignty of the people" with some other democratic enthusiasts. They believe that there is a divinely established order of nature which conditions society and which limits the choice of action open to the state. Within these limits, however, they see the people as supreme and government of the people, by the people, as the most desirable of political arrangements. Probably the most important consideration for democratic thought as a whole is that the best and most persistent Argentine Catholic tradition recognizes no force as superior to the people and no authorities to be preferred over those that the people select.

This does not mean that Argentine Catholic writers have attributed an absolute function of decision to the people. There seems to be, rather, a fundamental trust in the people's ability to recognize the "order of nature" and to operate politically within it. In Catholic thought it is impossible, of course, to eliminate the Church as the custodian of revealed truth. Where the Church officially exercises this function with consequence for political issues, the charge may be made that the authoritarian body is interfering with the democratic process. It will be seen in Chapter VI that when the Argentine hierarchy as a whole has spoken authoritatively on specific issues, its directives have been limited to reiteration of traditional Catholic positions or doctrines. The scant number of such directives cannot be cited to eliminate a problem of authority-versus-democracy. The relative rareness with which the function is exercised, however, both reduces the problem and suggests that the official Church shares the general trust which Catholic writers have placed in the democratic process. The problem will be examined in detail in the following chapter.

The democratic thought and endeavors of Argentine Catholics

have shown both strength and weakness. There is a good deal to suggest that both qualities have been to a certain extent colored by the national character and the purely national historical currents.

For example, it seems to the present writer that the glaring weakness of the Argentine Catholic position has been a failure to grasp the essential relation between effective democracy and free and open elections. While this has been an Argentine weakness rather than a strictly Catholic one, this circumstance does not entirely excuse the Catholic omission. Estrada alone seems to have had a full understanding of the fact that government of the people (which all Argentine Catholics seem to want) cannot be real if the people do not have an unhampered opportunity to select their authorities. Frías, and some other men of good will, have, as we have seen, been content to accept *"candidatos de transacción"* in practice, or to surround the exercise of the suffrage with restrictions and limitations. Argentina has rarely enjoyed honest elections. To the mind of this critic, the Catholic emphasis on morality should have made more of a dent on this problem.

The excuse will doubtless be offered that the Catholics who have preached morality in public life have been teachers, writers, and Church ministers. By the nature of their personal situations they can do little more than lift their voices. If the people will not heed them, it is the people's responsibility, not theirs. In connection with the last three decades of Argentine history, they will say, specific Catholic interests have been under attack, and the attack has forced Catholics to concentrate their efforts in defense so that they have had little time and few resources to devote to a general problem. These excuses are valid and historically true, but they do not go far enough. Given the wide acceptance of the Catholic religion by the Argentine people (a fact Catholic writers are prone to emphasize now and then) the best possibility for arousing the spirit to sustain electoral reform and to "moralize" the electoral process would seem to lie in an appeal to the Catholic conscience. Such an appeal probably could not normally emanate from ministers of religion without reviving the never-entirely-dormant charges of "clerical interference." But Catholic lay forces do not apparently recognize either the possibility itself or the compelling necessity of their response to it.

If Catholic thought has been weak in this respect, it has been strong in others. Its theoretical defense of democracy and its attempts to relate the theory to the Argentine realities have been no small accomplishments. Whether the efforts have been those like Gorriti's or Esquiú's in appealing eloquently to religious doctrine to solidify the Argentine people into a system of self-rule, or like Estrada's in founding a scientific discipline of politics and in inspiring a generation of intellectuals, the Catholic sources have had important consequences in Argentine development.

At this point in Argentine history it seems that the Catholic social thought which has continued from the past might well join forces with the much more recent welfare consciousness that is symbolized by Andrea's work. This combination might then begin to make good the promise that is implicit in the whole stream of Argentine Catholic thinking. Performance in accordance with this promise might take the form of a union of forces under the label of Christian Democracy. Or more exactly, that promise has apparently been made explicit in the formation of various Christian Democratic parties which have grown out of the 1955 political crisis and its aftermath. It is still too early to evaluate these parties, and the division of Christian Democratic sentiment into more than one camp does not bespeak any fundamental unity in Argentine Catholic thought at this time.

In this writer's opinion, which is naturally subject to revision as more concrete evidence of the parties' development becomes available, that which calls itself the Christian Democratic Party is the most promising. This belief rests principally on the fact that the original formulation of the party's position was a very conscious reflection of the historical influence of Catholic social thought, and showed an awareness of the resources which this historical development has made available. Above all, the party's original statement demonstrated a firm democratic commitment in accordance with the best of the Argentine Catholic tradition. Allowing for the fact that a Christian Democratic party cannot be a Catholic party or have any organic connection with the Church, a party of this sort is likely to draw on Catholic teachings and to find its basic inspiration in Christian doctrine. In the case of the Argentine party the appeal is both Christian and strongly national, as the excerpts quoted directly below from the party's

July 1955 manifesto make plain. The party's ideological orientation is stated in the following terms:

Man is the only eternal being in Creation; everything will pass away; he will never pass away. Therefore he is the center of all; the state, society, family, school, economy, syndicate are at his service.

Abandonment of the principles of Christianity has brought the modern world to the situation in which it finds itself. It is not by abandoning them further that we shall save ourselves, but by returning to their rule in spirit and in action. Only through the really Christian concept of man, family, civil society and state, shall we constitute the new society in order that it may be productive of individual and community realizations which may benefit all.[70]

The party's relation to the Church is stated thus:

Far be if from us to think of forming a confessional movement in which only Catholics take part; we do not want it, and we repudiate it at the political level. The Church does not direct us, not only because it does not want to—in keeping with the indifference with which it regards all regimes—but also because we resolutely and loyally wish to leave it [the Church] at the margin of civic contentions so that it may fulfill its own mission.

A distinctly national ancestry is claimed for the party:

This movement comes from afar: it appears in the Men of May; it is manifested in the Assembly of 1813 and the Congress of Tucumán; it lives in Gorriti, and in the most fundamental of the symbolic words of the *Asociación de Mayo;* [71] Rosas negates it, and his tyranny; it glows splendidly in the Constitutional Convention of 1853, whose President, Zuviría, proclaimed himself democrat and Christian . . . it is word, light and guide in Esquiú, Frías, Estrada and their legion, whose teaching and testimony of life have formed our minds and inspired our conduct. It can be said that whenever the Republic has followed the historical direction which today we represent, there have been peace and progress, and to the degree that it has been evaded, abandoned, or denied, calamities have rained upon the country.

There is an obvious peril in closing a chapter with extensive citation from a source whose value is so much more hypothetical

70. These excerpts are translated from the text of the manifesto which appear in the Chilean monthly publication *Política Y Espíritu,* Año XI, no. 139 (August, 1955), pp. 15–18.

71. The *Asociación* can hardly be claimed as a part of the Catholic tradition, but apparently the party leaders do not wish to limit their traditional ties to the strictly Catholic movements.

than real. Hypothetical values can disappear more rapidly than do words on paper, while the writer can be haunted by the consequences of the disappearance. The formulation of policy and objectives which the above quotations suggest is, however, probably the most logical consequence that the Catholic democratic tradition in Argentina could produce. If the party matures into a full-fledged political organization, it will provide an important test for the validity of that tradition.

CHAPTER VI

Social and Political Conflicts

IN KEEPING with what has been presented in the preceding chapter, most Argentine Catholics would be content with two basic claims concerning the relationship between their Catholicism and their status as members of the Argentine commonwealth. One is that between the dogmatic religion that they profess, and the politics of order and liberty to which they are in the main committed, there is no essential conflict. The other is that Christian moral doctrine has helped to form the Argentine civic conscience, which in turn has been guided and enlightened by the social philosophy which has sprung from Catholic sources. In brief, it would be claimed that, in the march toward democracy, Catholicism has been a major asset.

This claim will be challenged in many quarters. Two types of challenge will be noted and examined here. One is of the general sort that issues from a distrust of the influence of an authoritarian Church. It has been formulated in various ways and in connection with various developments in Argentine history. Ingenieros offers an example in his attitude toward Catholicism under the Rosas Restoration, which is noted above.[1] Basic to this view is the idea that Catholicism cannot survive in a society dominated by the spirit of free inquiry which is necessary for democracy. A corollary to this idea is that when anti-democratic forces show their strength they will inevitably attract Catholic support to their position. It has been claimed that precisely this has happened in modern Argentina when the institutions of constitutional democracy have been beset by crisis.

The other kind of challenge rests on more specific grounds

1. See Ch. III, p. 58.

which allege that Catholicism seeks to curtail freedoms essential to democratic citizenship. Freedom of conscience is one of them. Catholicism in Argentina, it is alleged, has a long record of opposition to this freedom in its insistence upon a program of compulsory religious instruction in the public school system. Marriage and family formation are also appropriated by the Catholic Church as subjects of its own authoritarian teaching and control, whereas it is asserted that greater freedom to the parties involved can be offered in civil regulation and control.

What challenges of both kinds seem to establish is that there are points of conflict between Catholicism and other organized forces which profess to offer a course of action that is more thoroughly in keeping with democratic principles. Let us look at some concrete instances of conflict in recent Argentine history.

Those which the first kind of challenge bespeak are most readily to be found in a decade which could be regarded as closing in 1946 or 1947. The decade began with a period in which Argentine democracy was functioning imperfectly under the auspices of the *Concordancia*. Traditional democratic concepts were then under assault in Argentina partly from pressures for drastic economic reform, partly as a local response to the international appeal of European fascism. The period closed with the revolutionary developments which began on June 4, 1943, and which concluded with the consolidation of Perón's quasi-totalitarianism in the October 1945 crisis and in the national elections of the following February.

This is a period which has attracted the best efforts of many writers and social scientists in a search for the explanation of the collapse of democracy and the success of Peronism. Among them have been several North American scholars and professional journalists. Several of these have suggested or asserted that the transition from the feeble democracy of the Ortiz-Castillo administration to the rampant authoritarianism of Perón is in part to be explained in terms of an anti-democratic Catholic influence which merged into a general stream of pro-fascist forces.[2]

2. Ysabel F. Rennie, *The Argentine Republic* (New York, 1945), pp. 268–270; Robert Alexander, *The Perón Era* (New York, 1950), p. 125 *et seq.*; George I. Blanksten, *Perón's Argentina* (Chicago, 1953), details (p. 237 *et seq.*) the activities of the "right wing" of the Argentine clergy.

THE "RIGHTIST" CLERGY

The Catholic influence is reported to have been exercised through two fronts: a rightist clergy attacking liberal democracy in the press and in the pulpit; the "ostensibly non-political" lay organization, *Acción Católica Argentina*. The clergy's attitude has been attributed to a variety of origins including among others the authoritarian formation of their own professional character, their ardent Hispanophilism, their anti-Marxism, their fear of a Bolshevist world conquest, an element of anti-Semitism after Perón's triumph,[3] and a general belief that the Spanish Caudillo Franco had perfected in his country a social and political organization which was worth duplicating in Argentina because it met the needs of modern society and at the same time was a bulwark against international Communism.

It is probably not difficult to find among the clergy of the period men whose social ideas were colored by one or more of these factors. It is somewhat more difficult, however, to establish on the basis of data offered a generally anti-democratic attitude which would make the clergy as a group effectively subversive of the existing political order. The scope of the indictment is too broad,[4] even if strong individual cases can be presented.

Even the individual cases appear to contain weaknesses in the light of subsequent movements in Argentine and world history. For example, one author cites the Catholic editor, Monseñor Gustavo Franceschi, as the "most intelligent spokesman for the Catholic fascist clergy."[5] Monseñor Franceschi, who died in 1957, had been an outstanding producer of Catholic apologetic works since the days of World War I, and in the early thirties he had become editor of the Catholic weekly *Criterio*. Monseñor Franceschi's pro-fascist views are alleged to have developed in the course of his work as editor.

In the early thirties the new Spanish Republic became one of

---

3. Felix J. Weil, *Argentine Riddle* (New York, 1945), pp. 48–51 deals with the element of anti-Semitism which he characterizes as the "native Catholic variety."
4. Almost all treatments of the subject make exceptions of specific clergy and laity whom they identify as strong partisans of democracy. In this connection the name most frequently cited is that of Monseñor Miguel de Andrea, Titular Bishop of Temnos. For further mention of Bishop Andrea see below, pp. 205–206.
5. Rennie, *op. cit.*, p. 269. Other writings are in general agreement.

his many interests, and like most Catholic writers he found much
to criticize in the Republic. With the outbreak of the Civil War
in 1936 Franceschi declared himself a partisan of Franco, and
immediately put his literary talents to work in defense of the Spanish Nationalists. In the midst of the war he made a trip to Spain,
and out of this trip came more published articles which vividly
confirmed the position he had originally taken.

Franceschi's principal writings on Spain were later published in
a collection entitled *En El Humo Del Incendio*[6] (*In the Smoke
of the Fire*). This volume has been offered as evidence of its
author's basically fascist outlook. In the same connection there
have been citations of other periodical writings from Franceschi's
pen, including a prolonged journalistic exchange with the leader
of the Progressive Democratic Party in 1937.[7] (This polemic did
not relate directly to the Spanish Civil War, but involved some
basic apologetic matters of socio-historical import ranging from
the Second Century to the Twentieth.)

An examination of Monseñor Franceschi's writings on Spain
show that his position was determined principally by a conviction
that the alternatives in the struggle were either a Nationalist victory under Franco or a Communist victory which would implant
the rule of Moscow on the Iberian Peninsula. On the outcome of
the war hung the "future of Communism in the world."[8] Franceschi sought to arouse his Argentine readers about the consequences
that a Communist triumph in Spain would have for Latin America. He insisted that too many Latin Americans had complacently
believed that a "deep Catholic tradition" was in itself a sufficient
protection against the Communist threat. The events in Spain
ought, he believed, to have awakened them to a realization of how
false a hope this was. In his view what was at stake in Spain was
"in good part the fate of the Hispanic-American continent."[9]

That the Communists were not the only people fighting against
Franco, Franceschi was quite willing to concede. But the other
anti-Franco elements were, he asserted, victims and dupes of a

6. Buenos Aires, 1938.
7. Franceschi's contributions were subsequently published under the title *Res-
puestas a de la Torre* (Buenos Aires, 1937); de la Torre's in *La Cuestión Social Y
Un Cura* (Buenos Aires, 1943).
8. *En El Humo*, p. 217.
9. *Ibid.*, p. 107.

Moscow-inspired and directed movement to which the label "Popular Front" had been attached.[10] For these other elements Franceschi had little sympathy. They were nineteenth century types of liberals and opportunist socialists whose blindness and pride had made them ready dupes of the Moscow technique. This characterization of the Popular Front was not limited to the Spanish version, but was explicitly extended to the French and Chilean forms as well.

This appraisal has been rejected by numerous students of the Spanish Civil War, both contemporary and subsequent. Many Catholic writers have agreed with it, but by no means all of them. Franceschi's stand attracted the attention of a Catholic audience outside of as well as within his own country. The distinguished French Catholic Jacques Maritain was one of those who publicly took issue with Monseñor Franceschi. Franceschi's reply to Maritain is contained in the long article *El Movimiento Español Y El Criterio Católico*.[11] The article provided its author with an opportunity to seek to identify his own position as a Catholic one. In it he concedes, after paying tribute to Maritain as an "eminent Christian" and after calling him a "personal friend," that the Maritain position probably cannot be attacked on questions of doctrinal orthodoxy.[12] But he argues that Maritain's position is one of practical error and that considerations of fact destroy the applicability of Maritain's theory. Franceschi is confident that the facts are on his side and that they render his position a Catholic one. This facts-versus-theory stand demonstrates the difficulty that Catholic writers had in finding a common ground on which to argue this extremely complicated question. The challenge of a famous Catholic philosopher was one which Franceschi could not ignore, yet Maritain's challenge did not move Franceschi the least bit from his position.

In the light of his pre-Civil War writing it may be said that Franceschi had reached this position slowly but, perhaps, inevitably. His concern with the politics of Spain and the relationship between the political and the religious in that country did not begin with the Civil War. A few months before its outbreak he

10. *En El Humo*, pp. 108–109.
11. *Ibid.*, p. 217 *et seq.*
12. *Ibid.*, p. 219.

had stated that conditions in Spain had become such that "from the strictly Catholic point of view" the problem of Spain was less a "political question" than one of the "apostolate." [13] The basic questions were those of moral and spiritual regeneration and indoctrination which were antecedent, in his view, to any political solution. He lamented the decline of the acceptance of Christian doctrine in the influential places in Spanish society, recognizing that this decline had begun much earlier than the birth of the Republic. Most specifically, he deplored that certain "directing classes" in the Spanish population were ready enough to be on the side of the Church, because they wanted to "shield themselves" and their private interests behind certain doctrines and positions of the Church, which suited their convenience. Thus the Church's position on the right of private property had been invoked to defend the "incontestable abuses of certain land-owners." [14]

In summary, then, Franceschi saw two forces at work on the higher echelons of Spanish society and to both of them he attributed potentially dire consequences for that society. One was the de-Christianization of a large part of the upper classes. The other was a misplaced enthusiasm for Catholicism not as a spiritual force but as a defender of mundane interests. As a remedy for both he called for a renewed Catholic apostolate among all classes of people. There was a suggestion that the model to guide the Spanish apostolate might well be that of France. French Catholicism, he said, had not too many years earlier faced similar problems. De-Christianization had been a strong force in certain quarters, while in others a movement of "throne and altar" had led many French Catholics into untenable positions. From these problems French Catholicism had escaped by means of a renewed apostolate which had been free of any political considerations and which had produced, in Franceschi's judgment, admirable effects.[15]

This attitude would indicate that Franceschi did see the Spanish problem as a Catholic problem but that as late as February 1936 his solution was in terms of anything but the violence of armed struggle. Indeed, what appeared most feasible to him then

13. *En El Humo*, p. 51.
14. *Ibid.*, p. 54.
15. *Ibid.*, pp. 56–57.

was a religious revival of the sort of which Maritain, his future opponent, was himself both a product and an active agent. The factor that moved Franceschi from this position was in all probability a new appreciation of the immediacy of the Communist threat. This was the single issue in terms of which he and the other "rightist clergy" viewed the whole complicated Spanish matter.

Whether this view was justified is something that can still be debated, and the debate is probably complicated rather than simplified by the changing appraisals which Communism has undergone in Western liberal thinking since 1934. At the time of Franceschi's writing, many serious students of world politics who had no ideological sympathy with Moscow looked upon Communism in terms of its value as a bulwark against fascism. This was a value which Franceschi refused to acknowledge. Many of the same students have taken in the post-World War II years a view of world Communism very close to that upheld by Franceschi and his associates between 1934 and 1939. This reappraisal may not of itself deny the anti-fascist value once attributed to Communism, but it recognizes that the anti-fascism was a tactical maneuver designed, not to keep free societies from becoming the prey of fascism, but rather to advance the Communist world revolution. From this reappraisal Monseñor Franceschi's group could undoubtedly draw some major *post-facto* consolation, but an unqualified justification of their position would be possible only if the tactical necessities of the democracies in the period were similarly the subject of a total reappraisal. There has been no generally-agreed-upon re-evaluation of this sort, and hence the debate can go on indefinitely.

To acknowledge this, however, is not to beg the question of the reality of the fascist threat, which was clearly serious at the time. It is therefore quite in order to ask two questions about the position which Franceschi was holding: (1) Was he, as charged, a fascist sympathizer? (2) Did he and his group strive for the implantation of a fascist system in Argentina?

Both questions have been faced by Franceschi in his own writings, the first explicitly, the second by implication. In the reply to Maritain he admitted that his previous articles had resulted in his being called a fascist. He also noted that there was a related charge that this represented a complete reversal of his earlier stand, which, he wrote, had been generally regarded as pro-democratic. He insisted, however, that his thinking had undergone no change and that his social ideas were the same as he had held before the Spanish Civil War. He stated that he could not talk about fascism except in concrete terms. The concrete form of fascism was in Italy, but as an abstraction, particularly as one of epithet, the word *fascist* had been stretched to cover too much. Fascism was the "concrete political form" of contemporary Italy. "Far be it from me to discuss here if it is that which is best for that nation." "But I believe our [Argentine] inheritance of tradition and idiosyncrasy to be so different that I judge the aforesaid concrete form to be inadequate for our country." [16] In the same passage, though there is an expression of qualified admiration for Mussolini as a person, there is a strong suggestion that Italian fascism is not a model to be copied anywhere else. Franceschi did not believe that Franco could or would pattern the Spanish system after it. The model he urged for Spain was that which Salazar had followed in Portugal. The merit of the latter, Franceschi argued, was that it rejected the fascist notion of "permanent" dictatorship and merely used the dictator as a "temporary remedy." [17]

As for other movements of the time which were tagged as fascist, Franceschi touched them now and then with a suggestion of sympathy but without sufficient attention to identify himself as their partisan. He was, moreover, careful in these cases to state that these movements were not Catholic—in complete contrast to his attitude toward the Spanish Nationalists. For example, in his brief treatment of Belgian Rexism he voiced an undeniable note of approval of the movement because, in his opinion, Rexism had been the determining factor in preventing the establishment of a Popular Front government in Belgium.[18] At the same time, however, he was frank enough to point out that after he had stated his judgment that the question of Rexism was "outside the religious problem," the Belgian hierarchy had specifically condemned "attitudes and tendencies" of the movement.[19]

16. *En El Humo,* p. 218.
17. The most durable non-Communist dictatorship in Europe to date has been that of Salazar.
18. *Ibid.,* p. 66.
19. *Ibid.,* p. 65, footnote 1.

With regard to the most consequential form of what was then called fascism, German Naziism, Franceschi was specific and unequivocal in his denunciation. Writing from Paris in 1937 he equated the Nazi and Communist movements as "two forms of an identical materialist doctrine," [20] and he pointed out that both movements had been condemned in Papal encyclicals.

In connection with the various movements which were frequently grouped together as fascist and of which, certainly, none represented anything that could be called traditional democracy, Monseñor Franceschi's record then is as follows: Naziism is denounced, Italian Fascism is rejected as unsuitable for export, though there is a word of praise for Mussolini. Belgian Rexism is praised for a specific accomplishment attributed to it, but the condemnation of the movement by ecclesiastical authority is noted. Salazar's authoritarian system is held up as a model worthy of imitation at least in Spain, and Franco's dictatorship is regarded as salvation from Communism. In general the record does not bespeak what would normally be considered a strong commitment to democracy.

On the other hand, it does not indicate conclusively the intention to overthrow the existing order and implant in Argentina a dictatorship of the right, an intention which has frequently been ascribed to Franceschi and his associates. It is undeniable that these men were critical of the state of affairs in Argentina. So too were many articulate liberals. A charge of subversive intent is no more justified in the one case than in the other. Both sides would plead that they wanted to take steps which would strengthen Argentine society in its traditional modes, but they did not share a common view of what was traditional. Franceschi specifically pleaded that what was basically necessary was the perpetuation of Argentine constitutional tradition. He argued that the Constitution itself contained all the necessary means to protect the country and to promote its welfare.[21]

To recognize that the general charges against a "rightist clergy" have been overdrawn does not, of course, eliminate the possibility that the clerical ranks included specific individuals who were frank totalitarians. But the central question for Argentine Cathol-

20. *En El Humo*, p. 199.
21. *Ibid.*, p. 24 *et seq.*

icism at this time is whether, if totalitarian clergymen to the number of one or more existed, they represented a social attitude which could be operative on Catholic citizens, *qua* Catholics. Assuming the loyalty of practicing Catholics to episcopal authority within the Church, one can say that the possibility is very slight. For in their collective pastoral of 1938 the Argentine bishops most specifically pointed out two doctrines that "have merited the just condemnation of the Church." These were the "doctrine of the totalitarian state," and the "doctrine of racism."

The pronouncement would appear to make clear that any would-be remakers of the Argentine state in the totalitarian model had already earned the condemnation of the Argentine Church. Within the traditional framework of Roman Catholicism it is, of course, unthinkable that, in spite of individual sacerdotal aberration, any significant number of clergy would defy so clear a directive.

If this is so, it must be asked why, then, so many objective observers of obvious good faith found in the Argentine clergy of this period a subversively anti-democratic force. Any answer must be somewhat speculative, but the following probably offers a general, if not altogether complete, explanation.

The decade of the 1930's and the World War which followed formed a period of continuing crisis for the survival of free men and free institutions in all of Western society. Hardly any country, least of all Argentina, was spared the onslaught of economic dislocation, for the amelioration of which exotic and drastic political innovations were offered both by zealots and by thoughtful and temperate men. Many of the clergy—Monseñor Franceschi is a major example—were deeply concerned about the hardships of the poor and the working classes. Their sympathy led them to examine and sometimes to espouse some of the exotic remedies offered. Many of them, moreover, did not stop here. The Catholicism of which they were the ordained ministers had for many years been under attack by certain kinds of liberals, materialists and upholders of *laissez-faire* economics. The attackers had frequently sought to identify themselves as the sole agents of progress and democracy. Some of them had ridiculed Catholicism as an obstacle to progress and had emphasized traditional religion's lack of success as a social force in modern society. Now their own "success," or what

they had claimed as such, had in large part vanished in the face
of the increasingly complex problems of Western Civilization in
the period between the wars. There is little doubt that many
Catholics, including clergy, were now gleefully returning the
scorn and the ridicule with which a once-successful *laissez-faire*
liberalism had formerly assaulted them. In terms of solving the
immediate problems before the nation they could have used their
talents to better purpose, but some undoubtedly thought that it
was important not to lose the opportunity to demonstrate that
the "opposition" no longer commanded an impregnable fortress.

There were also, as has been suggested above, many sincere
persons within the liberal ranks who were earnestly seeking the
salvation of liberal democracy in terms of its own tradition. These
persons, with a point of view often extremely remote from the
clergy's, could find no common ground with the latter. Both—
clergy and liberals—were sincere in their protestations that they
did not want to change the existing order, only to save it. But they
could agree on scarcely any mutually acceptable means to save it.
Exchanges of antagonism between the two probably helped some
of the clergy to acquire the undeserved classification of fascist.

Especially was this true in the light of the factor that international Communism introduced into the argument. To the clergy it
was an immediate and pressing danger which would become more
grave as the social discontent of the period increased. To liberals
—certainly not to all, but to some—Communism was a remote
factor, inconsequential in terms of any revolutionary changes that
it could work in Argentine society. At the same time Communism
had the merit of being anti-fascist, especially after 1941 when the
Soviet Union and Germany went to war. Some liberals could
accordingly look upon Communism as a force for democracy, and
the apologetics for this view could find in Soviet Communism
"lessons" for the progress and advancement of the traditional
democracies of the West. To the clergy all these ideas were
anathema. They had opposed Communism in the Popular Front
era. They found it no more acceptable as an ideological ally in
the period in which democracy was under crushing attack from
the fascists.

World events since 1946 have given most liberals a different
concept of the threats of Communism to Western Civilization. It

is true that in retrospect few would concede that any other course of action than alliance with the Soviets was possible for the democracies during World War II. Yet to recognize the practical necessity is not to deny Communism's abiding ideological threats and the long-range revolutionary aims that priests like Franceschi foresaw. A difference of opinion about the threats and the aims, a difference which has not proved permanent, earned these priests the label of pro-fascists. They probably deserve it about as much as the honest liberals who once called for cooperation with the Soviets deserve the pro-Communist reputation which has been accorded to many of them.

ACCIÓN CATÓLICA ARGENTINA

If pro-fascist charges against the clergy are at best insubstantial, there still remains the allegation of a like bias among large sectors of the Catholic laity. Specifically, the lay organization, *Acción Católica Argentina*, has been singled out as the apparatus through which anti-democratic and pro-fascist trends were made effective in the critical years 1938–46. Before the question of this organization's anti-democratic commitment [22] is examined, a brief inquiry into the general character and purpose of the organization will be useful.

Acción Católica is the Argentine manifestation of the worldwide movement known as Catholic Action. The movement was consolidated by Pope Pius XI following efforts to organize lay activity both by himself and by his recent predecessors. Pius XI defined Catholic Action as the "laity's participation in the hierarchical apostolate of the Church." [23] Though his call was for a universal movement, the decision about the time and circumstance of any national organization of Catholic Action was left to the bishops in each country. The Argentine hierarchy established

22. The charges of anti-democratic influence are persistent, though the basis of the charge differs from one time to another. The original charge was one of pro-fascism. Perón, however, said in his last years that the organization was collaborating with Communists. After the revolt of June 16, 1955, Peronist sources returned to the original accusation that the organization was pro-fascist and had planned to follow the revolt with a "fascist dictatorship." See below, p. 212, footnote 84.

23. A study which is apposite to some of the questions raised in the present context is by Raymond Francis Cour, C.S.C., *Catholic Action and Politics in the Writings of Pope Pius XI*, unpublished doctoral dissertation, University of Notre Dame, 1952.

Acción Católica Argentina through a collective pastoral of December 1, 1928.[24] The episcopal statement and the subsequently drafted statutes of the organization dedicate the national movement to "action of the spiritual order." An elaboration by the *Junta Central* of the organization in 1943 asserts that the dedication means that a certain "social action" is inescapable on the part of *Acción Católica* because it seeks to defend and develop religious principles which will have an effect upon "the individual, the family and society."

All the directives affecting *Acción Católica Argentina* from the first Papal pronouncement to the organizational statutes are explicit, however, in insisting that the social action envisaged cannot and must not include any form of partisan political activity. The organization cannot be allied with any political group, and its work must be entirely "outside of and above" the national political parties. Nor, in the light of specific Papal prohibitions, can *Acción Católica* turn itself into a party which submits candidates of its own for election or offers a platform of proposed political action.

At the same time, the whole body of authoritative statements dealing with Catholic Action make plain that the prohibition on partisan political activity is entirely organizational in its application. So far as the individual member is concerned, Catholic Action offers him a special channel for religious work, which in part at least may also be social work. It is not intended, however, that his membership in the organization should close to him the other normal channels of action, such as political parties, through which he may also work for social ends. The individual is free to join any political party he chooses provided that the party is not explicitly opposed to "Catholic doctrine or morality."

In all probability the obvious difficulty of keeping distinct the individual's participation in *Acción Católica* and his participation in the affairs of a political party helped to create the impression of a political stand on the part of the Catholic organization itself during the period under discussion. Members would more readily appreciate the distinction than non-members, and at the same

24. The terms of this letter as well as of a later one of April 5, 1931, are discussed by Juan Casiello in *Iglesia y Estado en la Argentina* (Buenos Aires, 1948), pp. 272–280.

time one cannot ignore the possibility that members were also in the best position to abuse the distinction, if they so chose. Whether there was widespread abuse is an open question, but a statement of the *Junta Central* in the critical year 1943 suggests that there may have been some.[25] Re-emphasizing both the absence of partisan commitment on the organization's part and the freedom of the individual member to adhere to the party of his choice, the *Junta* vigorously stated that any political activities on the part of individual members could not be linked with *Acción Católica*. The statement further asserted that Catholics in public life had no right to speak in the name of the Church or of Catholics in general.

In addition, some confusion may have arisen in non-Catholic quarters from a misunderstanding of the historical origins of *Acción Católica Argentina*. In a strict sense its immediate origin is in the bishops' letter of December 1928. However, the inauguration of the movement brought to a close, or at least thoroughly transformed, some organized lay activity that had preceded *Acción Católica* and which in certain phases of its history had sought specific ends through political activity.

The earliest Catholic lay organization which had a political involvement probably was the *Asociación Católica de Buenos Aires* which was headed by José Manuel Estrada in 1884. Its frank purpose was to arouse and organize Catholic opinion against the laicizing trends of the Roca administration.[26] This branched out into a country-wide organization and its directing group included several prominent politicians, who later occupied legislative and ministerial posts, and it also included at least one future president. The members of this group sought to oppose certain specific measures as well as a general trend. It would be difficult to regard their activity as other than political.

In later years the questions originally involved lost some of their immediate importance, and so did this particular Catholic organization. However, up to and including the period of World War I there were various Catholic lay developments, whose ancestry could be traced to this organization, and which pursued definite political objectives. There was even a short-lived political party,

25. Casiello, *op. cit.*, pp. 285–286.
26. See above, Ch. III, pp. 99–100; also below, pp. 190–194.

la Unión Demócrata Cristiana. After 1919 Catholic lay organizations were less concerned with winning political objectives than they were with propagandizing the recent social teachings of the Papacy. This shift in emphasis was marked by the emergence of a new entity, *la Unión Popular Católica Argentina.* This was organized with the express approval of the national episcopate.[27] The "assessor" named to advise the organization was Bishop Andrea, who had already begun the social work which has been treated in Chapter V.[28]

The *Unión Popular Católica* worked much more definitely under the auspices of Church authorities than had the earlier more or less spontaneous lay organizations. It had been approved by the episcopate, where the strictly lay organizations had not, even though they had obtained demonstrations of sympathy from individual prelates. The *Unión Popular* did not work for immediate political ends, but sought to arouse the conscience of the individual into social action. It was clearly a very different venture from the earlier organizations, although much of its support came from identical sources.

The *Unión* ceased to exist when *Acción Católica* came into being. In many eyes the latter would seem to be the heir of the former, although in reality *Acción Católica* represents something quite different. Moreover, critical eyes might tend to regard the later movement as heir to the political action organizations which had flourished much earlier. This may be another origin of the mistaken opinion regarding the political proclivities of *Acción Católica Argentina.*

Beyond this, however, there is a final point in the allegations of political activity on the part of *Acción Católica's* members which should be examined. This is the charge that since *Acción Católica* operates under the direction of the bishops, the large membership of the movement provides the hierarchy with a block of votes which can be swung one way or another as the bishops may decide, and hence the organization is a means of episcopal interfer-

27. Casiello, *op. cit.,* p. 272.
28. Mons. Dr. Miguel de Andrea, *El Catolicismo Social Y Su Aplicacion* (Buenos Aires, 1941), p. 22. Bishop Andrea's account follows the same line as Casiello's, but is less specific. Andrea also records that the *Unión Popular Católica* was founded at the indication of Pope Pius X. If the dates given are accurate, there seems to be a considerable time lapse between the Pope's indication and the formation of the organization, since Pius X died in 1914.

ence in the electoral process. This charge cannot be disposed of merely by referring to the ban on partisan political activity which limits the organization, or to the statement that any Catholic is in conscience free to join any political party which does not offend against "Catholic doctrine or morality."

For, it is alleged, the bishops are the interpreters of what constitutes offense in this regard, and since they are free to make interpretations at any time they can direct the faithful in and out of parties as ecclesiastical interests may indicate. The hierarchy has not been lavish with its directives on this point, and to date it has established six criteria which limit the Catholic individual's vote. The official statement, first issued in 1931, declares that "no Catholic can affiliate himself with parties or vote for candidates who inscribe in their programs the following principles": (1) the separation of Church and State; (2) the suppression of the legal dispositions which recognize the rights of religion and particularly the religious oath; (3) a laicized system of education; (4) legal divorce.[29] To these four the bishops later added the two injunctions, noted above,[30] against the doctrine of the totalitarian state and racism.

Obviously, not all of these criteria will be cited as evidence of an anti-democratic intent. The full significance of two of them, the school question and divorce, will be examined in later pages in the chapter. The first two listed must be evaluated in terms of what has been presented in Chapter I on Church-State relations. The complaint has been that these instructions from Church authority are prejudicial to certain parties, and many party spokesmen have registered such complaints, although none so loudly as the Peronistas in 1955.

The purpose, however, of the pronouncements is clearly not to penalize any particular party nor to "swing" elections at a given time. That this is the most remote intention implied in the statement is made evident if a single fact is considered. This is that practicing Catholics have already committed themselves in conscience to the principles of which the bishops in their declaration make specific applications. The declaration, therefore, is not designed to wean Catholic votes away from parties or candidates

29. Casiello, *op. cit.*, p. 281.
30. See above, p. 178.

that are openly anti-Church in their principles and program, because the votes of practicing Catholics are not likely to be cast in
this direction anyway. The detail and specification given, however, suggest that the declaration is meant to clarify, for the
Catholic, party positions which could create some confusion. The
most apparent problem arises here in those cases where a candidate may take a stand which is offered as "Christian" or "Catholic"
in order to win Catholic votes, but which is the candidate's own
conception of what is Catholic. In these cases the hierarchy will
insist that for the Catholic laity, the authoritative concept of what
is Catholic must come from the Church. In the latest crisis in
which these instructions became an issue, Perón and various
Peronista leaders were insisting that they were the truly effective
teachers of Christian principles, not the Church.[31] From their
side the bishops answered with a reiteration of their 1931 declaration. It is beyond question that the declaration seeks to defend
long-range Church interests, as the bishops see those interests.
The suggestion, however, that the declaration may be used ca-
priciously to gain immediate and temporary advantages is not
warranted, because it would attribute to the Church a more direct
participation in the dynamics of politics than it has ever sought.

Thus far this chapter has dealt with two aspects, the clerical
and the lay, of the general question of the presence of an organized anti-democratic force within Argentine Catholicism. Before attention is turned to more specific questions in the succeeding sections, it will be well to summarize here any conclusions
which can be drawn with regard to this question. So far three
rather narrow conclusions seem justified, and while they do not
dispose of the question, they may prove useful in future discussion
of it.

One is that the charges of anti-democratic intent, especially in
terms of a pro-fascist attitude, have been exaggerated. No one can
deny the possibility of anti-democratic individuals within the
Catholic fold, but that such individuals command an organized
political force, composed of Catholics, is a false belief. A second
conclusion is that there is probably a need for re-examination of

31. See *Hechos E Ideas*, Año XV, Tomo XXVII, nos. 126/127 (October–November,
1954), pp. 386–387. Perón himself, in keeping with one of the long anti-clerical
traditions of the Latin world, stated that he was defending the doctrine of Christ
against the sort of priests who for two thousand years had corrupted it.

much of the Catholic position between 1935 and 1946 when a great many of the criticisms leveled against it were colored by a view of Communism which most of the critics no longer hold. A third is that specific utterances and movements on the part of Catholics have from time to time come into conflict with other positions sustained by other groups in Argentine society. From the point of view of democratic politics, clashes of this sort are not likely to be absent from any society that is dedicated to maintaining free and open conditions for human existence, and the mere presence of these conflicts is not conclusive evidence that one of the parties to them is behaving undemocratically.

THE SCHOOL QUESTION

In certain quarters it might be conceded that these limited generalizations are possibly true, but, it would be contended, they apply only in those areas where in the nature of things the full power of the Catholic Church cannot be used to attain specific advantages. The Church cannot be rigid in the application of its authority to matters where the outcome will be determined by ballots cast in secret and by the overlapping pressures to which policy-makers are sensitive. Therefore, it is suggested, the Church is willing enough to have members of *Acción Católica* belong to any party, to have Catholic laymen and clergy write articles and make speeches and to leave the broadest area of citizen activities free from any ecclesiastical supervision. When, however, the concrete institutional interests of the Church are in question, then, so it is asserted, the Argentine hierarchy behaves differently and in violation of the accepted rules of democracy.

The issue that is most often cited in evidence here is the school question, or, more specifically, the question of "compulsory" religious instruction in the public schools. This, it is contended, is the main evidence to show that Argentine Catholicism is anti-democratic in its influence. The Church wants to mold the conscience of the citizen while it is still in the pliable condition of immaturity. To have access to the school children the Church will, it is suggested, make deals with political authorities whenever such deals are feasible, and these deals run counter to the basic tenets of democracy because they fail to respect freedom of belief and worship. One North American writer characterizes the reintroduction of religious doctrine classes into the public school system in 1943 as the "crux of an understanding" between the revolutionary (and undemocratic) government that had seized power in that year and the Roman Catholic hierarchy.[32]

The school question has been a major, perhaps *the* major, bone of contention between civil and ecclesiastical authority in Argentina for three-quarters of a century. The central issue at stake has been whether or not religious instruction shall be offered in the public schools as a part of the regular curriculum and within the normal hours of daily attendance.[33] In brief, the history of this question has been the following. Religious instruction was a customary part of the public school system until 1884. In that year the practice was done away with by a statute which removed religious instruction from the regular curriculum.[34] Until 1943 the practical effect of the statute was that no religious instruction was offered in the public schools. At the latter time the revolutionary government decreed that religious instruction would be reintroduced into the regular schedule of all the federally supported schools.[35] This decree was confirmed by a statute passed by the Argentine Congress in 1947.[36] This statute, in turn, was first suspended and then repealed in 1955, and religious instruction was removed from the classroom. There the matter stands at the date of writing (1957).

In summary, then, out of the 71 years between 1884 and 1955 religious doctrine has been a required subject in the public school curriculum for slightly less than eleven. This represents a little better than a fifteen per cent success for the Catholic position, a degree of success which is in itself not very impressive. However, the development of that position as well as that of the much more successful opposition should be examined in detail. Such examination is required both by the gravity of the charge that freedom of conscience is exposed to violation, and by the allegation of behind-the-scenes machinations on the part of the hierarchy.

32. Alexander, *The Perón Era*, p. 126.
33. The discussion of this issue is in terms of the federal laws and the federally supported schools. Provincial schools have tended to copy the various phases through which the federal schools have gone. Private schools, including those maintained by religious denominations, are not directly affected by the laws.
34. Law no. 1420 of 1884.
35. Decree no. 18411 of December 31, 1943.
36. Law no. 12978 of April 29, 1947.

Before going into the historical details involved in the question, two points which are related only by the fact that they have caused embarrassment to non-Argentine Catholics dealing with the matter should be noted. One is the characterization of the system as "compulsory." The term has been used in North American treatment of the question, but not in the treatment given by Argentine Catholic writers. The term is probably too broad. The decree of 1943 called for Catholic instruction as a part of the "ordinary material" in the curriculum. This would seem to make the instruction "authorized," but the exceptions in the decree's application, which will be treated below, do not sustain the view that the instruction was "required." [37]

The other point raises a consideration *ad hominem,* which may not be of basic importance but which certainly cannot be passed over in silence. Gustavo Martínez Zuviría, the Minister of Education who promulgated the 1943 decree, was a man whose reputation has not been enhanced by the conflicting evaluations to which it has been subjected. In certain circles he has been regarded as an exemplary figure of contemporary Argentine Catholicism. A popular, though not critically acclaimed, literary craftsman writing under the pseudonym of *Hugo Wast,* he is said to articulate in his books an Argentine Catholic point of view. In other circles *Hugo Wast* has been accused of popularizing the anti-Semitism which his own Church, among other forces of decency, has explicitly condemned. A fame for anti-Semitism on the part of the public official who was the formal agent of restoration of religious instruction to the school system has been a point of attack on the system which the decree established. This consideration, however, like the preceding one, may emerge with less importance in an examination of the whole history of the question.

The practice of religious instruction in the Argentine schools seems to have originated in the post-1853 period more in the tendency to honor a strong tradition than in anything else. It was a general practice, sustained in provincial and federal decrees and statutes, but it probably rested more definitely on custom than on legal dispensation. Historically, the religious institutions and the schools had been closely tied. "Civilizing" the masses of the people was the great task to which the governments of the post-

37. See below, p. 196.

1853 period were dedicated, and religion was looked upon as a civilizing force.

Questions of freedom of conscience do not seem to have bothered the strong and not very self-critical minds of the leaders of the Organization period, even when as individuals they were not notably fervent in their own religious commitment. Sarmiento furnishes a good example. On the national political stage he was a firm upholder of the rights of freedom of belief and worship. As noted above, he opposed the proposal of amendment to Article 2 of the federal constitution which would have put the article in a more strictly Catholic context.[38] Yet Sarmiento as Director of the Department of Education in the Buenos Aires Provincial government did not display any concern for the freedom of belief of the pupils under his supervision. He laid down precise stipulations about how religious observances were to be conducted in the schools. These included daily prayers, Catholic catechism and weekly attendance at Mass. Moreover, the Director's instructions provided that there could be no exceptions for either teachers or pupils. The teachers, he wrote, "must be persuaded to fulfill these simple duties of worship, which are means of education because of the serious ideas which they awake in the soul and because of the moral effect the presence and numbers of the pupils may have on the centers of population." [39]

It is not unfair to Sarmiento to suggest that he was less interested in perpetuating the cult to which his decree committed all public school personnel than he was in the "serious ideas" and the "moral effects" which would raise the tone of the communities. It would, however, be unfair to Sarmiento to suggest that he had no respect for freedom of belief or that he was incapable of a tolerance which would respect a diversity of creeds. The only reasonable inference is that the question of freedom of belief simply did not arise because of the credal unanimity of the population and because custom gave support to Sarmiento's stand.

A decade later the devout Catholic José Manuel Estrada occupied the same post in the Buenos Aires government. Estrada's instructions on the same subject show a much more scrupulous re-

38. See above, Ch. I, p. 14.
39. Casiello, *op. cit.*, pp. 329–330, notes both Sarmiento's attitude and the contrasting one of Estrada which came later.

gard for freedom of belief than did Sarmiento's. Estrada circularized his teachers with the directive that they could not oblige any student to attend religious instruction classes if the student's parents belonged to any other religious communion and if they indicated that they did not want the child to have religious instruction.

The contrast between the two men in the same post dealing with the same subject reflects in part the vast differences in the psychological make-up of the two. Sarmiento with his extraordinary ego and his absolute lack of self-doubt was not given to consideration of exceptions to a determined course. Estrada with his introspective tendencies and his habits of caution was. The contrast also shows that by the time of Estrada's tenure of the post the question of freedom of belief had arisen in connection with the public school curriculum. The religious solidarity of the nation may have begun to be affected slightly by the immigration movement, although at this time, as well as later, the vast bulk of immigration was originating in the Catholic countries of southern Europe. Whatever the cause for Estrada's directive may have been—a part of it certainly was to be found in his own just and sensitive conscience—it is worth noting that the man who was to become the chief symbol of Argentine Catholicism in his later life was the first to insist on official respect for freedom of belief and diversity of creeds in the public school system.

Difficulties over the question of religious instruction in the school system seem to have arisen as the pedagogical body began to develop a professional coherence and status. Normal schools were established to provide teachers with the technical qualifications for their work. Professional standards began to be emphasized and preparation for a teaching career came to include more technical and specialized content than it had in the earlier years. The professionalization of the teachers may have helped to polarize differences and even antagonisms between them and the clergy which had lain dormant as long as the clergy was the group with the superior formal education.

In 1882 a national Pedagogical Congress was held under the auspices of the Ministry of Education. Its purpose was to bring together all the teachers who could help in improving public instruction through a coordination of methods and standards. Participation in the Congress was limited to lay persons, clergy and religious being excluded.[40] Out of this Congress came demands for removal of the religious instruction classes. These demands were met in the law enacted two years later.

Before the law was enacted severe tension had grown up between the ecclesiastical and civil authorities of the country, and the tension had stirred up reactions in the body politic. Tensions and reactions came to a head more or less simultaneously with the passage of the law. To begin with, Catholic spokesmen in the early 1880's became concerned with a "naturalist" trend which was coming more and more into prominence in professional educational circles. As usual, the most balanced and informed criticism of this trend from the Catholic side came from Estrada, then at the pinnacle of his career.[41] In Estrada's view the naturalists in the school system were limiting the function of education to one of unfolding to the students the marvels of scientific progress. The enthusiasm for science was something that Estrada could share. He admired it no less than they, but, he insisted, science by itself was inadequate to explain human existence. He did not want any less science in the curriculum. He urged the naturalists, however, to recognize the limitations of science and the necessity for moral instruction based on values beyond and above those that could be established by experimental methods. His tone at this point was friendly, but full of concern.[42]

A few years later this same author voiced what had become a general worry of Catholics over the showing of secularist strength in the Roca cabinet. He expressed the belief—also apparently common among Catholics—that the President was not himself a

40. Casiello, op. cit., p. 331, suggests that the exclusion of the clergy and religious was a deliberate move on the part of the Minister of Public Instruction. What he does not specify is the kind of credentials that were required for admission of the lay persons, and the present writer has so far been unable to ascertain just what they were. A certain kind of credential might throw a different light on the exclusion, although there seems to be little doubt about the long-range intentions of the Roca administration.

41. El Naturalismo Y La Educacion, Obras, Vol. XII, p. 207 et seq.

42. It is a matter of curiosity that in this article as well as in several other pieces of this period Estrada makes frequent reference to the writings of St. Thomas Aquinas, although the revival of the study of St. Thomas had not yet become general in the Catholic Church.

party to the rising anti-clericalism within his official family, but he regretted that this influence was increasing.[43]

Concurrently there was a charge against the Catholics that they wanted to use the school system to impose their own creed on everyone. Estrada again was the principal agent of an endeavor to refute this charge. His argument was that the record of religious toleration in the school system did not justify the accusation [44]—he made no mention of the fact that he himself had inaugurated the observance of religious toleration in the Buenos Aires school system. His principal point was simply that this was a false issue to introduce into the debate on laicization of the schools.

In other quarters the clashes grew sharper. To staff and direct the normal schools the federal government had brought a number of "maestras protestantes" from the United States. These women were regarded with some hostility by bishops who feared that to place Protestants in the direction of the schools would jeopardize the continuance of the traditional Catholic instruction. In 1884 the diocese of Córdoba was without a bishop, and the administrator sede vacante was the Capitular Vicar Jerónimo Clara. Clara issued a pastoral instructing the laity within his jurisdiction that it was not licit for Catholic parents to send their children to the normal schools where they would be exposed to the influence of Protestant teachers. The government ordered Clara's suspension and threatened him with arrest. A complete crisis was averted only by the fact that the newly appointed bishop took over the see shortly thereafter, thus terminating Clara's jurisdiction and the questions involved in the government's action against him.

Before this had happened, however, Bishop Risso Patrón of the Salta diocese publicly allied himself with Clara's stand. For this the government decreed the "destitution" of Monseñor Risso Patrón from his episcopal see. At the same time two Vicars Forensic were decreed out of office for similar reasons. Risso died before the affair could be settled. A general conflict in principle, however, developed between the government and the Catholic hierarchy as a whole. The Roca government, endeavoring to make

43. *Obras*, Vol. XI, p. 119.
44. *Ibid.*, p. 247 *et seq.*

its position clear, sent information copies of its decree removing Bishop Risso to all the other bishops. Without exception, the latter replied that they could not recognize the decree as valid, since the government was presuming to remove a person from an office which it was not within its competence to confer. This, of course, raised the old and still unsettled question of the *patronato*.

The relations between hierarchy and government were further exacerbated by the abrupt expulsion of the Apostolic Delegate from the national territory. The Delegate, Msgr. Mattera, had gone to Córdoba, the point of origin of the recent difficulties. His activities there resulted in his being handed his passport and given 24 hours to leave the country. Evaluations of the Delegate's activities at Córdoba differ considerably. A biographer of President Roca wrote that Mattera wanted to encourage "episcopal rebellion." [45] Estrada states that all the Delegate did at Córdoba was to give "confidential advice" to the parents in the hope of toning down the bitterness that was becoming more prevalent.[46] A North American scholar reports that at Córdoba Mattera had an interview with the Protestant lady in charge of the normal school. The interview appears to have been entirely amicable, with the Delegate advising the director that the difficulties would be cleared up if she would announce that it was not her intention to proselytize for Protestantism in the school, and that she had no intention of interfering with the regular religious instruction to the pupils.[47] According to the same account, the government looked upon this advice as interference in internal affairs on the part of a foreigner. Whatever the causes the government may have found, Msgr. Mattera was expelled as a result of his Córdoba visit.

The year 1884 was clearly a year of great turmoil for Argentine Catholicism. All its articulate sectors were aroused. Certain members of the hierarchy were in open defiance of the government. The hierarchy in general refused categorically to acknowledge a jurisdiction the government claimed. Relations with the Holy See were critically strained. The large body of the Catholic laity was engaged in a struggle to organize itself into an instru-

45. Mariano de Vedia, *Roca* (Paris, 1928), p. 119.
46. *Obras,* Vol. XII, p. 465.
47. Mecham, *Church and State in Latin America,* pp. 294–296.

ment of protest—a struggle that was without success. The symbol of both the gravity of the conflict and the Roca administration's eventual victory was the dismissal of Estrada from his academic posts.[48]

A defender of the Roca policy has conceded that in this action the government was taking a grave risk.[49] Estrada was too popular a figure to be removed from the scene without serious repercussions. Many opposed the dismissal *per se*. Many others, partisans of the official policy, feared that it was not a politically prudent act. But, Vedia later explained, no other course was open to the government. Emotions were running high, and Estrada had made himself the spokesman of the Catholic position. From his university chair he was a threat to the stability of the regime, and there was no other way of allaying the threat than through dismissal.

Estrada suffered a fate that many other academic persons in Argentina and elsewhere have experienced. He upheld a position to which his own intellectual efforts had brought him. The position was in criticism of a prevailing public policy and it earned him the mark of a subversive. Estrada was not interested in trying to impose his own creed on anyone. His insistence was that in Argentina the religious instruction was a traditional part of education for an overwhelmingly Catholic population. He would force no one to submit to that instruction, but he believed that it was only consistent with national tradition to offer the opportunity of the instruction to all who wanted it. In the Córdoba fight and its aftermath in Salta he was not a bigot slashing out against Protestants, but he insisted that until the situation was clarified Church authorities must have a right to speak, and that their right did not depend upon permission from the civil authorities.

The Education Law itself did not strictly outlaw religious instruction from the schools, and from this fact both parties to the dispute were able in later years to derive some meager satisfaction. What the law provided was that religious instruction could be given only outside the regular school hours. Casiello states that the genuine advantage to the laicist position came in the ad-

48. See above, Ch. III, p. 100.
49. Vedia, *op. cit.*, pp. 120–122.

ministrative regulations attached to the law by the Ministry of Public Instruction. They provided that

> When the ministers of the different faiths desire to give in the public schools lessons on religious education they will approach the School Councils so that the latter may designate the place and time, it being prohibited to give those [lessons] if there is not an attendance of more than fifteen pupils.[50]

The administration of these regulations was, in Casiello's view, the real obstacle to continuing a religious instruction program outside of regular class hours, because the School Councils would not cooperate in the undertaking. It may also be worth noting that, as Estrada had prophesied,[51] the new law did little to protect the beliefs of the small Protestant minority. The obvious difficulty for persons of this faith was the requirement of an attendance of more than fifteen pupils, a requirement which would frequently be impossible to meet even if they could obtain a designation of time and place from the educational authorities. In spite of these obstacles, the government could claim, as it did in later years, that the law did not outlaw religion from the schools.

There is some irony in the fact that the regime which reversed the situation in 1943 made a similar claim. The decree of December 31, 1943, stated that the 1884 law "has not abolished religious instruction, but in assigning it an inconvenient schedule has made it impossible." [52] The decree also contended that if the purpose of the law had been anti-Catholic, it would be unconstitutional, and it would not be binding upon the "citizens to observe it or on the government to maintain it." [53] But, the decree states, "it is not thus." Therefore religious instruction may be restored to the schools, without violating the law, merely through changing the administrative regulations. This is obviously a very loose construction of the 1884 statute in view of the attitudes taken by both its proponents and its opponents at the time of its enactment.

50. Casiello, *op. cit.*, p. 331.
51. *Obras*, Vol. XI, p. 228.
52. Casiello, p. 334.
53. This may not be a water-tight juridical argument, since precedents on whether an anti-Catholic statute is constitutional could be cited both ways, depending upon the interpretation of *anti-Catholic*.

The critical points in the 1943 decree are in the first article, which in translation reads:

> In all the public schools of primary, post-primary, secondary and special instruction, the teaching of the Catholic religion will be imparted as ordinary material in the respective plans of study.
> There will be excluded from this teaching those pupils whose parents manifest express opposition by reason of belonging to another religion, thus respecting freedom of conscience. To these pupils moral instruction will be given.

The following three articles provide that the program of religious instruction shall remain under government control, but its content shall be determined in consultation with ecclesiastical authority. For this consultation and supervision a special administrative entity is created.

The decree itself is alleged to have been the coin in which the Roman Catholic hierarchy was paid for its support of—or at least its lack of opposition to—the revolutionary government, over which in the immediately succeeding months Perón was to establish his domination. Perón's government was notoriously undemocratic and quasi-totalitarian. Hence, it has been alleged, the decree demonstrates conclusively that the bishops were ready to cooperate with an anti-democratic program and to use the revolutionary conditions of 1943 to gain an advantage for their creed, an advantage which sixty years earlier had been denied through constitutional procedures.

A few years ago the present writer ventured the opinion that this view, which was then prevalent, was probably not justified.[54] He argued that this view implied an element of choice that was in reality not available to the bishops. The hypothesis was offered that the more probable circumstances had been that the hierarchy recognized in 1943 the totalitarian nature of the new regime, because the Catholic Church had by this time had no little experience in dealing with totalitarian governments imposed by revolutionary means on Catholic populations. The Church, it was noted, had had to face the fact that one of the characteristic acts of such regimes was to obstruct opportunities for the religious training of the young. The new Argentine government offered one avenue of religious instruction for the school-age children, and

54. *The Review of Politics*, Vol. 14, No. 1 (Jan. 1952), p. 135.

the bishops, not knowing when other normal avenues of instruction might be closed off, took up the offer. This thesis was meant to suggest that the decree of December 1943 was not necessarily the result of a dark plot between reactionary bishops and military adventurers.

In that sense the thesis may still have some limited validity, but further study has convinced the writer that in the main it is wrong. Its first error consists of the fact that it treats the problem almost entirely in terms of the 1943 situation, and pays no attention to a steady, though unavailing, Catholic demand for revision of the school laws from 1884 onward. A second error springs from attributing to the hierarchy even a passive role in the decision which is embodied in the decree. A more careful appraisal has shown that the bishops played no part at all in the decision-making. The decree was issued by the revolutionary government on its own volition. It was in all probability designed to gain Catholic lay support for the new regime, but there is nothing to indicate that the decree was a product of "political compromise" with ecclesiastical authorities.

It is true that in a collective pastoral early in 1944 the hierarchy greeted with enthusiasm the re-establishment of religious instruction in the public schools. The bishops claim no credit for the decree, however, and they attribute its origin to the "Catholic tradition" of the Republic. A year later two prelates, the Archbishop of Santa Fe and the Bishop of Rosario, specifically rejected the suggestion that the religious education program had resulted from any official ecclesiastical endeavors. They noted that ever since 1884 Catholics had worked as citizens to obtain changes in the law, but so far as the 1943 settlement was concerned, "neither the Church as an institution, nor *Acción Católica* in official representation of Argentine Catholics as an organization, has asked for or influenced directly and formally the Decree Law by which the Revolutionary Government established religious instruction." [55]

55. Castello, *op. cit.*, pp. 338–339. In a collective statement of June 13, 1955, the hierarchy as a whole repeats the declaration made by these two ordinaries that the decree was in no sense their work, even though they were happy to see it. Peronists, who had not attacked the 1945 statement of the two ordinaries, rejected the 1955 statement with ridicule. See *Hechos E Ideas*, Año XVI, Tomo XXVII, nos. 134/135 (June–July, 1955), p. 488.

The emphatic quality of the statement may lead some of its readers to dismiss it with a demurrer or to discount it as too obviously self-serving. Public reaction to the decree, however, would seem to confirm the bishops' claim that they did not ask for the decree, at least in the sense that it was not necessary for them to ask for it. If it is borne in mind that the decree was administered with careful regard for the religious preference of the school-children's parents,[56] the response would appear to justify in large part what various Catholic sources have claimed for the decree, namely, that it was little more than the reassertion of a national tradition.[57]

In the years immediately following the decree more than 97 per cent of the primary-school children were in the religion classes, while an average of 92 per cent of the secondary-school group chose the religious instruction.[58] At the same time the number of students not enrolled in the classes is large enough to show that coercion was not a factor in determining the choice.

The motivation of parents in their response to the decree cannot be analyzed here. Some allowance must be made for the fact that the initial response occurred in an atmosphere of crisis, which does not exclude the possibility of an element of hysteria or of herd-like acceptance of a new situation. Even with this allowance, however, it is difficult to regard the widespread acceptance of the new system as other than a largely spontaneous response to a program which must not have appeared too strange or unexpected to the majority of the population.

The situation is admittedly one which North Americans, of any religious commitment, find difficult to understand. In the United States no government would, of course, impose religious instruction as an integral part of the school curriculum. Any state or federal administration attempting to undertake such a course would be flying in the face of a firm national tradition, and the

56. Casiello, p. 339, stresses that no child was required to enter the religion classes and that all means were available to parents to indicate their preference.
57. *Ibid.*, p. 332, footnote 25, records doubts expressed by prominent secularists during the 1920's about the wisdom of the 1884 exclusion of religion from the schools. These doubts naturally did not reflect a concern for credal interest, but rather for the "moral effects" that Sarmiento had talked about in the last century.
58. *Ibid.*, p. 339. The statistics are presented in tabular form which shows the heaviest concentration of non-participation in the religion classes in the public schools in the city of Buenos Aires.

measure would be contested in the courts and widely opposed, even by those who endorse a voluntary program of religious instruction as a part of primary and secondary education. Argentina, however, has a different tradition. The tradition is not primarily operative in tolerance and respect for diversity of creeds for the reason that there is so little diversity. Rather the major problem confronting the religious element in the Argentine national tradition is survival in the face of a non-religious opposition which frequently becomes an anti-religious opposition.

The 1943 decree undoubtedly appeared to most Catholics as a promising means for survival of religion. Later difficulties with the Perón administration have probably given many Catholics second thoughts on the subject, and the eleven years of experience with the arrangement may indeed not prove that this kind of measure justifies the hopes that Catholics originally placed in it. What is probably more important, however, is that Argentine Catholics will not cease to search for the means which, they believe, best protect the kind of Catholicism they have traditionally known from the kind of attack they believe they have reason to fear most. Future quests for such means will in all probability be undertaken. Whether they focus on the schools, on some other points, or on a combination of several, no search is likely to be basically conditioned by a regard for the practice of religious toleration, as it is known in the United States. This is not to imply that it will be conditioned by intolerance, either, but rather that the problem of diversity of creeds is not a major one in Argentine society.

As for the Argentine hierarchy's relation to the government's decision in 1943, North American parallels may be cited in a way that throws some light on the hierarchy's situation. In the United States, spokesmen for religious bodies, Protestant, Catholic and Jewish, offer from time to time pronouncements on what they consider to be specific moral issues involved in questions of public policy. Roman Catholic bishops, for example, have made statements in recent years on such matters as dissemination of birth control information, so-called right-to-work proposals, and racial segregation. From time to time the point of view which these statements have upheld has turned out to be largely identical with the one that becomes dominant in the formulation of public policy.

It would, however, be too much to claim that these statements have by themselves determined the course of public policy. The situation of the Argentine bishops on the school question, while not identical, is similar. After 1884 the bishops did not abandon their stand that religious instruction should be in the schools. They publicized their stand on several occasions, and they acclaimed the 1943 decree. Yet they were not the effective and responsible decision-makers of the policy promulgated in that decree.

Insisting on the absence of a fundamental problem of religious toleration and dispelling the aura of conspiracy attributed to the bishops do not, however, dispose finally of the question of freedom of religion that has been raised in connection with the 1943 school measure. Two considerations remain. Did the government's act violate in principle this freedom? Did Argentine Catholicism endorse such a violation? These questions obviously cannot be answered in terms of the overwhelming majority response to the decree, since the specific freedom involved is one for which majority rule has no value.

To transfer the problem into the realm of the purely imaginary, it is readily seen that if in the United States the religious doctrines of the Protestant majority were offered as "ordinary material" in the "plans of study" of the public schools, a vigorous protest would immediately be made by the Roman Catholic minority to the effect that freedom of religion was being violated. It is unlikely that the protest would be any less vigorous if there were a provision that Catholics and other non-Protestants could be excused from the religious doctrine classes at the indication of their parents. The protests would still center on the point that Protestant doctrines were considered worthy of becoming "ordinary material" in the classroom, while those of other faiths were not.

To make the protest effective there would be recourse on the part of Catholics to the judicial process, and the outcome would undoubtedly turn on the First Amendment. The Argentine Constitution contains nothing that corresponds to the First Amendment of the Constitution of the United States. On the contrary, numerous constitutional provisions beginning with Article 2 invest the state with authority to regulate and legislate in the field of religious observance and practice. It is true that the Constitution also guarantees everyone the freedom of belief and worship.[59] These latter provisions, however, combine with those authorizing state regulation to produce a total situation which is radically different from that obtaining in the United States under the First Amendment. The 1943 decree did not violate this totality in terms of constitutional principle. In strict logic, then, the second consideration noted above may be disposed of by the fact that there was no violation for Catholics to endorse. This is an answer which may seem to beg the question, but within the Argentine terms of reference no other seems possible.

The latest chapter in the history of the school laws will be treated in a later section.[60]

The Marriage Laws

The conflict between civil and ecclesiastical authorities on matrimonial laws and regulations follows a course parallel to that of the school question. Here the Church has not been accused of a desire to repress rights or of failure to respect liberty. Nevertheless, the historical development of the conflict began at about the same point as it did over the schools, and through the years similar antagonisms between the Catholic position and the official one have been generated. It is therefore appropriate to note this development in connection with any study of the social and political conflicts in which Argentine Catholicism has been involved.

The basic statute governing marriage in Argentina is the *Ley de Matrimonio Civil* of 1888.[61] The law does not prohibit a religious ceremony for marriage, but requires that its legal validity be established in a civil ceremony which is made obligatory for all marriages. It also provides that no religious rite may take place until the civil requirements have been met. For violation of this provision the original statute imposed rather severe penalties, but it does not appear that the penalties have been customarily applied in recent years.

Catholic opposition to the law has been both general and specific. The origins of the law are in the laicizing movements

59. The pertinent articles are, in the 1853 Constitution, numbers 14 and 19; in the 1949 revision, article 26.
60. See below, p. 208.
61. Law no. 2393 of November 12, 1888.

of the Roca and Juárez Celman administrations, which Catholics regarded from the beginning not as movements designed to expand the area of individual freedom, as their proponents claimed, but as part of a piece-meal attack on Catholicism as a religious and social force. The same lay Catholic organizations which tried unsuccessfully to combat the education law of 1884 struggled with equal lack of success against the Civil Marriage Law. Here again Estrada, now out of his professorship and a member of the Chamber of Deputies, was a principal leader.

As he voiced it, contemporary Catholic opinion saw in the law a "totalitarian" threat.[62] In keeping with Church tradition, Catholics insisted that the status and rights of the family as a social unit are distinct from those of the state and cannot have their origin in the authority of the state. The creation of the family originates in the marriage pact. If the pact is made exclusively dependent upon the State, the Catholics argue, the state is establishing and controlling a social unit whose establishment has been already provided for by natural and divine dispensations. As in nearly all Catholic treatment of this question, opponents of the law took care to specify that the state was not prohibited by Catholic doctrine from regulating in the field of the "civil effects" of marriage. Their main point was simply that for the state to claim to be the exclusive origin of the creation of the family through marriage was a denial of the divine and natural origins of the institution.

In defense of their measure, the proponents took a different view. They argued that the proposal did not prevent Catholics and other religious believers from following their own consciences, since they were free to honor their own concept of the divine origin of matrimony through a religious ceremony, once they had satisfied the civil requirements. Moreover, the law would make marriage easier for non-Catholics and unbelievers. Finally, they argued, the simplicity of the civil law would encourage the spread of legal marriage among the classes of the population who were living in concubinage. Legalizing the status of these unions would extend the security of the family institution into areas where currently it did not exist.

Catholic replies on these points were specific enough, but

62. *Obras,* Vol. XII, p. 418.

they took the argument away from the main field of interest for the Catholics.[63] Marriage of non-Catholics was already provided for in law, and no Catholic was interested in suppressing the right of these persons to marry and form families. With regard to concubinage, Estrada, for one, was quite willing to recognize that the practice was prevalent in certain rural areas. But, he said, the new law would not curb the practice. Correction of this condition must be brought about by many forces which it was beyond the power of a mere statute to generate. The task was to raise the level of moral habits to the point where the responsibilities of marriage would be respected and accepted. This law, in the Catholic view, was not raising the standards of morality, but rather lowering those of marriage to put them within such easy reach of concubinage that the difference between that and marriage might cease to be noticeable.

More recent Catholic treatment of the 1888 law has questioned its constitutionality.[64] The argument has been that by imposing a penalty on the parties to a Catholic ceremony, if that ceremony occurs prior to the civil rites, the law in effect imposes a penalty on the free reception of a Catholic sacrament.[65] Since the federal constitution explicitly declares that the state supports the Roman Catholic religion, any act which undermines a sacrament is a violation of the spirit of the constitution.

These arguments on specific points, however, have only served to underscore the basic Catholic opposition to the Civil Marriage Act. The complaint has been not that the law makes civil marriage available to those who want it, but that it makes it obligatory for all. This is regarded as an interference with the free exercise of religion, and since 1888 Catholics have continued to protest the obligation.[66]

63. The Catholic position is stated in detail in two speeches by Estrada in the Chamber of Deputies on October 18 and October 20, 1888. They are reprinted in *Obras*, Vol. XII, p. 595 *et seq.* and p. 627 *et seq.*
64. So far as the present writer knows, the argument has been entirely theoretical and has not been presented in judicial proceedings dealing with concrete cases. See also footnote 53 above.
65. Casiello, *op. cit.*, p. 299.
66. The suggestion has been made that the Argentine requirement of the civil ceremony is largely for the purpose of public record, and violates the free exercise of religion no more than does the requirement of a marriage license in the various states of the United States. It has been noted that the state legislation establishing certain standards governing the issuance of the marriage license has not been

The protests have been quite unavailing, and the Perón regime before it was finished carried the conflict with Catholic opinion over the marriage question still further. This came with the enactment of a divorce law in 1954.[67] Until this time divorce was unknown to the Argentine law. Agitation for divorce legislation had existed in certain "advanced" sectors of the political groupings, and the idea had found favor with certain political leaders. There appears, however, to have been very little chance of enactment of such legislation at any time prior to Perón's second term.

It is probably a reasonable speculation that the Peronista divorce law was less of a measure to satisfy widespread popular demands than it was a political weapon to end the struggle with ecclesiastical authority which by 1954 had reached an acute stage. It was hardly to be expected that Argentines would begin to flood the court with petitions of divorce. It was probably intended, however, that the Catholic hierarchy would take note of the power which Perón commanded in securing passage of a law which defied not only the doctrine of the Church but also a specific instruction which the Argentine hierarchy had repeated for the benefit of Catholics on several occasions since 1931.[68] Similarly, the law was probably an invitation to laymen to take note of the seeming impotence of Catholic opinion in the face of the challenge offered by the bill.

CONFLICTS IN THE PERONIST PERIOD

The Church policy of the Perón government was never entirely clear in all its details during the time that government was in power. In the two years since its overthrow circumstances have not been propitious for historical clarification of this and other policies of the regime. For this reason hard and fast judgments about Perón's relations with Catholicism are not now possible.

protested by religious bodies in the United States. The comparison, however, is inexact. In Argentina the civil ceremony leaves the parties married in the eyes of the law. In the United States the license by itself has no such effect. It is a prelude to a civil or religious ceremony by which the marriage of the parties is established.

67. The President signed the measure on December 22, 1954. See *The New York Times,* December 23, 1954, p. 8.

68. See above, p. 184.

Nevertheless, the external attitudes both of the regime and of Catholicism during the 1943–1955 period may be noted, and from them some logical, if tentative, deductions may be made.

First, and most obviously, it seems reasonable to believe that as the military regime founded in 1943 began to evidence the character which Perón infused into it, the new political movement met with little significant opposition from any of the elements of Argentine Catholicism. Some North American writers have suggested that there was a polarization of Catholic forces at the time, with certain clergy and laity avowing an enthusiastic support for the new state of affairs while another set of Catholics opposed it. Here the emphasis is generally placed on the heroic Bishop Andrea as the spokesman for the opposition.[69]

The present writer shares all the sympathy which other North Americans have lavished on this elderly prelate, but he believes that the case for the existence of a genuine opposition is somewhat overdrawn. It was as a distinguished individual that Andrea voiced his criticism of the new government. Although a bishop, he possessed only a see in partibus, and he was without any authority over a diocese in Argentina. This statement is not offered to belittle the worth of a meritorious individual, but merely to emphasize an important fact. Had Andrea been governing a diocese, his attitude would probably have been the same, but his freedom of action as an individual might have been much less. The diocesan bishops were in a quite different position. It has never been consistent with the character of the Argentine hierarchy to offer general opposition to any government in power. Opposition to specific points of public policy or of proposed programs has, of course, been voiced, sometimes by individual bishops, other times collectively. The difficulties with the Roca and Juárez Celman administrations provoked this kind of opposition, but it was all in terms of specific issues involving Church interests or doctrine. Before Perón's time was up, he too had stimulated such opposition, but in the beginning he did not offer any challenge in terms of the interests which it is the obligation of bishops to defend.

Bishop Andrea, immersed for more than thirty years in the

69. See above, footnote 4.

social action programs of Argentine Catholicism, saw—and, in this writer's opinion, with admirable accuracy—the thoroughly unsavory character of the rising power structure. He was free to speak out against it. If diocesan bishops had similar insights, as long as there was an absence of specific issues they were not free to speak. This is not to suggest that bishops will necessarily remain silent except when the threat to their Church is direct and extreme. Nor is it intended to suggest that the peculiar pattern of Church-State relations in Argentina leaves the hierarchy in a position of subservience to the state, from which they can escape only at the price of rebellion. Estrada's fight and the attitude of the hierarchy in Bishop Risso Patrón's case have shown that this is accepted by neither clergy nor laity. It is, however, obvious that the responsibilities of active ecclesiastical authority pose for its possessor questions of prudence much more far-reaching than those which confront other clergy and the Catholic laity.

Some who concede that the foregoing is true will, however, inquire why then the hierarchy felt obliged to commend the new regime and take collective action on its behalf. The action alleged consists of two pastorals, the first in February 1944 acclaiming the re-introduction of the religious instruction in the schools,[70] and the second during the 1946 electoral campaign. In the latter there was a reiteration of the standards which the hierarchy had since 1931 made binding on the Catholic conscience in the matter of voting.[71]

With regard to the first, the episcopal attitude must be understood not in terms of a single incident in the Perón regime, but rather in the light of the history of the school question as it has been summarized above.[72] In 1943–44 some Catholic opinion was dubious about whether the new regime's action had solved or settled the long-standing question. The hierarchy, however, saw in the education decree, if not a solution, at least a step in the direction of a solution. Subsequent history did not confirm their hopes, but their attitude must be understood in the light of the history of the sixty years that preceded the decree.

70. See above, pp. 197–198.
71. *Ibid.*, p. 184.
72. *Ibid.*, pp. 186–188.

The second pastoral involves a quite different matter. The criteria enunciated were the same that the bishops had begun to stress fifteen years earlier. In 1946 it was alleged that they favored the Peronistas. Eight years later the Peronistas were complaining that the same criteria discriminated against them.[73] The only alternative available to the hierarchy at any of the times when the statement had been reiterated was silence. Since silence would be widely interpreted as retreat on matters which the bishops have claimed in terms of doctrine or ecclesiastical interest, it has never been a real possibility.

To suggest that the bishops' pronouncements were motivated more by historical factors than by a desire to support the military dictatorship in 1944, and later the Perón presidential candidacy, does not dispose of the question of whether the effect of the statements was actually to aid first the dictatorship and then the candidacy. Objectively, it is impossible to ascribe a different effect to them. They did not oppose the dictatorship or Perón. This obvious answer, however, may be less important in the long run to Argentine Catholicism than is the equally obvious demonstration of the weight of historical factors in the hierarchy's judgment. The reassertion of positions which had been formulated long before the Perón crisis was bound to be interpreted in many quarters as an endorsement of Peronism. Events of the next decade must indeed have led members of the hierarchy to lament that this was the effect produced. It is unlikely, however, that a contrary effect could have been achieved except through retreat from traditional positions.

The unchanging position of the Argentine hierarchy suggests the second tentative conclusion that may be drawn in connection with civil-ecclesiastical relations during the Perón period. This is that when Perón's dispute with the Church began, and as it later developed in a general fight with various segments of Catholicism, the difficulties arose precisely in those areas where the Argentine Church's position has been most consistent.

By the time of the first uprising against Perón in 1955, his government had taken certain actions which ran counter to almost every one of the hierarchy's points. Divorce legislation had

73. See below, p. 211.

been enacted in 1954. The religious instruction in the schools was suspended on April 14, 1955,[74] and outlawed by statute on June 2.[75] In its place a program of instruction in "morality" was inaugurated. Peronista spokesmen explained these and other measures not approved by the Church, such as the legalization of a system of prostitution, as necessary steps in social progress, the taking of which had hitherto been prevented only by "clerical prejudices." In the last months of the Perón regime there was also a plan for calling a Constitutional Convention, and it was made clear that the chief revision that the convention would undertake would be to "separate" Church and State. All these steps involved points on which the position of the Church had been clear, and since 1931 no one had been left in any doubt about how Catholics had been instructed to regard political issues revolving around them.

Needless to say, Perón himself did not see his fight with the Church in these terms, nor did the leaders of the Peronista Parties. The two principal discourses of later 1954 [76] in which Perón attacked the problem of Church relations show that for him the problem was one of "infiltration" of Catholic forces into the "popular movements," especially the labor organizations. The purpose of this infiltration was believed to be to subvert the loyalty of the members of the organizations and turn them away from Perón. At the time of these speeches the quarrel had not reached the extreme stage achieved six months later, and though the texts are full of confusion and contradiction they probably represent with some accuracy Perón's basic attitude.

On both these occasions Perón insisted that he had no quarrel with the Catholic Church, only with a "few clergy" and with certain prominent Catholic laymen. To bolster his claim that he had no quarrel with the Church, he referred to the recent official visit of the hierarchy as a group, in accordance with the custom whereby the bishops at the close of their annual meeting make a formal call upon the President of the Republic. During this visit

74. *The New York Times*, April 15, 1955, pp. 1, 8.
75. *Ibid.*, June 3, 1955, p. 4.
76. *Hechos E Ideas*, Año XV, Tomo XXVII, nos. 126/127 (October–November, 1954), p. 389 *et seq.* for the speech of November 10 to the Governors of the Provinces and the "Representatives of the popular forces," assembled together; p. 397 *et seq.* for the speech of November 25 to the mass meeting in Luna Park of the *Confederación General de Trabajo* and the Peronista parties.

Perón discussed the problem of the priests and laymen who were infiltrating the popular movements and disturbing public order with their attacks on the Peronista positions. Perón said that the bishops agreed with him that these persons should not speak as Catholics and that the bishops promised to take action which would prevent their doing so. Perón's reporting, however, does not seem to rest on very certain factual grounds. For, though both texts refer to his interview with the bishops, in the second he indicated his lack of patience with the bishops for not taking any action, and promised that now he would let the full force of the law fall on these disturbers of the peace whether they were clergy or not. The implication is that he had given the bishops their chance and they had failed to take it.

His speech to the Governors shows a most peculiar contradiction on the point of relations with the hierarchy. After an insistence that he and the bishops were still friends, he gave a name by name denunciation of certain bishops and priests. Three bishops were singled out as "open enemies of the government." [77] One bishop was recognized as a "Peronista," [78] but the President apparently could not claim any other members of the hierarchy as his own.

As for the laymen, Perón left neither of his audiences in doubt that he took a dim view of the supposedly non-political *Acción Católica Argentina*. The organization was filled with men who worked "with all hypocrisy" to give the impression that they were not political agitators, but who were really availing themselves of a religious organization to upset public order. He advised the Governors especially to watch out for these men and to take action against them.

In his second speech Perón carried his charges against *Acción Católica* further. The Catholic leaders were, he asserted, in a conspiracy with the Communists to destroy the existing government. The evidence offered to support this was scanty, but it included the report that the Vice President of *Acción Católica* had been arrested while he was closeted in unlawful meeting with four Communists.

77. The ordinaries of Córdoba, Santa Fe and La Rioja. Numerous priests were given the same classification.
78. The Bishop of Catamarca. Even this designation is rendered somewhat dubious by the unanimous stand of the hierarchy six months later.

Two other items in the speeches should be noted. One is the claim that Catholic subversion was not of recent origin or limited to the labor organization. Years before, Perón had begun to receive complaints that the clergy were trying to work against him. His attitude, however, had been to disregard these complaints, and he had not paid any serious attention to them until three months before the speeches, when representatives of four principal organizations approached him with a bill of particulars on Catholic interference. The four organizations were the *Confederación General de Trabajo, la Confederación General de Profesionales, la Confederación General Económica,* and *la Confederación General Universitaria.* Catholics were therefore trying to seize control of labor, professional life, business and the universities, and bring all of them under clerical management. These reports confirmed the earlier ones which Perón now regretted having disregarded. The infiltration could not be tolerated, and he promised that it would be stopped.

The other is the ironic statement of tolerance promised to a still hypothetical Christian Democratic Party. If Catholic forces wanted to organize this kind of a party, Perón indicated that he and his government would not stand in the way. Though the tone is one of sour jesting, one can read into the text evidence of Perón's belief that he would find such a party a comfort and a convenience. The party would, he knew, attract only four kinds of followers: the Conservatives, some nationalists, Communists and Clericals. In terms of internal composition no group could present a better collection of targets for the Peronistas to aim at.

Approximately seven months after these speeches came the unsuccessful revolt of June 16, 1955. The revolt owed its origin to more than Catholic opposition to the regime, although Catholic antagonism had by this time been thoroughly aroused.[79] A formal decree of excommunication against Perón [80] undoubtedly helped to consolidate Catholic opinion at the very time that the revolt was in process. By September, when the successful revolt took place, the Catholic element in the anti-Peronista drive was certainly no less than it had been in June. Nor had the issues over

79. Arthur P. Whitaker, *Argentine Upheaval* (New York, 1956), offers a good evaluation of the forces opposed to Perón in these uprisings.
80. *The New York Times,* June 17, 1955, pp. 1, 14.

which Catholic opinion was exercised been to any degree settled.

It is appropriate to ask at this point whether these events of 1955 show Argentine Catholicism as a political factor capable of turning the balance in the national society. Beyond that, does the total history of Perón in power show Catholicism as a potentially disruptive force, a force to be cajoled by administrations that desire to retain office and to be opposed by political leaders only at their own peril?

In a strict sense the answers are negative. Though the repetition is trite, it is still true that the official Church in Argentina has not sought quarrels with any regime. For a quarter of a century, however, it has stipulated certain guides for the Catholic conscience in political matters. Some articulate sectors of the population do not agree with these stipulations, and, more importantly, do not accept the idea that ministers of religion should provide any guides to political decisions. A very large part of the population, however, does accept such guidance, which they believe has the weight of a tradition of a "Catholic society" to support it. In 1955 the official Church, through the Permanent Commission of the Argentine Episcopate, reiterated and re-emphasized the stipulations that had originally been formulated in 1931. The Commission also examined and made some statements on the specific problems then pending between the civil and ecclesiastical authorities.[81] Nothing in the declaration signified a departure from the standing position of the Church. In Peronist circles, however, the reaction was as though the Commission had innovated an entirely new course for the purpose of battling Peronism.[82] Now, the Peronists began to charge, the affair was no longer one of a "few priests," but of a whole Church which had turned subversive. In July there was a collective statement from the hierarchy as a whole, which again represented neither departure nor innovation, although it did include specific protests of certain recent acts of the government.[83]

The consistency of the hierarchy's stand, a consistency which is not disturbed in times of gravest crisis, would therefore tend

81. *Ibid.*, April 16, 1955, p. 23.
82. *Hechos E Ideas,* Año XV, Tomo XXVII, no. 131 (March, 1955), p. 193 *et seq.* (The March date indicates sequence, but not the actual time of issue, since many of the events discussed occur much later.)
83. *The New York Times,* July 14, 1955, p. 7.

to support the claim that the Argentine Church in its official manifestation is not a politically intrusive force. Like other religious bodies the world over, it takes positions in accordance with the doctrine it preaches. These positions may have social and political effects, and these effects may on occasion produce conflicts with the government or with other forces in society. The cause of these conflicts cannot be removed by the simple expedient of charging that the religious body has become political. In an extreme sense, the only absolutely certain way of removing the cause would be to deny any and all functions to organized religion.

Manifestations of Catholicism are not, of course, limited to official pronouncements of the hierarchy, and in terms of informal but sensitive Catholic opinion, any answers to the above questions are considerably less definite. While it is illogical to think of any sector of Catholic opinion that would work at cross-purposes to the hierarchy or which would defy Church authority, the area of social thought and action where Church authority commands compliance is necessarily one that is authoritatively defined. In practice, definitions have not pre-empted a general field of social concern to Catholics. It is therefore entirely possible that Catholic opinion, that is to say a cohesive body of opinion sensitive to Church interests and to the implications of Christian doctrine in a given social context, may react, not in disharmony with, but beyond the limits of, an official Church position.

It is probable that through the 1955 uprisings in Argentina the large body of lay Catholic opinion, considered in the sense of the foregoing comment, was a consciously active factor in the overthrow of Perón. A Catholic reaction merely in terms of support for the minimal stipulations of the hierarchy would probably not have gone so far. It should be noted that the Perón government had done much to provoke from Catholics a reaction exceeding this minimum. Representatives of Catholicism, clerical and lay, had been excoriated as "infiltrators" and "subversives." Where their critics had once called them fascists, Perón himself sought to brand them as "Communists" and "fellow-travelers." [84]

84. After the June 16 revolt, the Peronistas revived the old charges of fascism against *Acción Católica*. See *Hechos E Ideas,* Año XVI, Tomo XXVII, nos. 134/135 (June–July, 1955), pp. 483–484.

They were committed to a general way of life which they thought had long been sanctioned by Argentine custom and law, but they found themselves labeled "enemies of the government." Their choice of revolutionary action is accordingly not surprising.

The final events in the Perón period therefore seem to show that there is a body of Catholic opinion in Argentina which may become a politically active factor. It is probably only the gravest crisis that can render it active or fundamentally decisive. In contrast, in the day-to-day routine of politics it may appear so quiescent that any respect paid to it must be in terms of a potential, not an overt, force. Certainly, it is not manipulatable, and it is not to be controlled by gadgets that turn it on and off. It is rather a vital, though frequently artless, force that can be evaluated in the following terms:

Catholicism in Argentina has had a relatively undisturbed history for more than a century. Conflicts at the official level between civil and ecclesiastical authorities have not been unknown, but they have been infrequent and limited. Catholicism's status in society is supported by official dispensations of the Constitution and the laws. A very large body of public opinion approves for various reasons and with varying degrees of intensity the position which this support provides for Catholicism.

One element in this national tradition is the inheritance from Spain of regalism, which is acclaimed by many Argentines as a basic cause of the general harmony between the two authorities. While strongly committed Catholics do not share this enthusiasm, the established pattern of Church-State relations has met with a rather general acceptance. One effect of this general acceptance is that the civil power is not generally regarded as being without competence to legislate in matters of common concern to both Church and State. The exercise of this competence will not normally arouse serious Catholic antagonism. Tradition makes for a *de facto* tolerance of specific acts even in those quarters where the competence is questioned in principle.

This tolerance, however, does not extend to acts which, to the Catholic mind, put the established status of Catholicism in jeopardy. When such acts occur there is a Catholic reaction, as in the Perón administration or as in Roca's to a lesser degree. There is obviously a deeply permeating public sentiment which finds satisfaction in the religious *status quo*. Acts of the civil power which come to be regarded as threats to the *status quo* call this sentiment into active play as a political force. The force may fail in winning its goals, as it failed in the 1880's. It may be a decisive element in the outcome of a struggle, as it proved to be in 1955. This force in all probability will continue to be an occasional source of aggravation to future Argentine governments, unless or until they find the means to reverse the weight of a rather complicated national tradition.

A CONCLUDING COMMENT

It is not entirely inappropriate to end this study of Argentine Catholicism in a chapter dealing with conflicts. Catholic social thought has been at odds with many intellectual currents of the modern age, and the polemics in which recent Catholic spokesmen have engaged in Argentina have been duplicated in many other parts of the world. From an Argentine point of view, however, this duplication contains a paradoxical element, since the status of Catholicism on this particular national scene is unique, and quite different from the position which Catholicism has in most of the other countries, especially the Latin American and Mediterranean countries, where similar conflicts have occurred.

Argentine Catholics claim again and again that the national tradition is on their side in these conflicts. Their claims have been challenged in important non-Catholic quarters, and, as we have seen, some of those challenges have been effective in the formulation of certain public policies. While they have produced no major institutional dislocations for Catholicism as a religion, one of their chief results has been to put Catholic social thought on the defensive. Defensiveness has frequently produced a kind of Catholic negativism, which has an undeniable strength but which is not the creative force that the Catholic thought of an earlier period was.

Catholics will say that they have been forced into a defensive position because of the peculiar nature of the challenge they have had to meet. There has been no grand-scale assault on Catholicism which might have stimulated a creative Catholic reaction on an equal scale. Instead, from the challenging camp have come isolated and sporadic skirmishes which have penetrated through the wall of the Catholic tradition without ever actually pulling it down. To repel these invading parties has been a major task for the Catholic spokesmen, and they can plead that the task necessarily absorbs most of their energy.

Earlier generations of Catholic thinkers, however, were not spared a defensive role nor did they shy away from polemics with their opponents. Frías gloried in them. Estrada was no stranger to them. Yet these men did not limit themselves to a defensive role. The expansion of the nation and the development of its human and material resources gave them opportunities to demonstrate that the Catholic religion could inspire and sustain free men in the making of a good society out of the elements which Providence has specially provided in the River Plate region. Their judgment was not infallible, and some of them were not innocent of an occasional pursuit of the trivial. But they entered whole-heartedly into the task of building the nation, drawing on the special resources which they commanded.

Their successors in the present century are no less convinced that Catholicism in Argentina continues to have an important social function to discharge. It does not seem possible for them, however, to define that function in the same sweeping terms that their predecessors used. The more recent environment may not indeed provide the same kind of affirmative and creative opportunities that the earlier period offered to Catholic thinkers. It does not offer them to any school of thought. But the problems in the contemporary era of Argentine history ought to call forth the best and most productive talents of any group. If contemporary Catholics are to respond to this stimulus, then certainly they must find a way to reassert the creative tradition which nineteenth century Catholicism established. If this tradition produced a "Catholic orientation," then those who dedicate themselves to perpetuating that orientation must re-examine its origins to discover just what their peculiar strength was and whether it is applicable to present conditions. Mere verbal repetition of a tradition will not keep it vital indefinitely.

These are the conclusions of a foreign, but sympathetic, student of some manifestations of Argentine Catholicism. They are not meant to deny or belittle the significant and truly effective accomplishments that are the substantial part of the Argentine tradition in Catholic social thought. Yet it seems inescapable that the main task in social thought confronting twentieth century Argentine Catholicism is to reassert the strength of that tradition in terms that are generously meaningful to the present era.

INDEX